VITAL RECORDS

OF

GRAY
MAINE

TO THE YEAR OF

1930

Howard G. Black, Jr.

HERITAGE BOOKS
2019

HERITAGE BOOKS

AN IMPRINT OF HERITAGE BOOKS, INC.

Books, CDs, and more—Worldwide

For our listing of thousands of titles see our website
at
www.HeritageBooks.com

Published 2019 by
HERITAGE BOOKS, INC.
Publishing Division
5810 Ruatan Street
Berwyn Heights, Md. 20740

Heritage Books by the author:

Headstone Inscriptions: Gray, Maine
Howard G. Black and Sharlene Black

Vital Records of Gray, Maine to the Year of 1930

International Standard Book Numbers
Paperbound: 978-1-58549-886-4
Clothbound: 978-0-7884-6943-5

Thank you to all the town employees that take the time from their daily workload to help us with our family research. Also to my wife Shelly for her help and understanding.

This compilation is meant as a guide to the vital records of Gray, Maine. As there may be errors or omissions in this work, original records should be used as a source for research. The death records list place of birth if known.

Contents

BIRTHS

ADAMS, Viola 22 Oct 1865

ADAMS, male 4th 5 Jan 1892 to Chas. S. Adams farmer, Amanda
E. Skillin, West Gray

ADAMS, Frank F. Adams 12 May 1876

ADAMS, male 5th 22 May 1895; Charles S. Adams, farmer and
Almeda E. Skillings

ALLEN, Pearl M. 30 Nov 1888 Mother Hattie Allen

ALLEN, infant of Andrew Allen 22 Jan 1877

ALLEN, ? Oct 1878

ALLEN, female 2nd 8 May 1895; Josiah W. Allen, farmer and Ida
M. Field

ALLEN, stillborn 18 Mar 1899 female 2nd; Eugene Allen, farmer
and Sadie Frank

ALLEN, Emily Louisa 6 Oct 1899 female 1st; Ernest Allen,
carpenter and Grace Blake

ALLEN, Lawrence R. 8 Aug 1905 male 1st; Roscoe G. Allen,
blacksmith and Grace G. Hipper

ALLEN, Lena Mabel 27 Dec. 1905 female 3rd; Eugene F. Allan,
laborer and Sadie F. Frank

ALLEN, male 2nd 13 Oct 1906; Roscoe G. Allen, blacksmith and
Grace G. Hipple

ALLEN, stillborn 15 Nov 1912 male 1st; Ernest H. Allen and
Dorothy M. Rogers

ANDREWS, female 1st 29 Oct 1893; William B. Andrews, teacher
and E. Marion Sanborn

ANDREWS, John & Egbert twins 2 Mar 1904 males 1&2; Anson
M. Andrews, physician and Carolyn M. Southard

BAILEY, John Allen 23 Aug 1898 male 6th; George Allen Bailey,
laborer and Mary O. Morse

BAILEY, female 1st 13 Apr 1906; Leroy M. Bailey, farmer and
Elizabeth F. McConkey

BARBERICK, female 11 Aug 1902; William Barberick, laborer
and Susie M. Hall

BARBERICK, Winona 10 Oct 1904 female 3rd; William T.
Barberick, laborer and Susie M. Hall

BARBOUR, Willie R. Barbour 26 Nov 1876

BARBOUR, Emerson S. 20 Aug 1897 male 5th; William L.
Barbour, farmer and Emma M. Smith

2

BARKER, Herbert F. 17 Feb 1915 male 1st; Herbert F. Barker, laborer and Sadie Winslow

BARKER, Nathan Phillip 30 June 1916 male 3rd; Herbert F. Barker, laborer and Sadie R. Winslow

BARKER, female 1st 7 May 1922; Phillip E. Barker, laborer and Elizabeth E. Swinnington

BARTON, Phillip 8 Mar 1896 male 2nd; Fred W. Barton, laborer and Mary H. Sawyer

BARTON, male 3rd 9 Apr 1906; Fred W. Barton, laborer and Mary H. Sawyer

BARTON, Frederick 11 Apr 1918 male 2nd; Philip W. Barton, laborer and Viola M. Weymouth

BARTON, female 2nd 24 June 1918; E. Clifford Barton, merchant and Myra L. Frank

BARTON, female 3rd 24 June 1919; Philip W. Barton, laborer and Viola Weymouth

BARTON, Virginia Mae 9 May 1924 female 4th; Philip Barton, farmer and Viola M. Weymouth

BEASLEY, male 3rd 11 June 1917; Percy E. Beasley, laborer and Margaret T. VanIderstine

BECK, Henry Walter Jr. 5 Jan 1930 male 1st; Henry W. Beck, physician and Annie Mae Scrutton

BEEDE, female 4th 31 Mar 1905; William W. Beede, lumberman and Esther M. Tatis

BENNETT, Laura Charlotte 24 Mar 1920 female 1st; James E. Bennett Jr., laborer and Alice M. Smith

BENSON, George Elbrige 8 July 1851 son of George W. and Elizabeth A. Benson

BENSON, Jabez Woodman 22 Mar. 1853 son of George W. and Elizabeth A. Benson

BENSON, John Albert 13 Mar. 1855 son of George W. and Elizabeth A. Benson

BENSON, Charles Edwin 18 Dec. 1857 son of George W. and Elizabeth A. Benson

BENSON, Melvin Haskell 4 July 1860 son of George W. and Elizabeth A. Benson

BENSON, Margaret Benson 5 Feb 1878

BERRY, stillborn 7 Jan 1900 female 4th; George Berry, laborer and Lizzie May

BERRY, twin boys 12 Feb 1902 male 5th & 6th; Geo. W. Berry, laborer and Emma E. Berry

BERRY, female 1st 19 July 1904; George F. Berry, laborer and Georgie Carpenter

BERRY, Florence H. 19 Nov 1905 female 2nd; George F. Berry Jr., laborer and Georgie Carpenter

BERRY, female 1st 23 Oct 1906; Ralph Berry laborer and Emma L. Thompson

BERRY, Richard Chase 7 July 1929 male 1st; Chas. Everett Berry, service-salesman and Doris E. Chase

BISBEE, Eleanor Miriam 15 Oct 1922 female 2nd; F. Wilbert Bisbee, farmer and Eleanor Stover

BISHOP, Julia Hunt 15 Sept 1898 female 3rd; Stanley Bishop, farmer and Martha A. Carpenter

BISHOP, Mildred E. 18 Oct 1914 female 4th; Henry F. Bishop, fisherman and Edith N. Poor

BLACK, Charlotte Ledora 5 May 1895 female 4th; Wallace Black, laborer and Ada M. Skillin

BLACK, Lizzie 17 May 1898 female 2nd; George F. Black, laborer and Alice J. Brown

BLAKE, Gertie Blake 1878

BOELILKE, male 6th 12 Sept 1912; Paul H. Boelilke, farmer and Alice MacKinnon

BRACKETT, stillborn 17 Sept 1896 female 3rd; Charles Brackett, farmer and Hattie Edwards

BRACKETT, male 4th 14 Feb 1898; Charles Brackett, farmer and Hattie D. Edwards

BRACKETT, female 1st 23 Oct 1907; George T. Brackett, lumberman and Bessie M. Sawyer

BRACKETT, female 2nd 18 Feb 1913; George T. Brackett, laborer and Bessie M. Sawyer

BRAGDON, Adeline 31 May 1910 female 1st; Gilbert Bragdon laborer and Rosetta Verrill

BRAGDON, Benjamin Sherman 3 July 1914 male 2nd; Gilbert S. Bragdon, laborer and Rosetta Verrill

BRAGDON, female 3rd 27 Jan 1917; Gilbert S. Bragdon, laborer and Rosetta Verrill

BRAGG, Edward Ernest Jr. 14 Aug 1921 male 1st; Edward E. Bragg, auto mechanic and Lauris P. Snow

BRETTON, male 1st 8 Apr 1913; Alfred J. Bretton, laborer and Louise S. Lopeman

BRETTON, male 2nd 1 Feb 1915; Alfred J. Bretton, laborer and Sarah L. Lopeman

BROOKS, Allyn V. 22 Aug 1899 male 1st; J. Nelson Brooks, farmer and Ida Bliss

BROUGH, Joseph Emery 29 Oct 1920 male 4th; Vernon Brough, steam engineer and Mary C. Carr

BROWN, Clara Brown 9 Nov 1878

BROWN, stillborn 31 July 1897 female 6th; William H. Brown, laborer and Louisa Meyers

BROWN, female 7th 5 July 1902; William H. Brown, laborer and Louisa S. Maier

BROWN, Daniel 27 Oct 1911 male 2nd; William H. Brown, laborer and Bertha C. Sawyer

BROWN, stillborn 30 Oct 1916 female 1st; Frank J. Brown, lineman and Laura E. Randolph

BURGESS, male 5th 13 Feb 1906; Harry L. Burgess, laborer and Sarah M. Ward

BURNELL, Everett M. 13 Dec 1903 male 1st; William E. Burnell, blacksmith and Mary Charlotte Morse

BURNELL, male 2nd 22 Dec 1904; William E. Burnell, laborer and Lottie M. Morse

BURNELL, male 4th 11 May 1909; William E. Burnell, farmer and Charlotte M. Morse

BURNELL, Annie Elizabeth 19 Feb 1911 female 5th; William E. Burnell and Lettie Morse

BURNELL, male 6th 2 Aug 1912; William E. Burnell, farmer and Mary C. Morse

BURNELL, Alice A. 20 Apr. 1914 female 7th; William E. Burnell, laborer and Mary C. Morse

BURNHAM, male 2nd 22 Oct 1920; Harrison G. Burnham, laborer and Mary S. Chadbourn

BURNS, Bessie M. Burns 18 Feb 1890

BURNS, female 2nd 29 Nov 1892; Maurice P. Burns, laborer and Nellie G. Thompson

BURNS, Clifford M. 23 Jan 1895 male 3rd; Maurice P. Burns, laborer and Nellie G. Thompson

BURNS, Gladys Helen 16 Apr 1897 female 4th; Maurice P. Burns, laborer and Nellie G. Thompson

BURNS, Clifton W. 7 Sept 1899 male 4th; Maurice Burns, laborer and Nellie Thompson

BURNS, Kenneth H. 30 Mar 1905 male 6th; Maurice P. Burns, laborer and Nellie G. Thompson

CAMPBELL, male 1st 22 Feb 1900; Lindsay Cambell, farmer and Georgia Foster

CAMPBELL, male 1st 4 May 1902; John A. Campbell, farmer and Mary L. Osborne

CAMPBELL, Charles 19 July 1903 male 2nd; John A. Campbell, farmer and Mary E. Osborne

CAMPBELL, John J. 24 Apr 1906 male 3rd; John Campbell, farmer and Mary E. Osborn

CAMPBELL, Carolyn M. 24 Mar 1907 female 4th; John A. Campbell, farmer and Mary E. Osborn

CAMPBELL, female 5th 4 Dec 1908; John A. Campbell, farmer and Mary E. Osborn

CASTALL, Margie 2 Apr 1899 female 2nd; Bert Castall, laborer and Lillian Cummings

CASWELL, Willard 2 Oct 1910 male 1st; Claude E. Caswell, laborer and Alice M. Coffin

CASWELL, male 2nd 10 May 1913; Claude E. Caswell, carpenter and Alice M. Coffin

CASWELL, Hortense Asenath 2 Feb 1916 female 3rd Claude E. Caswell, carpenter and Alice M. Coffin

CASWELL, female 4th 25 Nov 1917; Claude E. Caswell, carpenter and Alice M. Coffin

CHILDS, Harold Lawrence 1 May 1898 male 1st; Herman Childs, clergyman and Dora Whittmore

CHIPMAN, Iva 4 Oct 1899 female 6th; William Chipman, farmer and Ella Shackford

CHIPMAN, Louise 12 Sept 1909 female 1st; Ernest F. Chipman, expressman and Della M. Haskell

CHIPMAN, Russell Shackford 26 Apr 1913 male 2nd; Ernest F. Chipman, farmer and Della M. Haskell

CHIPMAN, Eleanor Frances 6 Nov 1915 female 3rd; Ernest F. Chipman, farmer and Della M. Haskell

6

CHUTE, Richard 23 Aug 1922 male 4th; Lyman Chute, millman and Mary Dodge

CHUTE, Robert Erlon 14 July 1925 male 1st; Robert D. Chute, laborer and Jennie E. Foster

CILLEY, Bertha May 9 Dec 1921 female 1st; Bernard S. Cilley, laborer and Katherine C. Maxwell

CLARK, Jane Libby 18 Mar. 1855 dau. of Jacob and Lucetta Clark

CLARK, Harriett Humphrey 24 Nov. 1856 dau. of Jacob and Lucetta Clark

CLARK, Charles Jacob 27 Oct. 1858 son of Jacob and Lucetta Clark

CLARK, William Harris 31 Dec 1859 son of Jacob and Lucetta Clark

CLARK, Frank Laurence 2 July 1860 son of Jacob and Lucetta Clark

CLARK, Geneva 23 June 1894 female 2nd; Frank L. Clark, merchant and Artie E. Libby

CLIFFORD, female 1st 2 Nov 1920; John E. Clifford, electrician and Olive C. Thompson

COBB, Imogene 11 Sept. 1897 female 1st; Dwinal Cobb, laborer and Frederica Maiers

COBB, Marshie Mildred 12 July 1898 female 3rd; Marshall C. Cobb, farmer and Rosa Tripp

COBB, Bernise 19 Apr 1899 female 3rd; Dwinal Cobb, laborer and Fredrika Maier

COBB, stillborn 12 July 1899 female 4th; Marshall Cobb, laborer and Rosabelle Tripp

COBB, stillborn 24 Mar 1902 male 1st; Marshall Cobb, laborer and Jennie Small

COBB, female 2nd 1 June 1903; William A. Cobb, conductor and Mabel Knight

COBB, female 1st 7 May 1904; Marshall C. Cobb, farmer R. Small

COBB, Catherine A. 1 June 1906 female 1st; Albert D. Cobb, farmer and Edith M. Allen

COBB, Enoch Chipman 12 Mar 1907 male 5th; Marshall Cobb, laborer and Jennie R. Small

COBB, male 2nd 6 Mar 1909; Albert F. Cobb, farmer and Edith M Allen

COBB, Winnifred 8 Apr 1911 female 3rd; Albert F. Cobb, farmer and Edith M. Allen

COBB, Arline P. 28 Apr 1914 female 5th; Aaron D. Cobb, laborer and Frederica Maier

COBB, Glendon H. 25 Dec 1916 male 2nd; Stuart Cobb, farmer and Besse Libby

COBB, Clyde Stuart 7 Mar 1920 male 3rd; Stuart S. Cobb, laborer and Bessie L. Libby

COBB, Myrna Frances 27 Jan 1924 female 4th; Stuart S. Cobb, carpenter and Bessie L. Libby

COBB, Pauline Vera 30 Dec 1927 female 1st; Aaron D. Cobb, vendor and Vera C. Crawford

COFFIN, female 6th 21 Mar 1913; Silas A. Coffin, farmer and Selina Pierce

COFFIN, female 2nd 10 Mar 1898; Charles W. Coffin and Ruth Herrick

COLE, Ellen Frances 21 Mar 1907 female 1st; Hewett D. Cole, farmer and Jennie Cummings

COLE, Leonard C. 14 Apr 1908 male 2nd; Hewitt D. Cole, farmer and Jennie H. Cummings

COLE, male 3rd 8 May 1910; Hewitt D. Cole, farmer and Jennie H. Cummings

COLE, Warren S. 30 Jan 1917 male 4th; Hewitt D. Cole, farmer and Jennie Cummings

COLE, Merilyn Imogene 10 Dec 1926 female 5th; Hewett D. Cole, farmer and Jennie Cummings

COLLEY, Victoria 2 Mar 1866

COLLEY, Reina 28 Apr 1894 female 2nd; Charles W. Colley, farmer and Susie H. Edwards

COLLEY, male 3rd 5 Feb 1898; James H. Colley, farmer and Addie M. Ellis

COLLEY, Clifford 21 June 1903 male 2nd; Sturgis V. Colley, horse dealer and Dora L. Brown

COLLEY, Maynard 26 July 1905 male 3rd; Sturgis V. Colley, stable keeper and Dora L. Brown

COLLEY, male 1st 10 Feb 1920; True M. Colley, laborer and Thirza M. Huntress

COLLEY, James Alfred 13 Mar 1921 male 2nd; Harold O. Colley, fireman and Elizabeth M. Michaud

COLLEY, Helen Frances 22 Dec 1921 female 1st; True M. Colley farmer and Thirza M. Huntress

COLLEY, Dorothy 19 Sept 1925 female 3rd; True M. Colley, Hwy patrolman and Thirza Huntress

CONLEY, female 3rd 26 Apr 1896; Neil Conley, laborer and Gertie Witham

CONLEY, female 4th 6 Jan 1900; Neal Conley, laborer and Gertrude Witham

CONLEY, female 1st 11 Jan 1916; Fred W. Conley, laborer and Alice M. Searles

COOMBS, Charles James 19 Jan 1926 male 4th; Frank M. Coombs supt. of schools and Edith Hennessey

COOPER, Dorothy F. 5 May 1914 female 1st; John Cooper, clerk and Annie Traine

CORSEN, stillborn 18 Oct 1896 male 1st; Louville H. Corsen, farmer and Alice E. Ryder

COTE, Adelaide Florence 18 June 1912 female 1st Omer L. Cote, laborer and Mary L. Gimbault

COTE, Omer Nulbran 30 July 1913 male 2nd; Omer L. Cote, millman and Mary L. Guilbault

COTE, male 1st 3 Mar 1917; Raymond M. Cote, mill fireman and Mertie D. Libby

COTE, female 2nd 31 May 1918; Raymond M. Cote, laborer and Mertie D. Libby

COTTON, 2 June 1926 female 1st; Albert M. Cotton, mail truck and Eleanor F. Witham

COUSINS, Sanford B. 1 Oct 1898 male 6th; Edgar M. Cousins, clergyman and Ella M. Burnham

CROOKER, male 1st 9 Dec 1910; Joseph E. Crooker, attendant and Mary E. Thompson

CROSS, Elsie F. 18 Oct 1886 to W. B. and Isabelle Cross

CROSS, Helen J. 27 Feb 1891 to W. B. and Isabelle Cross

CROSS, Guy A. 5 Dec 1892 male 6th; Wm. B. S. Cross, farmer and Isabelle F, Libby

CUMMINGS, Franklin L. 5 Sept. 1838, son of Leonard F. and Hannah S. Cummings

CUMMINGS, Eliza H. 7 Mar. 1840, dau. of Leonard F. and Hannah S. Cummings

CUMMINGS, Samuel M. 16 Mar. 1842, son of Leonard F. and Hannah S. Cummings

CUMMINGS, Susan M. 21 Jan. 1844, dau. of Leonard F. and Hannah S. Cummings

CUMMINGS, Abbie F. 29 Dec. 1845, dau. of Leonard F. and Hannah S. Cummings

CUMMINGS, Alroy V. 21 Nov. 1848 son of Leonard F. and Hannah S. Cummings

CUMMINGS, Mary E. 10 Nov. 1850 dau of Leonard F. and Hannah S. Cummings

CUMMINGS, Frederick A. 23 Mar. 1853 son of Leonard F. and Hannah S. Cummings

CUMMINGS, Jennie 2 Nov 1887 to S. M. and Gene Cummings

CUMMINGS, Charles Cummings 20 June 1878

CUMMINGS, Irving Ellsworth 30 Oct 1916 male 1st; John E. Cummings, railroader and Nellie J. Grant

CUMMINGS, male 2nd 14 Apr 1920; John E. Cummings, R R employee and Nellie J. Grant

CUMMINGS, Milo Gay Jr. 17 Dec 1925 male 1st; Milo G. Cummings, carpenter and Lucy Merrill

CUSHING, Merrill Henderson 2 Mar 1900 male 1st; Lewis Cushing, dentist and Emma Merrill

CUSHING, Frances Louise 13 June 1902 female 2nd; Lewis Cushing, dentist and Emma M. Merrill

CUSHING, Aubigne 5 Dec 1909 female 3rd; Louis T. Cushing, dentist and Emma Merrill

DAVIS, Edith May 13 June 1907 female 1st; Elmer W. Davis, laborer and Caroline D. Leighton

DAVIS, female 2nd 20 May 1908; Elmer W. Davis, laborer and Caroline D. Leighton

DAVIS, George William 1 Nov 1916 male 4th; George F. Davis, section foreman and Margaret M. Watson

DAVIS, Jerald Laforest Pike 21 Nov 1918 male 1st; Franklin Davis, R R foreman and Eliza C. Pike

DAVIS, Norman James 17 Feb 1923 male 3rd; George F. Davis, R R track crew and Charlotte E. Pike

DAVIS, Harold Linwood 25 May 1925 male 4th; Geo. F. Davis, elec. R R master and Charlotte E. Pike

DAVIS, Earl Glendon 8 June 1928 male 5th; Geo. F. Davis, road master and Charlotte E. Pike

DENNISON, male 2nd 11 Mar 1921; Wm. V. Dennison, salesman and Julia W. Haskell

DIXON, James Everett 17 Feb 1930 male 1st; Everett N. Dixon, lineman and Mabel H. Tingley

DOLLEY, Frank E. Dolley 1 Feb 1877

DOLLEY, Zylphia Susie 13 Sept 1899 female 1st; Frank Dolley, laborer and Mertie Benson

DOLLOFF, Dorothy 14 Oct 1909 female 1st; Harry A. Dolloff, farmer and Lois B. Libby

DOLLOFF, Norman L. 3 Nov 1912 male 2nd; Harry A. Dolloff, farmer and Lois B. Libby

DOLLOFF, Maynard Curtis 12 Sept 1913 male 3rd; Harry A. Dolloff, farmer and Lois B. Libby

DOLLOFF, Abby Jeanette 15 Oct 1914 female 4th; Harry A. Dolloff, farmer and Lois B. Libby

DOLLOFF, Robert E. 22 July 1916 male 5th; Harry A. Dolloff, farmer and Lois B. Libby

DOUGHTY, Annie B. Doughty 4 July 1886

DOUGHTY, Warren Percival 14 Aug 1879 son of Charles H. and Carrie E. Doughty

DOUGHTY, Amy Gertrude 17 Aug 1885 dau of Charles H. and Carrie E. doughty

DOUGHTY, Grace Wilma 19 July 1888 dau of Charles H. and Carrie E. Doughty

DOUGHTY, Margurite Louise 10 Feb 1895 male 4th; Henry P. Doughty, farmer and Olive Strout

DOUGHTY, Carroll 18 Dec 1896 male 5th; Henry P. Doughty, farmer and Olive Strout

DOUGHTY, John Tappen 30 Dec 1898 male 1st; Henry C. Doughty, merchant and Jennie Merrill

DOUGHTY, Kathleen 21 June 1906 female 1st; Warren P. Doughty, stenographer and Elizabeth M. Perry

DOUGHTY, female 2nd 14 Oct 1907; Warren P. Doughty, clerk and Elizabeth M. Perry

DOUGHTY, Alice Constance 9 June 1912 female 4th; William E. Doughty, electrician and Ina E. Barbour

DOUGHTY, Olive Caroline 5 Feb 1914 female 1st; Carroll
Doughty, farmer and Lena Small
DOUGHTY, Edison A. 26 Sept 1915 male 5th; William E.
Doughty, laborer and Ina E. Barbour
DOUGHTY, Everett Wellington 31 July 1922 male 1st; Carroll
Doughty, laborer and Dorothy Sawyer
DOUGHTY, Bernard C. 20 Apr 1925 male 2nd; Carroll Doughty
R R trackman and Dorothy L. Sawyer
DOUGHTY, Janice Irene 24 Apr 1926 female 3rd; Carroll
Doughty, trackman and Dorothy L. Sawyer
DOUGHTY, Leonard Wayne 28 Mar 1928 male 4th; Carroll
Doughty, laborer and Dorothy L. Sawyer
DOUGLAS, Herbert Sydney 27 Aug 1928 male 1st; Wm. S.
Douglas, farmer and Marion L. Pollard
DOUGLASS, Elizabeth Emily 17 Feb 1903 female 1st; Frank N.
Douglass, lumber mfr. and Josephie E. Flint
DOUGLASS, William Sydney 7 May 1904 male 2nd; Frank N.
Douglass, millman and Josephine E. Flint
DOUGLASS, Louise Josephina 9 Jan 1907 female 3rd; Frank N.
Douglass, lumberman and Josephine E. Flint
DOUGLASS, Ethel Mabel 9 May 1909 female 4th; Frank N.
Douglass, lumberman and Josephine E. Flint
DOW, Philip H. 23 Aug 1892 male 2nd; William H. Dow, farmer
and Clara W. Pennell
DUNLAP, Malcom Orville 21 Sept 1924 male 2nd; Elmer E.
Dunlap, R R section foreman and Lucy L. Small
DUNN, Alfred W. 2 Jan 1898 male 2nd; Walter C. Dunn, farmer
and Elizabeth F. Whitney
DUNN, Mary Clay 1 Mar 1900 female 3rd; Walter Dunn, farmer
and Lizzie Whitney
DUNN, Walter Frederick 29 July 1911 male 1st; Moses T. Dunn,
plumber and Ellen F. Libby
DUNN, Hazel Matilda 18 Aug 1924 female 1st; Clifford K. Dunn,
soldier and Hazel L. Whitney
DUNN, Thomas Clifford 12 June 1926 male 2nd; Clifford Dunn,
laborer and Hazel Whitney
DUPLISEA, William A. 18 May 1921 male 1st; Arthur F.
Duplisea, dental mechanic and Margaret B. Dunbarm

DWYER, Mona Adele 13 Nov 1893 female 1st; Roscoe J. Dwyer, laborer and Annie A. Libby

DWYER, Alice Augusta 1 Mar 1897 female 2nd; Roscoe J. Dwyer, boxmaker and Annie A. Libby

DYER, Angie Lena 26 Dec 1900 female 5th; Frank Dyer, sawmill helper and Abbie Etta Record

EAGLES, male 1st 4 Jan 1907; W. W. Eagles, laborer and Ella L. Maier

EATON, Jane 2 June 1924 female 3rd; Carlton W. Eaton, forester and Mary Haskell

EDWARDS, female 9th 24 Dec 1892; William Edwards Jr., farmer and Estella Thurlow

EDWARDS, female 10th 29 Apr 1895; William Edwards, farmer and Estella Thurlow

EDWARDS, Inez Lila 10 Apr 1898 female 11th; William Edwards, farmer and Estella Thurlow

EDWARDS, Clarence Willis 6 June 1899 male 1st; Charles Edwards, farmer and Blanche Edwards

EDWARDS, Lester Purington 26 Sept 1900 male 2nd; Luther Edwards, farmer and Bertha Whitney

EDWARDS, female 2nd 12 Aug 1903; Charles Edwards, musician and Jennie M. Smith

ELLINWOOD, George Albert Jr. 29 Jan 1898 male 1st; George A. Ellinwood, physician and Helen M. Isham

ELLINWOOD, Everitt Eugene 28 Sept 1909; Geo. A. Ellinwood, physician & surgeon and Josephine D. Morrill

ELLINWOOD, Esther Irene 27 Mar 1921 female 1st; George A. Ellinwood Jr., laborer and Gertrude Luckings

ELLINWOOD, Helen Maude 1 Dec 1923 female 2nd; George A. Ellinwood, laborer and Gertrude Luckings

ELLINWOOD, stillborn 23 June 1929 female 1st; Geo. A. Ellinwood, laborer and Iva Webb

ELLIS, Maurice P. 21 Feb 1919 male 3rd; Dale M. Ellis, laborer and Grace L. Powell

ELLIS, Ashley Eugene 23 Dec 1921 male 4th; Dale M. Ellis, farmer and Grace L. Powell

EMERY, Geo. W. B. Emery 21 Apr 1886

EMERY, Florence Lorraine 5 Sept 1909 female 2nd; George W. Emery, farmer and Carrie B. Hall

EVANS, male 3rd 17 July 1913; Elmer E. Evans, laborer and Geneva E. Varney

EVELETH, ? June 1878

FARWELL, John B. Sept. 1843, son of Henry Farwell

FARWELL, Mary Jane May 1845, dau. of Henry Farwell

FARWELL, William Elbine 19 Apr. 1847, son of Henry Farwell

FARWELL, Anna A. 14 June 1851 dau. of Henry Farwell

FARWELL, Lizzie Farwell 15 June 1887

FARWELL, Martha Elizabeth 20 June 1887 to Edward L. and Emma Jane Farwell

FARWELL, female 4th 8 Feb 1901; Wm. E. Farwell, laborer and Mary A. Morey

FERGUSON, Dorothy Louise 14 Oct 1923 female 3rd; Harry Ferguson, motorman and Anna Von Deck

FIELD, male 2nd 23 July 1892; Fred l. Field, farmer and Maggie M. Sarbell

FIELD, ? Aug 1878

FIELD, Walter Leone 19 Nov 1893 male 3rd; Fred L. Field, farmer and Maggie R. Sarbell

FIELD, male 4th 22 May 1896; Fred L. Field, farmer and Maggie M. Sarbell

FIELD, Arthur E. 21 June 1897 male 1st; Ulysses G. Field, laborer and Addie E. Farwell

FIELD, Elsie Etta 27 Dec 1899 female 10th; Elias H. Field, laborer and Ella Morey

FIELD, Mary Caroline 5 Feb 1908 female 2nd; Edwin L. Field Jr., merchant and Susan M. Strout

FIELD, female 2nd 27 Apr 1914; Edward E. Field, laborer and Mary Ruth Webber

FIELD, Frances Isabel female 1st; Walter L. Field, auto mechanic and Isabel M. Coull

FIELD, Raymond Coull 29 June 1923 male 2nd; Walter L. Field, auto mechanic and Isabell M. Coull

FIELD, Geo. F. 11 Jan 1926 male 3rd; Walter L. Field, mechanic and Isabell M. Coull

FIELD, Phyllis May 17 May 1927 female 4th, Walter L. Field, garage owner and Isabel M. Coull

FIELD, Addie Elizabeth 4 May 1930 female 2nd; Artuhr E. Field, farmer and Ada E. Edwards

FOGG, Amanda 29 July 1865

FOGG, Edith E. 14 Mar 1889 to Frank and Margie Fogg

FOGG, Leroy 20 Apr 1894 male 5th; C. Frank Fogg, farmer and Margie E. Knowlton

FOGG, female 6th 23 Aug 1898; Charles Franklin Fogg, farmer and Margie E. Knowlton

FORTUNE, female 4th 12 Sept 1893; William Fortune, laborer and Hattie Boynton

FOSTER, Effie G. 1 Apr 1886 to Arthur and Nellie Foster

FOSTER, Effie 19 Apr to E. P. and Clara H. Foster

FOSTER, Annie J. 1 Dec 1887 to S. G. and Carrie Foster

FOSTER, Mildred 7 Aug 1888 to H. C. and Annie M. Foster

FOSTER, Bennie S. 8 Apr 1890 to S. G. and Carrie Foster

FOSTER, Bertha L. 29 Dec 1890 to Arthur and Nellie Foster

FOSTER, Carrie M Foster 18 Sept 1876

FOSTER, ? Oct 1878

FOSTER, male 3rd 24 Apr 1896; S. Granville Foster, farmer and Carrie J. Davis

FOSTER, female 1st 25 Dec 1903; Perley W. Foster, farmer and Nettie W. Small

FOSTER, female 1st 20 Feb 1910; Eugene Foster, merchant and Minnie E. Bohnson

FOSTER, Carroll Wescott 11 July 1910 male 2nd; Perley W. Foster, carpenter and Nettie W. Small

FOSTER, Silas Donald 13 July 1917 male 2nd; Eugene Foster, merchant and Minnie E. Bohnson

FOSTER, Edgar Jr. 4 Oct 1924 male 1st; Edgar Foster, farmer and Gladys Morrill

FRANK, Irvin E. 10 July 1889 to Orin and Eldora Frank

FRANK, Milton E. 26 Jan 1891 to Orin and Eldora Frank

FRANK, male 4th 7 May 1893; Orin L. Frank, butcher and Eldora Sawyer

FRANK, female 4th 8 May 1893; Vinton E. Frank, merchant and Jennie W. Hall

FRANK, Helen A. 31 Aug 1894 female 5th; Vinton E. Frank, merchant and Jennie W. Hall

FRANK, Lila M. 14 Nov 1895 female 7th; Orrin I. Frank, laborer
and Eldora Sawyer

FRANK, Mary Elizabeth 16 Mar 1898 female 1st; Augustas Frank,
laborer and Rosanna Hoye

FRANK, Annie W. 1 June 1905 female 1st; Hersey A. Frank,
farmer and Lizzie F. Cobb

FRANK, Orrin C. 6 Mar 1907 male 1st; Irving E. Frank, clerk and
Mildred S. Bailey

FRANK, John True 15 Feb 1909 male 3rd; Percy A. Frank, mill
man and Annette C. Merrill

FRANK, female 1st 27 Oct 1912; Percy A. Frank, clerk and
Elizabeth A. Tripp

FRANK, Ernest 10 Sept 1913 male 1st; Milton E. Frank, laborer
and Imogene M. Cobb

FREEMAN, James 26 Nov. 1888 son of James and Sarah
McGowan

FROST, Charles S. Jr. 27 June 1921 male 2nd; Charles S. Frost,
carpenter and Ada E. Sykes

FROST, Shirley May 16 Dec 1922 female 3rd; Charles S. Frost,
laborer and Ada E. Sykes

GERRY, Clyde B. 13 Sept 1894 male 1st; Harrison S. Gerry,
laborer and Sarah J. Searle

GILMAN, male 1st 23 Jan 1893; Lewis E. Gilman, carriage smith
and Mabel H. Cobb

GOFF, Jennie Goff 20 June1878

GOFF, Myra G. 9 Nov 1894 female 1st; Herbert Goff, laborer and
Sybil A. Quint

GOFF, Linwood E. 29 May 1895 male 1st; Melvin Goff, millman
and Ellionah J. Libby

GOFF, male 5th 28 Oct 1896; Frank E. Goff, blacksmith and Sarah
E. Hall

GOFF, Russell F. 22 Oct 1900 male 3rd Herbert L. Goff, laborer
and Sibyl A. Quint

GOFF, Alta Thayer 6 Feb 1927 female 1st; Willis W. Goff,
carpenter and Ruth P. Thayer

GOLDEN, Walter Henry 19 Oct 1924 male 2nd; Walter S. Golden,
laborer and Minnie Sanborn

GOLDEN, Clarence Herbert 16 Jan 1929 male 5th; Walter S. Golden, laborer and Minnie M. Sanborn

GOLDING, Lucy Kate 27 Oct 1921 female 1st; Walter S. Golding, laborer and Minnie M. Sanborn

GOLDING, Irving Scott 17 Apr 1927 male 3rd; Walter H. Golding, laborer and Minnie Sanborn

GOLDING, Nora Adeline 17 Apr 1927 female 4th; Walter H. Golding, laborer and Minnie Sanborn

GOODRICH, female 2nd 10 Nov 1913; Marcellus E. Goodrich, farmer and Hazel Owen

GOODRICH, female 3rd 23 Apr 1916; Marcellus Goodrich, farmer and Hazel Owens

GRANT, Margaret Leota 16 Sept 1925 female 1st; Sheldon S. Grant, carpenter and Winona M. Davis

GREEN, Shirley Lorraine 1 Jan 1924 female 2nd; Carroll Green, auto mechanic and Mary L. Smith

GROVER, Frank C. Grover 19 Aug 1889

GROVER, male 3rd 25 Sept 1909; David Lawrence Grover, laborer and Eva J. Libby

GROVER, stillborn 8 Mar 1911 twins female 1st & 2nd; Frank C. Grover, laborer and Bessie Crouse

GROVER, female 3rd 4 Oct 1912; Frank Grover, laborer and Bessie Crouse

GROVER, male 4th 31 July; Frank C. Grover, laborer and Bessie Crouse

HALL, Abbie S. 16 Feb 1869 dau of William T. and Julia Hall

HALL, Lizzie 6 July 1875 dau of William T. and Julia A. Hall

HALL, Carrie E. 26 Jan 1877 dau of William T. and Julia Hall

HALL, Joseph W. 6 Feb 1880 son of William T. and Julia A. Hall

HALL, Mary Susan 14 May 1886 dau of Cushman and Caroline H. Hall

HALL, Merton Scott 28 Dec 1894 male 2nd; Lester D. Hall, farmer and Bertha Morrill

HALL, Everard Eugene 30 Oct 1903 male 1st; Irving E. Hall, druggist and Emily H. Kidder

HALL, male 1st 24 Oct 1904; Lester D. Hall, farmer and Lillian G. Cobb

HALL, Donald Field 15 Mar 1924 male 2nd; Merton S. Hall, laborer and Sarah E. Field

HALL, Arnold Merton 27 Aug 1926 male 3rd; Merton S. Hall, farmer and Sarah E. Field

HALL, female 2nd 10 Dec 1928; I. Lloyd Hall, plumber and Emma E. Webster

HALL, Clifton Emerson 17 May 1929 male 4th; Merton S. Hall, farmer and Sarah E. Field

HALL, Arthur Webster 3 Aug 1930 male 3rd; Irasen Lloyd Hall, plumber and Emma E. Webster

HANCOCK, Lillian Thurston 4 Sept 1904 female 1st; Wilbur P. Hancock, merchant and Elizabeth V. Plummer

HANCOCK, Dorothy Plummer 13 Oct 1906 female 2nd; Wilbur P. Hancock, merchant and Elizabeth N. Plummer

HANCOCK, Sidney Martin 13 Dec 1910 male 3rd; Wilbur P. Hancock, merchant and Elizabeth V. Plummer

HANCOCK, John Thomas 3 Nov 1912 male 4th; Wilbur P. Hancock, merchant and Elizabeth Plummer

HANCOCK, Phyllis May 19 Apr 1914 female 5th; Wilbur P. Hancock, merchant and Elizabeth V. Plummer

HANCOCK, Ronald W. 8 Mar 1916 male 6th; Wilbur P. Hancock, landlord and Elizabeth Plummer

HANCOCK, Willis Kittridge 23 Dec 1920 male; Wilbur P. Hancock, clerk and Josephine T. Davis

HANNA, Annie 9 July 1915 female 1st; George Hanna, laborer and Annie McLeod

HANNA, John Angus 18 May 1918 male 2nd; George Hanna, farmer and Annie McLeod

HANSON, Byron 15 Oct 1902 male 1st; Orville Hanson, farmer and Susie M. Stiles

HARMON, Arthur 9 May 1911 male 1st; Orland C. Harmon, painter and Esther B. Hall

HARMON, Chester M. 27 Aug 1913 male 2nd; Orland C. Harmon, laborer and Esther W. Hall

HARRIS, Archie M. Harris 24 July 1878

HASTY, stillborn 23 Dec 1909 male 1st; Ralph Hasty and Ina M. Small

HAWKES, Marion 17 July 1910 female 1st; George E. Hawkes, farmer and Effie May Foss

HAWKES, Owen M. 12 Nov 1913 male 2nd; George E. Hawkes, farmer and Effie May Foss

HAWKES, Geneva Graham 6 Oct 1920 female 1st; Albert O. Hawkes, farmer and Alice M. Graham

HAYES, Stanley Howard 25 Mar 1918 male 1st; Francis Edward Hayes, laborer and Clara Mildred Thompson

HAYES, Katherine Augusta 14 Oct 1928 female 1st; Chas. E. Hayes, merchant and Verna Campbell

HEAD, Marion Merill 31 Mar 1895 female 7th; Charles C. Head, laborer and Jennie Mann

HEAD, Ruth Mae 4 Nov 1896 female 8th; Charles C. Head, laborer and Jennie McMann

HEAD, Lawrence C. 10 May 1898 male 9th; Charles C. Head, laborer and Jennie McMann

HEAD, female 1st 2 Jan 1911; Frank M. Head, laborer and Clara J. Goff

HEAD, Frances 6 Jan 1913 female 2nd; Frank M. Head, laborer and Clara J. Goff

HEAD, Glenys Katherine 7 May 1915 female 3rd; Frank M. Head, laborer and Clara J. Goff

HERMAN, Alta Read 9 Feb 1923 female 4th; John L. Herman, electrical eng. and Mabel M. Read

HERMAN, Rita Mabel 1 Oct 1925 female 5th; John L. Herman, electrician and Mabel M. Read

HERRICK, Peter 11 Apr 1892, male 2nd; Greenleaf C. Herrick, laborer and Lillian M. Harley

HICKS, female 4th 12 Aug 1929; Clarence W. Hicks, farmer and Wilma I. Edwards

HIGGINS, Mary Etta 23 Jan 1908 female 1st; Fred S. Higgins, farmer and Alma D. Savoy

HIGGINS, Carolina Sara 5 Sept 1917 female 2nd; Everett E. Higgins, laborer and Carolina Swenson

HIGGINS, Arthur Percy 28 May 1919 male 3rd; Edward E. Higgins, laborer and Caroline Swenson

HIGGINS, Helen Doris 17 Sept 1921 female 3rd; Edward E. Higgins, laborer and Caroline S. Swenson

HIGGINS, George Everett 10 Sept 1923 male 4th; Edward E. Higgins, laborer and Caroline S. Swenson

HILDRETH, Mary M. Hildreth 1878

HILL, James Frank 19 Dec to Luther and Mabel Hill

HILL, George T. 7 Apr 1891 to Luther and Mabel Hill

HILL, female 3rd 10 Feb 1897; Luther W. Hill , merchant and Mabel F. Cobb

HILL, Gladys May 23 Aug 1902 female 1st; Wilbur F. Hill, provision dealer and Celinda T. Nevias

HILL, Harry Wilbur 23 Aug 1904 male 2nd; Wilbur F. Hill, beef dealer and Celinda T. Nevins

HILL, Mary Esther 11 Jan 1910 female 4th; Luther W. Hill, merchant and Mabel F. Cobb

HILL, male 4th 1 Oct 1916; Wilbur F. Hill, farmer and Celinda T. Nevins

HILL, male 5th 24 Nov 1918; Wilbur F. Hill, butcher and Celinda T. Nevins

HILL, Alice Mae 27 May 1925 female 1st; Arthur W. Hill, RFD carrier and Bernice M. Nash

HILL, Evelyn Louise 25 Feb 1909 female 3rd; Wilbur F. Hill, provision dealer and Celinda T. Nevins

HILTON, female 1st 14 Oct 1911; Percy L. Hilton, lumberman and Lottie E. Burker

HILTON, Edgar Montise 30 Dec 1912 male 2nd; Percy Hilton, laborer and Lottie Barker

HILTON, Leon D. 21 Apr 1914 male 3rd; Percy L. Hilton

HITCHCOCK, Arthur Leroy Jr. 8 Nov 1923 male 2nd; Arthur L. Hitchcock, carpenter and Alice M. Brown

HITCHCOCK, Leon Willard 13 Oct 1925 male 3rd; Arthur Hitchcock, carpenter and Alice M. Brown

HITCHCOCK, Olive Louisa 20 July 1929 female 4th; Arthur L. Hitchcock, carpenter and Alice M. Brown

HODGKINS, Martha H. 19 Dec 1865

HODGKINS, female 6th 12 Sept 1896; Elisha F. Hodgkins, laborer and Abbie Tripp

HODGKINS, Irving Everett 4 June 1899 male 6th; Elisha Hodgkins, laborer and Abbie M. Tripp

HODGKINS, Alphonso Gilbert 26 Apr 1901 male 3rd; William E. Hodgkins, laborer and Margaret A. Smith

HODGKINS, female 8th 22 Apr 1902; Elisha Hodgkins, laborer and Abbie Tripp

HODGKINS, George Gilbert 30 Apr 1902 male 2nd; Elisha
  Hodgkins Jr., laborer and Georgianna D. Tripp
HODGKINS, Amos B. 10 June 1902 male 1st; Joseph Edward
  Hodgkins, laborer and Annie S. Hodgkins
HODGKINS, female 1st 15 May 1904; Whitman Hodgkins, laborer
  and Florence B. Hodgkins
HODGKINS, Frank A. 18 Aug 1905 male 9th; Elisha E. Hodgkins,
  laborer and Abbie M. Tripp
HODGKINS, Herman Henry 23 Dec 1905 male 1st; Harlan E.
  Hodgkins, laborer and Ethel S. Benson
HODGKINS, male 2nd 11 Dec 1906; Harlan Hodgkins and Ethel
  Benson
HODGKINS, Helen Louise 30 May 1908 female 2nd; Harlan
  Hodgkins, lab. and Ethel Benson
HODSDON, Kenneth York 25 Feb 1925 male 1st; Jos. Y.
  Hodsdon, laborer and Elva K. Pollard
HOGUE, Rosebud Marie 28 Sept 1919 female 1st; Orin E. Hogue,
  laborer and Ora Needa Chaput
HOLLOWELL, Elmer Eugene 21 Oct 1898 male 2nd; Geo. H.
  Hollowell, machinist and Mary W. Osgoog
HORR, Edwin Lucius 7 June 1906 male 1st; Harry B. Horr, farmer
  and Ina Libby
HORR, female 2nd 16 Jan 1908; Harry B. Horr, farmer and Ina L.
  Libby
HUMPHREY, Susie H. Humphrey 29 Apr 1878
HUMPHREY, Howard 25 Oct 1905 male 1st; George G.
  Humphrey, millman and Xena E. Verrill
HUMPHREY, Arvilla Fern 12 Dec 1921 female 1st; Gerald R.
  Humphrey, station agent and Daisy Johnson
HUMPHREY, Geraldine R. 28 June 1924 female 1st; Gerald R.
  Humphrey, R R station agent and Harriet L. Russell
HUMPHREY, George Lawrence 18 Jan 1929 male 1st; Howard L.
  Humphrey, auto mechanic and Doris M. Roberts
HUNT, Henry 26 Dec 1865
HUNT, Edith L. Hunt 4 Sept 1886
HUNT, Helen Hunt 15 Mar 1888
HUNT, Arline Merrill 14 Dec 1894 female 4th; James H. Hunt,
  farmer and Julia E. Merrill
HUNT, Harry Mason 14 Aug 1896 male 1st; Henry L. Hunt, farmer
  and Blanche A. Smith

JASON, Leroy Arthur 11 Oct 1911 male 1st; Arthur A. Jason, expressman and Blanche M. Emery

JOHNSON, Emmogene 28 July 1865

JOHNSON, Guy William 4 Aug 1893 male 1st; James L. Johnson, fisherman and Clara P. Goff

JONES, female 8th 11 Feb 1892; Levi Jones, woodchopper and Rosalana Berry

JONES, Oliver Gilman 22 July 1906 male 4th; Charles Leslie Jones, laborer and Bertha Whitney

JONES, Robert 30 Jan 1930 male 6th; Geo. Almon Jones, laborer and Florence H. Berry

JORDAN, Melba Wells 11 Nov 1919 female 1st; Sumner W. Jordan, farmer and Dora E. Leach

JORDAN, Sumner W. Jr. 25 June 1921 male 2nd; Sumner W. Jordan, farmer and Dora E. Leach

JORDAN, Norma Phyllis 7 Apr 1923 female 2nd; Sumner W. Jordan, farmer and Dora E. Leach

KENT, Beverly Pauline 19 May 1924 female 1st; Edward W. Kent, fireman and Dorothy H. Hancock

KENT, Donald Hancock 18 Dec 1928 male 3rd; Edward W. Kent, mailman and Dorothy H. Hancock

KENT, male 2nd 16 Oct 1925; Edward W. Kent, fireman and Dorothy H. Hancock

KIMBALL, Gerald Martin 22 Jan 1920 male 1st; Ernest M. Kimball, laborer and Mildred E. Sawyer

KIMBALL, Gordon Lester 10 Aug 1929 male 2nd; Ernest M. Kimball, R R section hand and Mildred E. Sawyer

KING, Charles Wesley 11 Feb. 1854 son of Joseph and Hannah King

KING, Ann Maria 9 Mar. 1855 dau. of Joseph and Hannah King

KING, George Washington 1 May 1857 son of Joseph and Hannah King

KNIGHT, stillborn 21 Sept 1892 male 1st; Alley R. Knight, carriage dealer and Flora B. Doughty

KNIGHT, Eveline Knight 1878

KNIGHT, Sylvia 2 Feb 1900 female 1st; Frank Knight, farmer and Maria Allen

KNIGHT, Charles Elmer 24 June 1905 male 1st; Charles C. Knight and Martha J. Campbell

KNIGHT, Phyllis June 23 June 1929 female 1st; Chas. E. Knight, farmer and Dorothy H. Durgin

KNOX, female 1st 11 Aug 1899 ; Herman Knox, teacher and Lizzie Morrill

KNUDSEN, David Warren 5 Jan 1928 male 3rd; Albert Knudsen, farmer and Helen Warren

LACHANCE, William 25 Nov 1914 male 1st; Frank Lachance, farmer and Alice M. Caswell

LAMB, Derril Oden 9 Apr 1925 male 1st; Derril O. Lamb, electrician and Florence Brown

LAMB, William Dexter 16 Mar 1927 male 2nd; Derrill O. Lamb, electrician and Florence Brown

LAMONT, Louis 20 Aug 1918 male 1st; William C. Lamont, laborer and Sadie E. Sawyer

LANE, Laura H. Lane 1878

LARRABEE, Philip 15 Apr 1892 male 2nd; Geo. H. Larrabee, teacher and Grace D. Evans

LATHAM, Levi B. Latham 24 Dec 1876

LATHAM, Frederick W. 8 Mar 1894 male 1st; James W. Latham, laborer and Wilhemina B. Hillman

LATHAM, Harold Francis 22 Nov 1896 male 2nd; James W. Latham, laborer and Wilhemina B. Hillman

LATHAM, male 3rd 1 Feb 1899; James Latham, laborer and Wilhelmina Hillman

LATHAM, male 4th 11 July 1901; James W. Latham, laborer and Wilhelmina B. Hillman

LATHAM, Mildred Ruth 4 Jan 1907 female 5th; James Latham, laborer and Wilhelmina Hillman

LATHAM, Leslie Eugenia Dec 1910 male 6th; James Latham, laborer and Wilhelmina Hillman

LATHAM, female 7th 4 June 1920; James W. Latham, laborer and Wilhelmina Hillman

LAUGHTON, John M. 1 May 1914 male 2nd; Ralph R. Laughton, laborer and Annie K. Hanson

LAWRENCE, Alice Maud 12 Mar 1901 female 4th; Henry L. Lawrence, stone cutter and Ada F. Mountfort

LAWRENCE, Estelle Merrill 7 May 1920 female 1st; Perley W. Lawrence, mechanic and Helen H. Merrill

LAWRENCE, Arthur Freeman 6 Aug 1922 male 1st; Charles H. Lawrence Jr., laborer and Marguerite Doughty

LEACH, Jennie Merle 22 Mar 1893 female 1st; Bela E. Leach,
    carpenter and Cora E. Wells
LEACH, Victor Wells 21 Jan 1895 male 2nd; Bela E. Leach
    carpenter and Cora E. Wells
LEACH, Dora Eveleth 18 Apr 1896 female 3rd; Bela E. Leach,
    carpenter and Cora E. Wells
LEACH, female 4th 1 Oct 1899; Bela Leach, carpenter and Cora
    Wells
LEACH, female 5th 15 Feb 1903; Bela E. Leach, carpenter and
    Cora E. Wells
LEAVITT, Hilda Jane 20 July 1897 female 2nd; George A. Leavitt,
    millman and Abbie J. Barrows
LEAVITT, Raymond H. 1 July 1900 male 1st; Francis Leavitt,
    farmer and Mary Hancock
LEAVITT, Alice Lucille 24 Aug 1918 female 1st; Clarence W.
    Leavitt, teamster and Henrietta Pritham
LEAVITT, Earl Cushman 15 Apr 1920 male 2nd; Clarence W.
    Leavitt, farmer and Henrietta E. Pritham
LEAVITT, Sidney Clarence 22 July 1922 male 3rd; Clarence W.
    Leavitt, farmer and Etta C. Pritham
LEIGHTON, Emnos Albert 16 Apr 1892 male 3rd; Edw. C.
    Leighton, carpenter and Annie M. Dunn
LEIGHTON, Walter E. 3 Aug 1893 male 4th; Edward C. Leighton,
    mechanic and Annie M. Dunn
LEIGHTON, Marion Elizabeth 2 July 1895 female 5th; Edward C.
    Leighton, carpenter and Annie M. Dunn
LEIGHTON, stillborn 2 Feb 1898 male 1st; Walter F. Leighton,
    expressman and Flora A. Philbrook
LEIGHTON, female 2nd 120 Jan 1907; Charles E. Leighton,
    farmer and Gertrude M. Stimson
LEIGHTON, Edward Gardner stillborn 21 Dec 1920 male 1st;
    Walter E. Leighton, auto mechanic and Stella M. Leighton
LEONARD, Edward Rhodes 21 Nov 1918 male 3rd; Wilfred R.
    Leonard, R R inspector and Rena M. Lapiere
LEONARD, Ernistine Minerva 27 Aug 1928 female 1st; Ernest W.
    Leonard, lineman and Ruth L. Farnham
LEONARD, Wilfred Eugene 18 Apr 1930 male 2nd; Ernest
    Leonard, fireman and Ruth Farnham
LESLIE, Harold 12 Sept 1892 male 1st; Ralph A. Leslie, carriage
    maker and Leo E. Field

24

LEWIS, male 7th 13 Nov1925; Earl W. Lewis, laborer and Marion
    H. Callahan
LIBBY, Linwood F. 12 July 1888 to J. Parker and Jeannette Libby
LIBBY, stiilborn male 2nd Herbert C. Libby laborer and Fannie A.
    Thayer
LIBBY, Minnie B. Libby June 1878
LIBBY, male 5th 1 May 1893; James P. Libby, farmer and Jeanette
    F. Small
LIBBY, Philip H. 5 July 1896 male 1st; Albert A. Libby, musician
    and Jennie L. Pennell
LIBBY, female 6th 14 Feb 1899; James P. Libby, farmer and Nellie
    F. Small
LIBBY, Lottie Emeline 15 Mar 1899 female 1st; John M. Libby,
    laborer and Annie Barrows
LIBBY, Louise Freeman 5 June 1899 female 3rd; Albert Libby,
    musician and Jennie Pennell
LIBBY, Karl E. 3 Jan 1901 male 3rd; Herbert Libby, laborer and
    Fannie A. Thayer
LIBBY, Milton S. 3 Jan 1902 male 1st; Harry L. Libby, clerk and
    Marion S. Merrill
LIBBY, male 4th 1 Feb 1902; Albert A. Libby, musician and
    Jennie L. Pennell
LIBBY, female 5th 11 Mar 1903; Albert A. Libby, musician and
    Jennie L. Pennell
LIBBY, Everitt Elwell 14 Aug 1903 male 1st; Charles A. Libby,
    farmer and Edith G. Thompson
LIBBY, Harold Thomas 11 Sept 1903 male 1st; Wilbert T. Libby,
    farmer and Eliza A. Small
LIBBY, Alice Margaret 29 June 1905 female 2nd; Charles A.
    Libby, farmer and Edith G. Thompson
LIBBY, George Edward 1 Sept 1905 male 1st; Fred B. Libby,
    laborer and Lillian G. Nickerson
LIBBY, Hattie 8 Oct 1905 female 4th; Orrin W. Libby, laborer and
    Eva N. Varney
LIBBY, Donald W. 15 Nov 1905 male 2nd; Wilbert T. Libby,
    farmer and Eliza A. Small
LIBBY, male 2nd 25 Sept 1906; Fred B. Libby, laborer and Lillian
    Goldie Nickerson

LIBBY, female 5th 26 Oct 1906; Herbert C. Libby, carpenter and
    Fannie A. Thayer

LIBBY, female 3rd 14 Feb 1907; Charles A. Libby, mill hand and
    Edith G. Thompson

LIBBY, Merrill & Hettie 15 Mar 1907 male & female 2nd & 3rd;
    Harry L. Libby, clerk and Marion S. Merrill

LIBBY, Marguerite 26 June 1907 female 3rd; Wilbert T. Libby,
    farmer and Eliza A. Small

LIBBY, female 6th 8 July 1908; Orrin W. Libby, laborer and Eva
    N. Varney

LIBBY, female 3rd 7 Mar 1909; Fred B. Libby, laborer and Lillian
    G. Nickerson

LIBBY, female 4th 15 Dec 1909; Wilbert T. Libby, farmer and
    Eliza Small

LIBBY, stillborn 26 May 1910 female 2nd; Clarence A. Libby,
    farmer and Mabel A. Hunt

LIBBY, Arnold Emerson 27 Apr 1911 male 5th; Wilbert T. Libby,
    farmer and Eliza A. Small

LIBBY, Barbara 15 Nov 1911 female 3rd; Harry L. Libby, farmer
    and Marion S. Merrill

LIBBY, male 7th 14 Apr 1913; Orin Libby, laborer and Eva
    Varney

LIBBY, Ella May 2 Apr 1914 female 5th; Fred B. Libby, laborer
    and Lillian G. Nickerson

LIBBY, Stella May 2 Apr 1914 female 6th; Fred B. Libby, laborer
    and Lillian G. Nickerson

LIBBY, female 7th 2 Nov 1916; Fred B. Libby, laborer and Lillian
    G. Nickerson

LIBBY, male 1st 17 Sept 1917; Raymond Libby, laborer and Edith
    C. Clark

LIBBY, male 8th 27 Jan 1920; Fred B. Libby, laborer and Lillian
    Goldie Nickerson

LIBBY, Clarence Raymond 21 Apr 1923 male 9th; Fred B. Libby,
    laborer and Lillian G. Nickerson

LIBBY, Esther Gertrude 23 Dec 1923 female 2nd; Leroy Libby,
    elec. station oper. and Bessie Burns

LIBBY, Karl Endine Jr. 6 June 1927 male 1st; Karl E. Libby,
    service man and Laura Chosa

LIBBY, Shirley Theresa stillborn 18 Apr 1930 female 1st; Harry
    Libby, mechanic and Lottie E. Cates

LOUGEE, female 3rd 3 June 1908; Frank R. Lougee, farmer and Georgie B. Thompson

LOVELETT, Phillip Gordon 31 Dec 1919 male 1st; Herbert W. Lovelett, salesman and Rose G. Kane

LOW, Eugene H. Low June 1878

LOWE, Frances L. 1 Feb 1900 male 1st; Christopher Lowe, farmer and Blanche Meguire

LOWE, female 1st 3 Apr 1910; Eugene H. Lowe farmer and Ellen J. Humphrey

LOWE, female 2nd 27 Nov 1911; Eugene H. Lowe, farmer and Nellie J. Humphrey

LOWE, Eugene H. Jr. stillborn 21 Aug 1922 male 1st; Eugene H. Lowe, farmer and Wilma Adelle Snow

LOWE, female 2nd 16 May 1924; Eugene H. Lowe, farmer and Wilma A. Snow

LOWE, George True 22 Aug 1925 male 3rd; Eugene H. Lowe, postmaster and Adele Snow

LOWE, stillborn 15 Jan 1928 male; Eugene Lowe, postmaster and Adelle Snow

LUNT, Ruth 27 Apr 1892 female 3rd; Meschach H. Lunt, laborer and Lavina Carter

MacDONALD, male 2nd 9 Feb 1901; James MacDonald, laborer and Lettie E. Barrows

MAIER, George Augustas 27 Sept 1906 male 1st; Augustas W. Maier, laborer and Linda M. Goff

MANCHESTER, Warren C. 11 Dec 1914 male 2nd; Leon C. Manchester, clerk and Grace W. Doughty

MANCHESTER, female 3rd 3 Apr. 1919; Leon C. Manchester, clerk and Grace Doughty

MANCHESTER, George Bernard 10 Aug 1926 male 4th; Leon C. Manchester, merchant and Grace W. Doughty

MANCHESTER, Marilyn Annie 4 June 1928 female 1st; Charles Manchester, R R mail clerk and Annie W. Frank

MANNING, John Hugh 8 Oct 1905 male 1st; Chester B. Manning, evangelist and Florence I. Smith

MARR, Arthur J. 28 Jan 1876 son of Edward A. and Martha S. Marr

MARR, Stanwood H. 7 Aug 1878 son of Edward A. and Martha S. Marr

MARR, George Wolcott 28 July 1923 male 3rd; Thomas P. Marr, salesman and Wilma A. Morton

MARTIN, male 5th 20 Dec 1913; George H. Martin, laborer and Alice Smith

MASON, male 3rd 9 Apr 1897; Frederick A. Mason, laborer and Ellen R. Blake

MAXFIELD, male 1st 29 June 1900; Frank Maxfield, painter and Maud Brooks

MAXWELL, James Franklin 9 May 1920 male 1st; George W. Maxwell, laborer and Virginia W. Morrill

MAXWELL, Edna Allen 5 Feb 1923 female 2nd; Geo. W. Maxwell, laborer and Virginia W. Morrill

MAXWELL, Emily 23 Aug 1926 female 3rd; George Maxwell, motorman and Virgie Morrill

MAXWELL, Delmar Hortense stillborn 30 Dec 1928 female 4th; Geo. W. Maxwell, motorman and Virgie W. Morrill

MAXWELL, Beverly Louise 12 Feb 1930 female 5th; Geo. W. Maxwell, motorman and Virgie W. Morrill

MAY, male 13th 27 Apr 1892 Rufus May , laborer and Martha A. Tripp

MAY, George Albert Jr. 23 Nov 1900 male 1st; George A. May, laborer and Flora E. May

MAY, Maggie 9 Mar 1901 female 3rd; Melvin May, laborer and Maggie May

MAY, Nellie F. 10 Apr 1902 female 2nd; George A. May, laborer and Flora May

MAY, female 1st 10 Aug 1903; Edwin May, laborer and Lucy Tripp

MAY, Chester 13 Aug 1905 male 5th; Melvin May, laborer and Maggie Castello

MAY, female 3rd 19 June 1906; Geo. A. May, laborer and Flora May

MAY, Edwin Gilman 28 Feb 1907 male 2nd; Edwin G. May, laborer and Lucy A. Tripp

MAY, Marion 26 Jan 1911 female 6th; Edwin J. May, laborer and Lucy Tripp

MAY, male 4th 7 Jan 1909; Edwin May, laborer and Lucy Tripp

MAYBERRY, Elwood 22 Aug 1894 male 1st; Herbert Mayberry, laborer and Susan M. Tenney

MAYBERRY, Orland Henry 15 Mar 1898 male 2nd; Herbert J.
    Mayberry, laborer and Susie M. Tenney
MAYBERRY, Lena Alice 29 May 1899 female 7th; Fred
    Mayberry, laborer and Ida Stanford
McCOLLISTER, male 2nd 12 Dec 1900; James McCollister, lab.
    and Julia E. Tripp
McCONKEY, Clarence L. McConkey 1878
McCONKEY, stillborn 11 Feb 1893; Will Henry McConkey,
    farmer and Fanny Doughty Pennell
McCONKEY, Thirza 16 June 1899 female 1st; John R. McConkey,
    farmer and Bertha Tripp
McCONKEY, Mary 2 Jan 1901 female 2nd; John McConkey,
    farmer and Bertha Tripp
McCONKEY, stillborn 31 Dec 1902 female 3rd; John R.
    McConkey, farmer and Bertha Tripp
McCONKEY, male 4th 24 May 1904; John R. McConkey, farmer
    Bertha E. Tripp
McCONKEY, Milo 11 Aug 1906 male 5th; John R. McConkey,
    farmer and Bertha E. Tripp
McCONKEY, male 5th 12 Dec 1907; John R. McConkey, farmer
    and Bertha E. Tripp
McCONKEY, Jeanne Maria 12 Jan 1925 female 1st; Geo. D.
    McConkey, laborer and Leona Taylor
McDONALD, Joseph Charles 25 July 1895 male 3rd; George T.
    McDonald, farmer and Jennie M. Davis
McDONALD, Catherine Alice 7 July 1924 female 1st; Roy C.
    McDonald, farmer and Ella Wagg
McDONALD, Doris Helen 25 Jan 1928 female 2nd: Roy C.
    McDonald, farmer and Ella Wagg
McGLAUGHLIN, Mildre Elenora 1 Feb 1898 female 1st; Laughlin
    McGlaughlin, motorman and Lizzie A. sawyer
McGOWAN, James F. B. H. McGowan 28 Nov 1888
McINNIS, John Warren 17 June 1914 male 1st; Hector W.
    McInnis, laborer and Martha P. Skillings
McINNIS, James H. 6 May 1915 male 2nd; Hector W. McInnis,
    laborer and Martha Skillings
McINNIS, George 14 Mar 1916 male 3rd; Hector W. McInnis,
    laborer and Martha P. Skillings

McINNIS, William Eugene 16 July 1917 male 4th; Hector W.
McInnis, laborer and Martha P. Skillings

McINNIS, Virginia 6 June 1919 female 5th; Hector W. McInnis,
laborer and Martha Skillings

McINNIS, Hector Jr. 25 Aug 1920 male 6th; Hector W. McInnis,
laborer and Martha P. Skillings

McINNIS, Flora Louise 1 Apr 1923 female 7th; Hector W.
McInnis, laborer and Martha P. Skillings

McINNIS, Robert 12 Nov 1924 male 8th; Hector W. McInnis,
laborer and Martha P. Skillings

McINNIS, Clayton Francis 19 July 1926 male 9th; Hector W.
McInnis, laborer and Martha P. Skillings

McKEEN, Leslie Milton 31 July 1920 male 2nd; Eugene L.
McKeen, painter and Florence E. Burnett

McKEENE, female 1st 30 Aug 1910; Eugene L. McKeene, painter
and Florence E. Burnett

McKENNEY, Adelbert McKenney 1878

McQUARRIE, Emeline Colley 10 Mar 1901 female 1st; Frank H.
McQuarrie, store clerk and Grace E. Knight

MEGQUIER, Hewit 13 Sept 1906 male 1st; Lawson Megquire,
farmer and Julia Edwards

MEGQUIER, Ellen Edwards 28 Jan 1912 female 2nd; Lawson
Megquire, farmer and Juliette Edwards

MEGQUIER, Lewis L. 16 Mar 1915 male 3rd; Lawson L.
Megquire, farmer and Julia Edwards

MEGQUIER, Ava Lucretia 31 May 1921 female 4th; Lawson
Megquire, farmer and Juliett Edwards

MERRILL, Eugene A. 9 Dec 1865

MERRILL, Priscilla B. 24 Jan 1891 to Ansel W. and Mary M.
Merrill

MERRILL, male 1st 8 July 1892 Emma M. Merrill

MERRILL, infant of Mark C. Merrill 22 Jan 1877

MERRILL, Gertrude Hersom 21 Mar 1893 female 2nd; Ansel .
Merrill, farmer and Mary Hersom

MERRILL, Helen Harmon 19 July 1894 female 3rd; Willard L.
Merrill, farmer and Elizabeth F. Tufts

MERRILL, female 3rd 17 Mar 1897; Ansel W. Merrill, farmer and
Mary Hersom

MERRILL, Annie 12 Oct 1897 female 4th; Willard L. Merrill, farmer and Elizabeth Tufts

MERRILL, Karl H. 1 Sept 1900 male 2nd; George E. Merrill, farmer and Mary E. Merrill

MERRILL, Eliza W. 27 Oct 1900 female 4th; Ansel W. Merrill, farmer and Mary Hersom

MERRILL, Marian Gladys 30 Nov 1900 female 1st; Harry Merrill, farmer and Katherine H. Libby

MERRILL, Cynthia M. 2 Sept 1912 female 4th; Harold W. Merrill, laborer and Cynthia A. G. Shanks

MERRILL, Elizabeth R. 9 July 1914 female 1st; Frank G. Merrill, farmer and Lena P. Stevens

MERRILL, Leo Libby 7 Aug 1914 male 4th; Clark L. Merrill, laborer and Bessie Robinson

MERRILL, Madeline 10 Oct 1922 female 1st; George D. Merrill, farmer and Ruby Wilson

MERRILL, Neal Wilson 14 Oct 1924 male 2nd; Geo. D. Merrill, farmer and Ruby R. Wilson

MERRILL, Richard Woodbury 27 Apr 1927 male 2nd; Ernest L. Merrill, civil engineer and Alice J. Stanton

MERRILL, George D. 13 Jan 1893 male 1st; George E. Merrill farmer and Mary E. Merrill

MITCHELL, Dolores 26 May 1928 female 1st; Percy R. Mitchell, stock manager and Welda P. Merrithew

MOREY, Kenneth Leon 3 Aug 1930 male 3rd; Herman D. Morey, painter and Addie I. Decker

MORRILL, Evelyn Adele 17 Mar 1920 female 1st; Gardner M. Morrill, farmer and Aldine A. Osgood

MORRELL, infant 12 Aug 1865 child of John T. Morrell

MORRILL, John W. Morrill July 1878

MORRILL, male 6th 29 May 1895; Matthew C. Morrill, millman and Mary J. McConkey

MORRILL, male 1st 29 June 1897; Hugh P. Morrill, merchant and Dora L. Brown

MORRILL, female 1st 24 July 1897; Jacob P. Morrill, farmer and Alma S. Martin

MORRILL, Geneva Angelia 18 Nov 1898 female 2nd; Jacob P. Morrill, farmer and Anna E. Martin

MORRILL, male 3rd 6 Jan 1900; Jacob P. Morrill, farmer and
Alma Martin
MORRILL, female 4th 24 Feb 1901; Jacob P. Morrill, farmer and
Alma Martin
MORRILL, John Anderson 12 Feb 1902 male 1st; John W. Morrill,
lumberman and Bessie W. Anderson
MORRILL, Marguerite 7 May 1903 female 2nd; John W. Morrill,
laborer and Bessie W. Anderson
MORRILL, female 5th 21 Aug 1903; Jacob P. Morrill, farmer and
Alma S. Martin
MORRILL, male 7th 16 Apr 1906; Jacob P. Morrill, farmer and
Alma S. Martin
MORRILL, female 8th 19 June 1907; Jacob P. Morrill, farmer and
Alma Martin
MORRILL, Everett William 26 Aug 1907 male 3rd; John W.
Morrill, laborer and Bessie W. Anderson
MORRILL, male 4th 26 Mar 1910; John W. Morrill, sheriff and
Bessie W. Anderson
MORRILL, John A. Jr. 4 May 1925 male 1st; John A. Morrill,
farmer and Ruth E. Morrill
MORRILL, Robert Eldon 23 Oct 1929 male 2nd; John Anderson
Morrill, farmer and Ruth E. Morrill
MORRILL, Nathan Clifford 27 Jan 1905 male 6th; Jacob P.
Morrill, farmer Alma S. Martin
MORRISON, Lloyd Randall 17 Apr 1929 male 3rd; Webster R.
Morrison, box maker and Elsie P. Hall
MORSE, Julia Cushman 4 June 1895 female 3rd; Joshua R. Morse,
farmer and Louella A. Sawyer
MOSES, female 4th 4 Aug 1909; Jonathan Moses, basket maker
and Emily Jerome
MUSHROW, Dorothy Louise 22 Sept 1926 female 2nd; Francis A.
Mushrow, laborer and Ida M. Ferguson
MUZZY, George Lufkin 16 Mar 1918 male 1st; Marcus W.
Muzzy, station agent and Doris B. Chapman
MUZZY, June Estelle 29 Sept 1919 female 2nd; Marcus M.
Muzzy, electrician and Doris B. Chapman
MUZZY, Carleton William 23 Aug 1923 male 3rd; Marcus M.
Muzzy, station agent and Doris B. Chapman

MUZZY, Mae Madeline 24 Feb 1925 female 4th; Marcus M.
   Muzzy, station agent and Doris B. Chapman
MUZZY, Marcus Morton Jr. 7 Aug 1928 male 5th; Marcus M.
   Muzzy, sub station operator and Doris B. Chapman
NASON, Mabel S. 21 May 1889 to Charles H. and Gertrude Brown
   Nason
NASON, Harold C. 20 Sept 1890 to Charles H. and Gertrude
   Brown
NASON, Walter A. 24 Feb 1895 to Charles H. and Gertrude
   Brown
NASON, Walter 24 Feb 1895 male 3rd; Charles H. Nason, laborer
   and Gertrude J. Brown
NASON, Mildred Louise 9 Oct 1897 female 4th; Charles Nason,
   engineer and Gertrude Brown
NASON, Kenneth E. 30 Nov. 1901 male 1st; Charles H. Nason,
   laborer and Carrie A. Emery
NASON, Delbert 22 July 1904 male 2nd; Charles H. Nason,
   laborer and Carrie A. Emery
NASON, stillborn 11 June 1909 female 7th; Charles H. Nason,
   laborer and Carrie A. Emery
O'CONNELL, male 1st 9 Apr 1898; Edward O'Connell and Ella
   Blake
OLDHAM, Gerald Sumner 18 Mar 1917 male 1st; Charles
   Oldham, blacksmith and Elizabeth Shaw
OLFENE, Ernest A. 20 July 1865
ORNE, Mary Francis 29 Nov. 1839, dau. of William G. and Sarah
   L. Orne
ORNE, Maria Jane 17 May 1842, dau. of William G. and Sarah
   Orne
ORNE, Frances Jane 24 Dec. 1843, dau. of William G. and Sarah
   Orne
ORNE, Charles L. 4 June 1846, son of William G. and Sarah Orne
ORNE, Rufus Henry 28 Dec. 1847, son of William G. and Sarah
   Orne
ORNE, Ann Elizabeth 22 Feb. 1850 dau. of William G. and Sarah
   L. Orne
ORNE, Ferdinand 10 Nov. 1852 son of William G. and Sarah L.
   Orne
ORNE, Isabella 6 Sept. 1854 dau. of William G. and Sarah L. Orne

ORNE, Charlotte L. 11 Oct. 1856 dau. of William G. and Sarah L. Orne

ORNE, William 19 Oct 1859 son of William G. and Sarah L. Orne

OSGOOD, Annie A. 14 May 1894 female 4th; Elmer L. Osgood, painter and Ina A. Harmon

OSGOOD, female 5th 13 Aug 1899; Elmer L. Osgood, painter and Ina A. Harmon

OSGOOD, Catherine Adelle 15 Dec 1923 female 1st; Wm. C. Osgood, carpenter and Laura S. Stickles

PALEY, infant 24 Feb 1866 dau of John Paley

PARKER, Lyle 4 Sept 1899 male 1st; Edward Parker, teamster and Elsie Leavitt

PARKER, Robert Allen 16 Feb 1922 male 3rd; Richard W. Parker, farmer and Virginia E. Small

PARKER, male 4th 22 Mar 1925; Richard W. Parker, farmer and Virginia E. Small

PARKHURST, female 3rd 19 Jan 1909; Arthur D. Parkhurst, teacher and Lillian L. Marsden

PEARSON, female 5th 14 Dec 1905; Frank Pearson, clergyman and Rosa Sanborn

PENNELL, George 24 Dec 1865

PENNELL, George Pennell Jan 1878

PERRY, Alberta Josephine 17 Mar 1909 female 2nd; Harry V. Perry, laborer and Maud B. Sawyer

PERRY, Hazel Maude 17 Jan 1913 female 3rd; Harry V. Perry, carpenter and Maude B. Sawyer

PETERSON, Robert Murchie 23 Sept 1930 male 2nd; Howard M. Peterson, truckdriver and Maude R. Chadbourne

PIERCE, Margaret Ruth 20 Oct 1925 female 2nd; Richard D. Pierce, laborer and Ruth M. Strout

PIERCE, female 6th 23 Oct 1925; Willis S. Pierce and Ethel R. Larner

PIERCE, Mae Ellen 30 Apr 1927 female 3rd; Richard D. Pierce, laborer and Ruth M. Strout

PIERCE, Kenneth Wayne 25 Nov 1929 male 4th; Richard D. Pierce, laborer and Ruth M. Strout

PLUMMER, Lindley 19 June 1856 child of George W. Plummer twin to Mary

PLUMMER, Mary 19 June 1856 dau. Of George W. Plummer twin to Lindley

PLUMMER, Bernard Isdora 19 Nov 1901 male 3rd; Daniel F. Plummer, farmer and Alwilda P. Weeks

POLLACK, Lester Leroy Berry 1 Jan 1924 male 2nd; Frank H. Pollack, printer and Florence H. Berry

POLLARD, Everett Vernon 28 May 1924 male 1st; Jas. W. B. Pollard, laborer and Sarah F. Hanson

POLLARD, Geraldine Frances 28 July 1925 female 2nd; Jas. Ward Pollard, laborer and Sarah F. Hanson

POLLARD, John Benjamin 26 Oct 1925 male 4th; Ira C. Pollard, laborer and Minnie E. Cannell

POLLARD, male 3rd 26 July 1927; Jas. W. Pollard, laborer and Sarah F. Hanson

POLLARD, Phillip Donald 10 July 1929 male 4th; Jas. Ward Pollard, carpenter and Sara F. Hanson

POLLARD, Gordon Chandler 5 June 1930 male 6th; Ira C. Pollard, farmer and Minie E. Cannell

POLLARD, Priscilla Irene 12 Nov 1930 female 5th; Jas. Ward Pollard, carpenter and Sara Frances Hanson

POOR, Fred W. 10 June 1916 male 3rd; Fred W. Poor, motorman and Beatrice Coldwell

POOR, Charles Lombard 16 Mar 1918 male 4th; Fred W. Poor, street car conductor and Beatrice Coldwell

PORTER, female 1st 11 Oct 1910; Wm. O. Porter, painter and Jennie Verrill

PRATT, male 4th 14 Oct 1910; Ernest H. Pratt, teacher and Edith O. Grover

PRATT, stillborn 4 June 1912 male 5th; Ernest H. Pratt, teacher and Edith O. Grover

PRIDE, Jane E. 22 Dec 1865

PRINCE, Sewall P. 6 Nov. 1888 son of Sewall B. Prince and Johanna Estes

PRINCE, Trueman L. 24 Dec. 1890 son of Sewall B. Prince and Johanna Estes

PRINCE, child 24 Oct 1902; Willis B. Prince, laborer and Anna Dow

PRINCE, female 3rd 17 Feb 1904; Willis B. Prince, laborer and Anna S. Dow

PRINCE, Gladys Isabell 19 Nov 1915 female 1st; Sewall P. Prince, laborer and Inez A. Burns

PRINCE, female 2nd 1 Aug 1919; Sewell P. Prince, laborer and Inez A. Burns

PRINCE, Richard Francis 3 Oct 1926 male 1st; Guy O. Prince, mechanic and Catherine S. Leavitt

PURDY, Sarah Edith 28 Oct 1901 female 1st; John Purdy, laborer and Dora F. Holmes

PURDY, male 2nd 24 Oct 1904; John Purdy, laborer and Dora T. Homes

QUINT, Arch. H. 19 Feb 1892 male 3rd; Frank A. Quint and Flora Morrill

QUINT, Harold Lewis 20 Sept 1897 male 1st; Lewis W. Quint, brick mason and Matttie E. Frank

QUINT, stillborn 29 Apr 1899 male 2nd; Lewis Quint, brick mason and Mattie Frank

QUINT, stillborn 11 Sept 1899 female 1st; Gilman Quint, brick mason, and Hattie Davis

QUINT, Susie 27 Dec 1900 female 3rd; Lewis Quint, brickmason and Mattie Frank

QUINT, Hazel 25 Dec 1901 female 4th; Lewis Quint, brickmason and Mattie Frank

QUINT, male 5th 28 Dec 1903; Lewis Quint, mason and Mattie E. Frank

QUINT, Clarence Morrill 2 Sept 1905 male 4th; Frank A. Quint, laborer and Flora Morrill

RACKLEY, male 4th 15 Oct 1917; Philip C. Rackley, clerk and Ora W. Garrett

RAY, Oren E. 2 Sept 1892 male 1st; Chas. Eugene Ray, farmer and Effie B. Humphrey

RAY, Gladys E. 21 July 1896 female 3rd; Charles Eugene Ray, farmer and Effie B. Humphrey

RAY, female 3rd 10 Aug 1898; Charles E. Ray, farmer and Effie B. Humphrey

REED, female 1st 21 June 1899; Roy C. Reed, laborer and Minnie Libby

RICHARDS, Orin E. 6 Mar 1897 male 4th; John Richards, farmer and Lillian Spencer

RICHARDS, male 31 Mar 1905; John Richards, laborer and Lillian Spencer

RICKER, stillborn 4 May 1901 female 1st; Clarence Ricker,
  laborer and Delinda M. Libby
RICKER, infant died 3 Feb 1928 male 1st; Basil Ricker, farmer &
  chef and Bessie Ricker
ROBERTS, female 6th 8 Mar 1909; Urban G. Roberts, farmer and
  Emma L. Veazie
ROBERTS, Urban G. Jr. 2 June 1918 male 8th; Urban G. Roberts,
  farmer and Emma L. Veazie
ROBINSON, Edith 6 Nov 1930 female 3rd; Frank Robinson,
  minister and Myra Wright
ROEHRIG, Verna Mildred 18 Nov female 1st; Walter Roehrig,
  soldier and Frances McIntosh
RUSSELL, Dana M. 14 June 1894 male 1st; William L. Russell,
  farmer and Julia Merrill
RUSSELL, Eleanor H. 14 Nov 1896 female 2nd; William L.
  Russell, farmer and Julia Merrill
RUSSELL, Edgar H. 16 Nov 1896 male 3rd; William L. Russell,
  farmer and Julia Merrill
RUSSELL, Mary 9 June 1898 female 4th; William L. Russell,
  farmer and Julia Merrill
RUSSELL, William 7 May 1903 male 5th; William L. Russell,
  farmer and Julia Merrill
RUSSELL, Harriet 7 May 1903 female 6th; William L. Russell,
  farmer and Julia Merrill
RUSSELL, Julia Eloise 13 Feb 1918 female 1st; Dana M. Russell,
  farmer and Arline Hunt
RUSSELL, Edith Hunt 3 Nov 1919 female 1st; Dana M. Russell,
  farmer and Arline Hunt
RUSSELL, James William 28 Jan 1921 male 3rd; Dana M. Russell,
  farmer Arline Hunt
RUSSELL, Martha Merron 8 Feb 1923 female 4th; Dana M.
  Russell, farmer and Arline M. Hunt
RUSSELL, Mary Merrill 8 Feb 1923 female 5th; Dana M. Russell,
  farmer and Arline M. Hunt
RUSELL, Helen Natalie 25 Feb 1924 female 6th; Dana M. Russell,
  farmer and Arline Hunt
RYDER, female 1st 7 May 1896; Austin M. Ryder, R.R. man and
  Jennie L. Edwards

SANBORN, Evelyn May 26 Nov 1909 female 1st; Werilock
Sanborn, laborer and Lilla M. Jones

SANBORN, William E. Jr. 14 Aug 1927 male 2nd; William E.
Sanborn, laborer and Blanche H. Kingsbury

SANBORN, Kenneth Edson 21 Dec 1929 male 3rd; William E.
Sanborn, riveter and Blanche H. Kingsbury

SAWYER, Blackie 6 Mar 1887 to Fred and Gertie Sawyer

SAWYER, Percie Winfield 18 Sept. 1880

SAWYER, Nettie Eva Sawyer 29 May 1884

SAWYER, female 1st 10 Feb 1893 James Herbert Sawyer,
carpenter and Alice E. Dorman

SAWYER, Henry Clifford 7 Mar 1893 male 3rd; C. Frank Sawyer,
farmer and Florence M. Low

SAWYER, Greenleaf F. 23 Sept 1893 male 3rd; George F. Sawyer,
farmer and Nettie E. Chase

SAWYER, Ralph White 19 July 1894 male 2nd; Horatio M.
Sawyer, merchant and Addie C. Staples

SAWYER, Velma Hazel 1 July 1894 female 3rd; John M. Sawyer,
laborer and Leonora Sawyer

SAWYER, Sadie Evalina 25 Nov 1895 female 7th; George F.
Sawyer, laborer and Nellie E. Chase

SAWYER, John Melton 29 Mar 1897 male 4th; John M. Sawyer,
laborer and Leonora Sawyer

SAWYER, male 3rd 9 Oct. 1898; Lewis E. Sawyer, laborer and
Alice E. Morey

SAWYER, Lucella Asenath 28 Dec 1899 female 5th; John M.
Sawyer, laborer and Lenora Sawyer

SAWYER, male 4th 31 July 1900; Lewis E. Sawyer, laborer and
Alice E. Morey

SAWYER, Bernard Levi 3 May 1902 male 1st; Ira P. Sawyer,
laborer and Mildred E. Foster

SAWYER, Harold J. 31 May 1902 male 2nd; James Herbert
Sawyer, laborer and Alice E. Damon

SAWYER, Roscoe Hall 5 Aug 1903 male 1st; Fernald D. Sawyer,
teacher and Susie A. Hall

SAWYER, James Irving 3 Mar 1904 male 5th; Lewis E. Sawyer,
laborer and Alice E. Morey

SAWYER, male 6th 2 July 1904; John M. Sawyer, laborer and
Lenora Sawyer

SAWYER, Eugene Fernald 5 Mar 1906 male 2nd; Fernald D. Sawyer, teacher and Susie A. Hall

SAWYER, male 7th 3 Sept 1906; John M. Sawyer, laborer and Nora Sawyer

SAWYER, male 6th 12 Oct 1907; Lewis E. Sawyer, laborer and Alice E. Morey

SAWYER, female 8th 18 Dec 1907; John M. Sawyer, laborer and Lenora Sawyer

SAWYER, Kenneth Horatio 22 Jan 1908 male 1st; Perley C. Sawyer, merchant and Jennie M. Bohnson

SAWYER, Isabelle C. 20 Sept 1908 female 1st; Joseph P. Sawyer, laborer and Emma Tweedie

SAWYER, female 7th 3 Jan 1909; Lewis Sawyer, laborer and Alice Morey

SAWYER, female 1st 24 May 1909; Hannibal W. Sawyer, laborer and Lucy A. Whitney

SAWYER, Elbert Carston 5 Jan 1911 male 2nd; Perley C. Sawyer, laborer and Jennie M. Bohnson

SAWYER, Philip Julius 11 Apr 1911 male 2nd; Hannibal W. Sawyer, laborer and Lucy A. Whitney

SAWYER, Mary Susan 18 Dec 1911 female 3rd; Fernald D. Sawyer and Susan A. Hall

SAWYER, Gladys Hazel 15 May 1912 female 8th; Lewis E. Sawyer, laborer and Alice Morey

SAWYER, Gwendolyn 4 Jan 1913 female 3rd; Hannibal W. Sawyer, laborer and Lucy A. Whitney

SAWYER, Frank Wilbur 29 Mar 1914 male 4th; H. W. Sawyer, laborer and Lucy A. Whitney

SAWYER, Charles Allen 16 Apr 1914 male 1st; Charles S. Sawyer, farmer and Ella A. Allen

SAWYER, female 5th 4 Mar 1916; H. W. Sawyer, R.R. section and Lucy Whitney

SAWYER, William Albert 26 Mar 1917 male 2nd; Charles H. Sawyer, farmer and Ella A. Allen

SAWYER, Charles Josiah 25 June 1919 male 3rd; Charles H. Sawyer, farmer and Ella Allen

SAWYER, Margaret Clair 29 July 1919 female 3rd; Perley C. Sawyer, farmer and Jennie M. Bohnson

SAWYER, Ralph Stanley 9 Jan 1921 male 1st; Ralph W. Sawyer, farmer and Evelyn L. Bishop

SAWYER, stillborn 15 Sept 1928 female 1st; Arthur M. Sawyer, laborer and Eleanor F. Witham

SAWYER, Louis Allen 18 Apr 1929 male 4th; Charles H. Sawyer, farmer and Apha Allen

SAWYER, Helen Irene 15 Dec 1930 female 3rd; Arthur M. Sawyer, farmer and Eleanor F. Witham

SAWYER, female 9th 10 Nov 1909; John M. Sawyer, laborer and Lenora Sawyer

SAYWARD, Stella Edith 24 Jan 1924 female 1st; Carroll E. Sayward, R R employee and Beatrice Varney

SAYWARD, Eugene Francis 19 July 1923 male 2nd; Carroll E. Sayward, R R employee and Beatrice E. Varney

SAYWARD, Dorothy May stillborn 11 Aug 1928 female 1st; Carroll E. Sayward, R R trackman and Bertha A. VanIderestine

SAYWARD, Kenneth E. 20 June 1927 male 1st; Henry E. Saywood, farmer and Iva M. Chipman

SEARLES, Ralph Melvin 10 July 1928 male 5th; Harold L. Searles, laborer and Gertrude M. Adams

SEARLS, Bertha Irene 11 Sept 1926 female 4th; Harold L. Searls, laborer and Gertrude M. Adams

SEARS, Warren Delancey 19 Dec 1913 male 1st; Raymond D. Sears, lumberman and Velma H. Sawyer

SEVERY, female 4th 9 Feb 1913; David T. Severy, farmer and Daisy E. Morse

SHAW, Granville 15 Aug 1919 male 3rd; Charles G. Shaw, laborer and Sophronia Manchester

SHAW, Charles Greenlief 15 Dec 1920 male 4th; Charles G. Shaw, laborer and Etta L. Sawyer

SIMPSON, Lewis A. 2 Sept 1864 son of Lewis A. and Henrietta C. Simpson

SKILLIN, Lucy E. Skillin 2 Sept 1876

SKILLIN, Bessie Estella 18 Mar 1894 female 1st; Joseph A. Skillin, laborer and Flora M. Colley

SKILLIN, Percy Warren 23 June 1896 male 2nd; Joseph A. Skillin, laborer and Flora M. Colley

SKILLIN, Eleanor Jane 5 May 1901 female 1st; Albert Skillin, farmer and Isabelle Hanna

SKILLINGS, Stanley M. 3 Dec 1886 to H. C. and Addie F. Skillings

SKILLINGS, Martha P. 18 Jan 1889 H. C. and Addie F. Skillings

SKILLINGS, Wallace A. Skillings 1878

SKILLINGS, male 1st 19 May 1894; Albert Skillings, farmer and Margaret A. Smith

SKILLINGS, male 8th 3 June 1896; Chandler Skillings, laborer and Addie F. Elwell

SKILLINGS, George Forest 31 May 1897 male 1st; Albert Skillings, farmer and Martha E. Smith

SKILLINGS, Elmer Atwood 10 July 1897 male 9th; Hewett C. Skillings, laborer and Addie Elwell

SKILLINGS, Edna Ethaleen 4 Apr 1898 female 3rd; Joseph Skillings, laborer and Flora Colley

SKILLINGS, Fred Ervin 7 Nov 1899 male 1st; Charles Skillings, farmer and Sadie Heckar

SKILLINGS, male 2nd 24 Nov 1902; Albert Skillings, farmer and Bella Hannah

SKILLINGS, Alice G. 22 Apr 1906 female 2nd; Charles Skillings, farmer and Sarah Jane Hechler

SKILLINGS, male 1st 24 Nov 1922; John A. Skillings, laborer and Catherine A. Cobb

SKILLINGS, Carlton John 3 Nov 1926 male 2nd; John A. Skillings, laborer and Catherine A. Cobb

SKILLINGS, Kenneth Stuart 8 Sept 1930 male 3rd; John A. Skillings, farmer and Catherine Cobb

SMALL, Lester H. 28 Mar 1889 to Walter and Carrie Small

SMALL, Ira Small 19 Nov 1889

SMALL, Florence 21 June 1891 to John H. and Nellie F. Small

SMALL, Ida May 21 Apr 1893 female 3rd; Levi G. Small, farmer and Hattie E. Libby

SMALL, I. Elizabeth 13 Sept 1895 female 4th; Levi G. Small, farmer and Hattie E. Libby

SMALL, Virginia 14 Feb 1896 female 3rd; Freeland M. Small, barber and Lucy J. Quint

SMALL, Lena Caroline 5 Apr 1896 female 1st; Walter S. Small, farmer and Carrie S. Sawyer

SMALL, male 5th 4 Jan 1897; Levi G. Small, farmer and Hattie E. Libby

SMALL, stillborn 1 July 1897 female 1st; Leon L. Small, tinsmith and Addie B. Stimson

SMALL, Edith Carro 9 June 1898 female 6th; Greenland Small, farmer and Hattie E. Libby

SMALL, female 16th 16 July 1900; Levi G. Small, farmer and Hattie E. Libby

SMALL, Freeland Evander 28 Oct 1900 male 2nd; Wilbur A. Small, teamster and Sadie M. Nichols

SMALL, female 1st 18 Nov 1900; Albert J. Small, farmer and Annie S. Mitchell

SMALL, male 2nd 13 Oct 1902; Albert J. Small, farmer and Annie Sophia Mitchell

SMALL, Forest L. 8 Aug 1904 male 3rd; Albert J. Small, farmer and Annie S. Mitchell

SMALL, female 4th 8 Feb 1907; Albert J. Small, farmer and Annie S. Mitchell

SMART, Lee Brackett 18 Apr 1924 male 2nd; Ernest H. Smart, farmer and Marion J. Strout

SMITH, stillborn male 5th, 15 Feb 1893; Lewis T. Smith, laborer and Titus Jackson

SMITH, female 2nd 3 May 1893; James E. Smith farmer and Thankful B. Whitney

SMITH, male 11th 18 June 1893; Ambrose G. Smith, laborer and Lucy Jackson

SMITH, male 11th 13 Dec 1895; Walter Smith, laborer and Ellen L. Strout

SMITH, Irving E. 14 Sept 1898 male 2nd; Charles C. Smith, laborer and Annie B. Thurlow

SMITH, Lester Allen 28 Dec 1899 male 3rd; Charles C. Smith, laborer and Annie Thurlow

SMITH, male 1st 9 Mar 1904; Carroll E. Smith, laborer and Pearl M. Small

SMITH, female 1st 10 Mar 1910; Henry Dennis Smith, woodchopper and Mabel V. Crouse

SNOW, Velma 18 Apr 1896 female 1st; George W. Snow, conductor and Jennie Leach

SNOW, Wilmer A. 4 May 1898 female 2nd; George W. Snow, hotelkeeper and Jennie Leach

SNOW, Lauris Percie 28 Aug 1899 female 3rd; George W. Snow,
   hotel keeper and Jennie Leach
SNOW, Nellie Velora 20 Aug 1905 female 2nd; Forest B. Snow,
   farmer and Florence D. Newell
SNOW, male 3rd 27 June 1906; Forest B. Snow, farmer and
   Florence L. Newell
SNOW, Clara Marshall 7 June 1920 female 1st; Winfield S. Snow,
   laborer and Laura C. Mountfort
SOPER, Helen Alvira 20 Oct 1924 female 1st; John Soper,
   carpenter and Hazel Whitney
SOUSY, male 2nd 22 June 1906; Fred Sousy, laborer and Annie
   Barren
SPILLER, Clarence F. Spiller 15 Feb 1876
SPILLER, Harold Augustat 1 May 1899 male 4th; Joseph Spiller,
   laborer and Flora Colley
STEEVES, Addison Elliot 5 Jan 1920 male 2nd; Earle R. Steeves,
   clergyman and Elizabeth C. Vosmus
STEEVES, Earle R. Jr. 19 Mar 1921 male 2nd; Earle R. Steeves,
   clergyman and Elizabeth E. Vosmus
STEEVES, Priscilla Elvina 1 Mar 1923 female 4th; Earle R.
   Steeves, clergyman and Elizabeth E. Vosmus
STEPHEND, female 2nd 8 Jan 1900; Wm. Stephend, laborer and
   Sisie Hale
STEVENS, stillborn 12 Feb 1905 female 2nd; Orin L. Stevens,
   solicitor and Mary Stevens
STEVENS, Lillian Morse 10 Apr 1906 female 1st; George M.
   Stevens, merchant and Elsie B. Morse
STEVENS, stillborn 7 Oct 1914 female 5th; Lester O. Stevens,
   express manager and Mary Stevens
STIMSON, Ciraine Covell 15 Oct. 1855 dau. of Theophilis and
   Caroline M. Stimson
STIMSON, Elmer Warren 13 Apr. 1858 son of Theophilis and
   Caroline M. Stimson
STIMSON, Carrie Wilmer 30 Oct. 1859 dau. of Theophilis and
   Caroline M. Stimson
STINCHFIELD, Muriel 31 Jan 1897 female 1st; Oscar C.
   Stinchfield, millman and Clara H. Doughty
STORY, female 1st 3 Mar 1909; Horace Edward Story, farmer and
   Tena Welena Mcleod

STORY, Hugh E. L. 26 July 1913 male 2nd; Horace E. Story, laborer and Tena W. McLeod

STROUT, female 1st 24 Dec 1894; Freedom H. Strout, laborer and Phoebe Verrill

STROUT, C. Harvey 19 Nov 1895 male 2nd; Freedom Strout, laborer and Phebe Strout

STROUT, Lewis Henry 4 Oct 1897 male 3rd; Freedom Strout, farmer and Phebe Verrill

STROUT, male 1st 17 Oct 1898; Prince E. Strout, laborer and Rachel M. Weeks

STROUT, female 4th 7 Dec 1899; Freedom Strout, farmer and Phebe Strout

STROUT, female 5th 13 Feb 1901; Freedom Strout, laborer and Phoebe Verrill

STROUT, stillborn 7 Dec 1902 male 9th; Dwinal F. Strout, laborer and Mary A. Frank

STROUT, Flisty N. 2 July 1903 female 1st; Ephraim P. C. Strout, laborer and Isabelle May

STROUT, female 2nd 13 Sept 1904; Ephraim P. C. Strout, laborer and Isabelle May

STROUT, Clifford Eugene 10 Apr 1905, male 6th; Freedom Strout, laborer and Phoebe Verrill

STROUT, Fredie Evelyn 15 Nov 1906 female 7th; Freedom Strout, laborer and Phoebe Strout

STROUT, Hazel A. 21 July 1907 female 3rd; Ephraim P. C. Strout, laborer and Isabelle May

STROUT, stillborn twins 16 Apr 1909 female 4&5; E. P. C. Strout, laborer and Isabell May

STROUT, Gladys Isabell 29 Apr 1911 female 4th; Ephraim P. C. Strout, laborer and Isabell May

STROUT, Vera Evelyn 2 Sept 1920 female 1st; Charles Harvey Strout, laborer and Bertha M. Young

STROUT, Reta Alberta 13 Sept 1921 female 2nd; Charles H. Strout, laborer and Bertha M. Young

STROUT, Lila Irene 3 Mar 1923 female 3rd; Charles M. Strout, laborer and Bertha M. Young

STROUT, Velma Almira 28 Nov 1924 female 4th; Chas. Harvey Strout, laborer and Bertha M. Young

STUART, Charles Frederick 13 Feb 1896 male 1st; Charles M. Stuart, farmer and Elsie J. Libby

STURGIS, male 1st 1 Jan 1917; Frank O. Sturgis, lumberman and
Josephine Bourgeois
STURGIS, male 2nd 1 Jan 1917; Frank O. Sturgis, lumberman and
Josephine Bourgeois
SWEETSER, Helen M. 17 July 1899 female 1st; Willard Sweetser,
merchant and Lenora Whitney
SWEETSER, Mary 1 Jan 1901 female 2nd; W. B. Sweetser,
merchant and Lenora Whitney
SWEETSER, Merton 9 June 1902 male 3rd; Willard B. Sweetser,
merchant and Leonora W. Whitney
SWEETSER, Alice 31 Aug 1903 female 4th; Willard B. Sweetser,
merchant and Lenora Whitney
SWEETSER, Kathryn 6 Aug 1904 female 5th; Willard B.
Sweetser, merchant and Lenora Whitney
TALBOT, Everett William Jr. 19 Aug 1921 male 1st; Everett W.
Talbot, laborer and Florence Roberic
TENNEY, Arthur L. 10 Aug 1893 male 1st; Fred A. Tenney,
oculist and Mary E. Snow
TENNEY, female 2nd 30 Mar 1895; Fred A. Tenney, oculist and
Mary E. Snow
THAYER, Ruth Perley 30 Jan 1892 ; female 1st, Chas. Thayer,
blacksmith and Sarah J Berry
THOMPSON, J. Herbert 21 Aug 1886 to Elisha and Emma
Thompson
THOMPSON, Oerley Thompson 23 June 1890
THOMPSON, female 2nd 6 May 1892 G. Willis Thompson,
laborer and Maude A. Mace
THOMPSON, Mary P. Thompson 1878
THOMPSON, Clara T. 6 Mar 1893 female 1st; Ebenzer B.
Thompson, laborer and Rhoda V. Verrill
THOMPSON, Howard 17 Oct 1894 male 2nd; Alice L. Thompson
THOMPSON, Harvey Floyd 3 July 3 July 1894 male 3rd; George
W. Thompson, laborer and Maud A. Mace
THOMPSON, Olive 31 July 1896 female 6th; Willis G. Thompson,
farmer and Maud A. Mace
THOMPSON, Harold Irving 4 May 1898 male 5th George W.
Thompson, laborer and Maude Mace
THOMPSON, male 1st 14 June 1906 Ida F. Thompson (out of
wedlock)

THOMPSON, male 1st 29 Aug 1909; Perley C. Thompson, laborer and Ida M. Hawkes

THOMPSON, Louise May 13 Oct 1911 female 2nd; Perley C. Thompson, laborer and Ida M. Hawkes

THOMPSON, Alice Thompson 19 Sept 1917 female 5th; Perley C. Thompson, laborer and Ida M. Hawkes

THOMPSON, Warren Alfred 11 Oct 1919 male 1st; Bertrand W. Thompson, RR section man and Mildred V. Prince

THOMPSON, male 7th 22 Apr 1921; Perley C. Thompson, laborer and Ida M. Hawkes

THOMPSON, Grace Evelyn 20 May 1922 female 2nd; Howard P. Thompson, laborer and Fannie E. Hawkes

THOMPSON, Laura Phebe 15 May 1922 female 1st; Frank M. Thompson, farmer and Elizabeth E. Swinnington

THOMPSON, Olive Alice 5 Aug 1929 female 5th; Howard P. Thompson, laborer and Fannie E. Hawkes

THOMPSON, Mirvin Richard 23 Mar 1920 male 1st; Howard P. Thompson, laborer and Fannie E. Hawkes

THURLOW, female 6th 6 Mar 1895; George W. Thurlow, laborer and Mary A. Frank

THURLOW, Nelson David 6 Mar 1895 male 5th; George W. Thurlow, laborer and Mary A. Frank

THURLOW, Clovis Gray 28 May 1897 male 3rd; Charles E. Thurlow, and Elizabeth A. Trask

THURLOW, John 3 Dec 1898 male 8th; G. Wilfred Thurlow, laborer and Mary A. Frank

HURLOW, Sewell Carlton 7 Oct 1916 male 3rd; Charles H. Thurlow, laborer and Hattie Strout

THURLOW, Wilfred Isaac 3 May 1921 male 2nd; Nelson D. Thurlow, laborer and Elizabeth Bubier

TINKHAM, male 1st 11 May 1904; Fred A. Tinkham, laborer and Bertha C. Maier

TINKHAM, Fred Leroy 10 July 1906 male 2nd; Fred Tinkham, laborer and Christina B. Maier

TINKHAM, Irene Viola 4 Jan 1909 female 3rd; Fred A. Tinkham, laborer and Christine Bertha Maier

TINKHAM, Doris Evelyn 2 June 1914 female 4th; Fred A. Tinkham, laborer and Christina B. Maier

TOTE, Ethel M. 29 May 1890 to Andrew J. and Mary E. Tote

TOWNSEND, Jacqueline 14 July 1923 female 6th; John P.
Townsend, auto mechanic and Elsie M. Jordan

TREMAIN, Joseph Arthur 26 July 1908 male 1st; Thomas J.
Tremain, laborer and Rosie Provoncher

TRIPP, male 3rd 10 Apr 1895; George B. Tripp, laborer and Emma
E. Tripp

TRIPP, female 4th 2 May 1897; George B. Tripp, laborer and
Emma Tripp

TRIPP, Erlon 27 Aug 1898 male 1st; C. Fred Tripp, laborer and
Philena A. Weld

TRIPP, stillborn 10 Jan 1908 1st; Fred Tripp, laborer and Mildred
E. Verrill

TRIPP, Perley M. 7 Mar 1908 female 2nd; Elliot Tripp, farmer and
Ellen E. Carpenter

TRIPP, Sydney Hayford 27 Oct 1915 male 6th; Alphonso Tripp Jr.,
farmer and Mildred E. Maxim

TRIPP, Charles E. 17 Aug 1917 male 1st; Herbert L. Tripp,
merchant and Julia C. Chipman

TRIPP, Glen 16 Mar 1918 male 7th; Alphonso Tripp Jr., laborer
and Mildred E. Maxim

VALIDARES, female 1st 29 Nov 1914; Maximo Validares, student
and Lucy E. Barker

VEAZIE, male 4th 16 Feb 1908; Charles E. Veazie, laborer and
Margaret J. Williams

VEAZIE, Wilbur C. 5 Oct 1910 male 5th; Charles E. Veazie,
laborer and Margaret Williams

VERRILL, John E. Verrill 8 May 1887

VERRILL, Charles L. Verrill 23 Nov 1889

VERRILL, Merle E. 14 July 1892 male 3rd; Howard D. Verrill,
farmer and Jennie E. Libby

VERRILL, male 4th 24 Feb 1894; Charles Verrill, laborer and
Flora Hodgkins

VERRILL, Lillian B. 19 May 1894 female 1st; Herbert A. Verrill,
laborer and Lydia A. Huff

VERRILL, male 3rd 18 July 1894; James Verrill, laborer and Cora
M. McGowan

VERRILL, Harland Everett 9 Nov 1894 male 1st; Dwinal Verrill,
laborer and Maria K. Strout

VERRILL, Albert 2 July 1896 male 2nd; Herbert A. Verrill, farmer
and Lydia A. Huff

VERRILL, male 2nd 5 May 1898; Dwinal Verrill, farmer and
Maria Verrill

VERRILL, male 4th 12 June 1898; Joseph Verrill, laborer and
Hattie Hodgkins

VERRILL, Nellie Laura 31 Aug 1898 female 3rd; Herbert A.
Verrill, coal burner and Lydia A. Huff

VERRILL, male 1st 5 Nov 1899; Lewis M. Verrill, laborer and
Annie O. Verill

VERRILL, female 4th 19 Oct 1900; Herbert A. Verrill, farmer and
Lydia A. Huff

VERRILL, female 5th 10 Feb 1901; Charles Verrill, laborer and
Florabelle Hodgkins

VERRILL, male 6th 24 June 1901; Joseph Verrill, laborer and
Hattie Hodgkins

VERRILL, female 5th 10 Nov 1902; Herbert Verrill, farmer and
Lydia Huff

VERRILL, female 9th 4 Dec 1902; Emmons E. Verrill, laborer and
Alice Field

VERRILL, male 2nd 19 Feb 1904; Lewis M. Verrill, laborer and
Omea O. Verrill

VERRILL, female 6th 30 Apr 1904; Herbert M. Verrill, laborer and
Emma G. Jackson

VERRILL, male 6th 30 Dec 1904; Herbert A. Verrill, laborer and
Lydia A. Huff

VERRILL, Anna Beatrice 13 May 1906 female 3rd; Lewis M.
Verrill, laborer and Anna O. Verrill

VERRILL, Lottie 17 Mar 1908 female 1st; Nathaniel Verrill,
laborer and Emma L. Thompson

VERRILL, male 1st 2 Jan 1909; Clark L. Verrill, farmer and Bessie
M. Robinson

VERRILL, male 3rd 22 Mar 1910; Clark S. Verrill, laborer and
Bessie Robinson

VERRILL, male 7th 28 July 1910; Herbert A. Verrill, charcoal
merchant and Lydia Huff

VERRILL, ? Lincott 12 Aug 1911 male 3rd; Clark L. Verrill,
laborer and Bessie Robinson

VERRILL, male 8th 21 July 1912; Herbert A. Verrill, charcoal merchant and Lydia A. Huff

VERRILL, male 1st 6 June 1915; John E. Verrill, laborer and Edna McGowan

VERRILL, female 2nd; John E. Verril, laborer and Eve E. McGowan

VERRILL, Aldine Margaret 28 Aug 1920 female 1st; Ernest C. Verrill, farmer and Eva I. Edwards

VERRILL, Donald Edwards 26 Feb 1922 male 2nd; Ernest C. Verrill, farmer and Eva I. Edwards

VERRILL, Albert Everett 10 July 1924 male 1st; Henry A. Verrill, laborer and Alfreda E. Strout

VERRILL, Catharine 5 Dec 1924 female 8th; Edw. E. Verrill, laborer and Jennie E. May

VERRILL, Elsie Gertrude 9 Mar 1927 female 2nd; Henry A. Verrill, laborer and Alfreda E. Strout

VERRILL, Irving Ernest 8 July 1927 male 3rd; Ernest C. Verrill, farmer and Eva I. Edwards

VERRILL, Harvey Lewis 10 Jan 1930 male 3rd; Henry O. Verrill, laborer and Alfreda A. Strout

WALLACE, male 2nd 6 Feb 1897; Charles H. Wallace, and Margaret A. Smith

WALLACE, Lafayette L. 3 May 1916 male 2nd; Levi A. Wallace Jr., fisherman and Hester E. Sanborn

WALLACE, male 3rd 2 May 1918; Levi A. Wallace, laborer and Hester E. Sanborn

WAY, Mary Olive 24 Mar 1923 female 6th; Eldon A. Way, laborer and Eva S. Caswell

WAY, Eva Adeline 13 Dec 1924 female 7th; Elden A. Way, lineman and Eva S. Cilley

WEBB, male 1st 15 Feb 1909; Roy F. Webb, laborer and Hattie H. Sawyer

WEBB, Nancy Adelaide 6 Oct 1917 female 2nd; Fred L. Webb, laborer and Mildred E. Colley

WEBB, Robert Greenleaf 2 Feb 1918 male 2nd; Roy Webb, clerk and Hattie H. Sawyer

WEBSTER, Louvelle 27 Mar. 1855 child of Armstrong and Ardelia M. Webster

WEBSTER, Albert 29 Aug. 1856 son of Armstrong and Ardelia M. Webster

WEBSTER, Florence Adele 26 Sept 1858 dau. of Armstrong and Ardelia M. Webster

WEBSTER, Julia Hortense 13 June 1862 dau of Armstrong and Ardelia M. Webster

WEBSTER, female 1st 12 Aug 1893; Frank W. Webster, farmer and Nellie L. Allen

WEBSTER, male 2nd 16 Dec 1895; Frank W. Webster, farmer and Nellie E. Allen

WEYMOUTH, Bernard Irving 1 Mar 1928 male 3rd; John Weymouth, laborer and Edith Andrews

WHITE, Louvelle Herbert 25 Apr. 1858 son of John L. and Harriett E. White

WHITE, R. Fred Lorenzo 7 Nov. 1859 son of John L. and Harriett E. White

WHITE, Nellie Gertrude 25 Oct 1863 dau of John L. and Harriett E. White

WHITE, female 4th 24 Sept 1921; Harry P. White, machinist and Merle J. Leach

WHITNEY, Carrie T. 1865

WHITNEY, Annie E. Whitney 19 Mar 1887

WHITNEY, Ethel M. 29 July 1889 to T. G. and Emma R. Whitney

WHITNEY, Albert N. Whitney 7 Nov 1889

WHITNEY, Harlan 28 June 1903 male 1st; Wilbert I. Whitney, barber and Ella F. Ramsdell

WHITNEY, female 1st 6 May 1904; Carl H. Whitney, laborer and Agnes Foster

WHITNEY female 4th 21 Sept 1904; Almon J. Whitney, laborer a   Conelley

WHITNEY, Beatrice 26 Apr 1905 female 2nd; Carl Whitney, laborer and Agnes Foster

WHITNEY, Almon Joseph 4 Nov 1905 male 5th; Almon J. Whitney, laborer and Anna N. Connolly

WHITNEY, Walter 4 July 1906 male 3rd; Carl H. Whitney, laborer and Marion A. Foster

WHITNEY, Lawrence 23 Mar 1907 male 2nd; Wilbert I. Whitney, barber and Ella F. Ramsdell

WHITNEY, Irving 22 Oct 1909 male 4th; Carl Whitney, laborer
and Agnes Proctor

WHITNEY, male 6th 3 Jan 1913; Carl H. Whitney, laborer and
Agnes M. Foster

WHITNEY, Oren Colley 11 July 1916 male 1st; Fred T. Whitney,
farmer and Reina Colley

WHITNEY, Earla Nora 9 Apr 1919 female 1st; Earl L. Whitney,
laborer and Margaret E. McIntosh

WHITNEY, John Thomas 1 Aug 1921 male 2nd; Earl L. Whitney,
laborer and Margaret McIntosh

WHITNEY, June Lenora 19 June 1924 female 3rd; Earl L.
Whitney, laborer and Margaret MacIntosh

WILLEY, Marguerite Elliot 18 Mar 1908 female 1st; Herbert N.
Willey, teamster and Lucy E. Webster

WILSON, male 1st 22 Aug 1896; Carl A. Wilson, farmer and Alma
J. Lunn

WING, Everett Judson 15 Nov 1901 male 1st; William H. Wing,
laborer and Helen E. Holland

WING, Major Augustas 10 May 1902 female 1st; Adelbert Wing
and Lydia Benson

WING, Fred H. 1 Dec 1903 male 2nd; William H. Wing, laborer
and Helen E. Holland

WING, Louise Georgie 21 Dec 1905 female 3rd; William H. Wing,
laborer and Helen E. Holland

WING, female 4th 27 Oct 1909; Wm. Herbert Wing, laborer and
Helen E. Holland

WING, Berdena Helen 21 Aug 1926 female 1st; Frederick H.
Wing, laborer and Bernice Ryeson

WING, Lloyd Eldon 27 June 1928 male 1st; Everett J. Wing, R R
trackman and Myra Chadbourne

WINSLOW, Nellie B. 11 Oct 1893 female 5th; Roscoe D.
Winslow, laborer and Cora E. Cobb

WINSLOW, Florence M. 15 Mar 1896 female 6th; Roscoe D.
Winslow, laborer and Cora E. Cobb

WINSLOW, Luther Freeman 7 Aug 1900 male 1st; Lyman E.
Winslow, laborer and Rachel Hodgkins

WITHAM, male 1st 22 July 1895; John Witham, laborer and Cora
Thompson

WITHAM, male 1st 15 Jan 1897; Otis Witham, farmer and Martha Frances Symonds

WITHAM, male 2nd 23 July 1898; Otis Witham, farmer and Martha Symonds

WITHAM, Viola Rosa 17 June 1905 female 1st; Orrin Witham, laborer and Elizabeth M. Farwell

WITHAM, female 3rd 29 July 1907; Otis Witham, farmer and M. Frances Symonds

WITHAM, Frank C. 11 Dec 1914 male 2nd; Leon W. Witham, wood moulder and Alberta P. Peterson

WITHAM, stillborn Dilys May 28 June 1922 female 1st; Stanley H. Witham, farmer and Annie Irving

WITHAM, Dorothy Frances 11 Nov 1923 female 2nd; Stanley H. Witham, farmer and Annie Irving

WOODBURY, Kenneth Foster 23 June 1901 male 1st; Harry F. Woodbury, shoe cutter and Edna V. Foster

WORTH, male 2nd 18 July 1922; Frank H. Worth, farmer and Elizabeth Goldwater

WORTH, female 3rd 11 Sept 1924; Frank H. Worth, farmer and Elizabeth Goldwater

YOUNG, stillborn 8 July 1899 female 6th; Samuel Young, laborer and Annie Tripp

YOUNG, male 2nd 24 Aug 1901; Charles M. Young, farmer and Emma L. Glantz

YOUNG, Jeanette Susan 1 Nov 1912 female 1st; Thaddeus Young, blacksmith and Alice Smith

YOUNG, Harold Orrison 12 Jan 1921 male 2nd; Samuel A. Young, laborer and Julia Thurlow

MARRIAGES

ADAMS, Joshua and Sabrina Skillins both of Gray 9 Sept. 1804 p.180

ADAMS, Susan and Moses Haskell both of N. Yarmouth 16 Oct. 1808 p.186

ADAMS, Abigail and John Hamilton both of Gray PUB. 24 June 1820 p.222

ADAMS, Simeon see Fluent, Caroline

ADAMS, Caroline and James Skillin both of Gray PUB. 10 Dec. 1825 p.243

ADAMS, Silas H. and Hannah Smith both of Gray PUB. 23 Apr. 1832 p.271, Md 13 May 1832 p.274

ADAMS, Silas L. and Kate A. Adams both of Gray Md 19 Mar. 1860

ADAMS, Charles S. and Almeda E. Skillin both of Gray Md 14 Dec. 1872

ADAMS, George see Cole, Hattie

ADAMS, Harriet see Emery, William

ADAMS, Fred L. and Cora E. Lawrence both of Gray Md 3 May 1880

ADAMS, Will Harton and Lizzie May Ryder both of Gray Md 13 Jan. 1893 in Canton p.7

ADAMS, Dolores and Milton B. Hallett both of Gray Md 3 Mar. 1923 in Portland p.137

ADAMS, Helen and Stephen Huston both of Gray Md 21 Mar 1856

ADAMS, Silas and Kate A. Adams both of Gray Md 19 Mar 1860

ADAMS, Kate see Adams, Silas

ADAMS, Benjamin of Gray and Elizabeth B. Chamberlin of Portland Md 11 Sept 1864

ADAMS, Isiah of Gray and Sarah J. Dwinal of New Gloucester PUB. 4 July 1841

ADAMS, Benjamin and Abigail Hatch PUB. 11 Aug 1844 p.294

ADAMS, Isaac of Gray and Elvira Allen of Portland PUB. 20 Dec. 1846

ALLEN, Caroline M. and Theophilus Stimson Jr. both of Gray 15Oct. 1854 at Auburn

ALLEN, Experience and John Webber both of Gray 2 Mar. 1855

ALLEN, Emery of Gray and Elizabeth Baker of Windham 4 Mar. 1856

ALLEN, Elisha see Young, Sarah

ALLEN, Elisha and Deborah Nash of Gray 12 Aug. 1804 p.178

ALLEN, Joseph see Emery, Doris

ALLEN, Joseph see Emery, Dorcas

ALLEN, Daniel of Gray and Mary Fenley of Windham PUB. 15 Mar. 1823 p.232

ALLEN, Josiah and Eleanor Frank both of Gray PUB. 6 Mar 1825 p.242

ALLEN, Sylvina and Stephen Blaisdell both of Gray PUB. 30 Mar.1828 p.256, Md 1828 p.253

ALLEN, Edward see Morse, Happiah

ALLEN, Hannah see Mountfort, Greenleaf

ALLEN, Statira of Gray and Abel Gossom of Poland PUB. 24 Sept. 1832 p.271, Md 25 Sept 1832 p.274

ALLEN, Emily and Theophilis Stimson Jr. both of Gray Md 25 July 1860

ALLEN, Emery of Gray and Susan W. Titcomb of Falmouth Md 14 Dec. 1860

ALLEN, Charles S. and Minnie J. Field both of Gray PUB. 14 Dec. 1888, Md 1 Jan. 1889

ALLEN, Abby D. and Edward Cobb both of Gray PUB. 24 Dec. 1867, Md 1 Jan 1868

ALLEN, Alonzo P. and Rachel H. Dole both of Gray Md 13 Oct. 1870

ALLEN, Alonzo P. and Caroline Allen both of Gray Md 17 Feb. 1872

ALLEN, Caroline see Allen, Alonzo

ALLEN, Katie E. and George D. Skillin both of Gray PUB. 19 Aug. 1872, Md 29 Aug 1872

ALLEN, Evelyn and George W. Libby both of Gray PUB. 15 Feb. 1875, Md 17 Mar 1875

ALLEN, John H. and Jennie O. Procter both of Gray Md 3 Feb. 1877

ALLEN, Andrew and Eunice Whitten both of Gray PUB. 11 Sept. 1877, Md 16 Sept 1877

ALLEN, Josiah W. and Ida E. Field both of Gray PUB. 25 Apr. 1883, Md 22 July 1883

ALLEN, Nellie L. and Frank W. Webster both of Gray Md 12 Feb. 1893 p.7

ALLEN, Eugene F. and Sadie Frank both of Gray Md. 8 Dec. 1897 in Windham p.23

ALLEN, Ernest H. of Gray and Grace Blake of Yarmouth Md.
Jan. 1899 in Yarmouth p 27

ALLEN, Winfield S. and Jennie O. Allen Md. 20 Mar 1905 p.49

ALLEN, Jennie see Allen, Winfield

ALLEN, Edith M. and Albert F. Cobb both of Gray Md. 28 June
1905 p.49

ALLEN, Frank E. and Lelia M. Bailey both of Gray Md. 11 Aug.
1906 p.57

ALLEN, Ella A. and Charles H. Sawyer both of Gray Md. 28 Oct.
1911 p.79

ALLEN, Ernest and Dorothy Rogers both of Lewiston Md. 1 Nov.
1912 p.83

ALLEN, Andrew see Twombly, Bertha

ALLEN, Caroline M. and Theophilus Stimson Jr. both of Gray Md.
15 Oct. 1854

ALLEN, Experience and John Webber both of Gray Md. 2 Mar.
1855

ALLEN, Emery of Gray and Elizabeth Baker of Windham PUB. 4
Mar. 1856 Md. 6 Mar 1856

ALLEN, Isaac see Bennett, Sarah

ALLEN, Mary S. and Roscoe G. Hall both of Gray Md. 17 Nov.
1856

ALLEN, Harriet E. and John L. White both of Gray PUB. 13 May
1857 Md. 6 June 1857

ALLEN, Edward see Bennett, Mary

ALLEN, Alvin of Gray and Angette Small of Windham Md. 31
Aug. 1858

ALLEN, Andrew and Harriett F. Knight both of Gray PUB. 7 Apr.
1859 Md. 9 Apr 1859

ALLEN, Valentine see Libby, Mary

ALLEN, Emily and Theophilis Stimson both of Gray Md. 25 July
1860

ALLEN, Emery of Gray and Susan W. Titcomb of Falmouth Md.
14 Dec. 1860

ALLEN, Charles see Foster, Clara

ALLEN, Charles B. and Cynthia J. Doughty both of Gray Md. 31
Oct 1863

ALLEN, Aggie see Leslie, Whitman

ALLEN, Cora see Maxwell, Frank

ALLEN, Alfred R. of Gray and Margaret S. Morse of New
    Gloucester PUB. 20 May 1838

ALLEN, Prudence and Robert Smith PUB. 2 Mar 1845

ALLEN, Elvira see Adams, Isaac

ALLEN, Sylvia of Gray and Joseph C. Moxcoy of Portland PUB. 2
    Nov 1852

ALLEY, Alice M. and Wilbur Sayward both of Gray Md. 17 July
    1915 in Windham p.95

ANDERSON, Abraham of Gray and Annah T. Waterman of N.
    Gloucester PUB. 10 Oct 1830 p.264

ANDERSON, Bessie and John W. Morrill both of Gray Md. 20
    Sept 1899 in Portland p.31

ANDERSON, Grace see Sawyer, Bernard

ANDERSON, Jennie T. of Gray and Charles M. Hopping of Mt.
    Vernon, N.Y. PUB. 8 Oct 1858 Md. 13 Oct 1858

ANDERSON, Hannah L. and Charles B. White both of Gray Md.
    12 Dec 1862

ANDREWS, Elbert T. of Gray and Emily C. Mills of Readfield
    Md. 23 May 1874

ANDREWS, Richard M. of Gray and Leila H. Thayer of Portland
    Md. 16 June 1902 in Cape Elizabeth p.37

ANDREWS, Lina see Carey, Albert

ARCHIBALD, Almeda see Foster, James

ARMITAGE, Fannie E. of Gray and Herbert W. Sargent of
    Rumford Md. 31 Oct 1922 p.133

ARMSTRONG, Alvin see Morrell, Silvia

ASH, Martha see Clough, Levi

ATWOOD, Ella see Barbour, Charles

AUSTEN, Elizabeth and Sam'l Rounds both of Gray 3 Feb. 1805
    p.180

AUSTIN, Minion and Sally Small both of Gray PUB. 21 Nov.
    1813 p.200

AUSTIN, Elizabeth see Cummings, Ira

AUSTIN, Sarah see Haines, John

AUSTIN, William see Hammond, Louise

AVERY, Annie see Doughty, Daniel

AYER, Susie see McCalmon, Edwin

BABB, Eunice and Jesse Young both of Gray PUB. 9 Apr 1826
    p.245

BABB, Abba see Low, Willard

BACHELDER, Amos and Lydia Lord both of Gray Md. 6 Nov. 1879

BACHELDER, John see Dutton, Mary

BACON, Mary see Cobb, Ebenzer

BACON, Matilda see Libby, Jonathan

BAGNALL, Isaac see Dill, Alice

BAILEY, George W. of New Gloucester and Irene Fogg of Gorham 12 Nov. 1854

BAILEY, Joel L. and Jane Foster both of Gray 25 Dec. 1855

BAILEY, Sarah J. H. and Silas N. Foster both of Gray PUB. 11 June 1860 Md. 17 June 1860

BAILEY, George A. and Bessie C. Hamilton both of Gray PUB. 19 Aug 1889, Md. 25 Aug 1889

BAILEY, Roy M. and Elizabeth M. McConkey both of Gray Md. 2 Sept 1905 p.51

BAILEY, Mildred S. and Irving E. Frank both of Gray Md. 1906 p.57

BAILEY, Lelia see Allen, Frank

BAILEY, Hanson L. and Velma D. Churchill both of New Gloucester Md. 29 Aug 1916 p.99

BAILEY, Joel L. and Jane Foster both of Gray PUB. 25 Dec 1855 Md. 25 Dec 1855

BAILEY, Mary A. and Charles D. Latham both of Gray PUB. 19 Apr 1856 Md. 19 Apr 1856

BAILEY, Sarah J. H. and Silas N. Foster both of Gray PUB. 11 June 1860 Md. 17 June 1860

BAILEY, Angie see Rich, George

BAILEY, George H. and Mary O. Morse both of Gray PUB. 15 Dec 1884 Md. 20 Dec 1884

BAILEY, Alexander Jr. and Miriam T. Doughty PUB. 13 Apr 1845

BAILEY, Dura see Brown, Sarah

BAILEY, Hannah and Salter Soper both of Gray PUB. 15 Nov 1827 p.250, Md. 1827 p.251

BAKER, Elizabeth see Allen,Emery

BAKER, Frank P. and Etta D. Hill both of Gray Md. 25 Apr 1880

BAKER, Elizabeth see Allen, Emery

BALDWIN, Charles A. and Lizzie J. Shaw both of Gray Md. 18 Nov 1896 p.19

BANGS, Edwin G. and Hannah F. Plummer both of Gray Md. 20 Nov 1858

BARBARICK, Theophilus and Mary S. Hall both of Gray Md. 3 Feb 1901 p.33

BARBER, Joanna of Gray and Nehemiah Porter of No. Yarmouth PUB. 13 Apr. 1782; 28 Apr. 1782

BARBER, Esther of Gray and Moses Bartlett of Sutbury, Canada PUB. 7 Sept. 1783; 21 Sept. 1783

BARBER, Mariam and Joseph Merrill both of Gray 12 Jan. 1786 p.137

BARBER, Lucy and Eli Stiles both of Gray 16 Oct. 1791 p.147

BARBOUR, Charles and Betty Loe both of Gray 29 Oct. 1801 p.165

BARBOUR, Mary of Gray and Capt. Wm. Leavitt of Portland PUB. 8 Apr. 1821 p.227

BARBOUR, Susan and James Robinson both of Gray PUB. 24 Nov. 1822 p.231, Md. 5 Dec. 1822 p.230

BARBOUR, Charles of Gray and Mrs. Joanna Cummings of Norway PUB. 8 Mar. 1823

BARBOUR, Mary S. of Gray and Charles D. Hamilton of Portland PUB. 31 Mar 1833 p.275

BARBOUR, Robert B. of Gray and Elizabeth Morgan of No. Yarmouth PUB. 20 Oct. 1833 p.276

BARBOUR, Martha A. and William H. Webster Md. 24 Sept 1860

BARBOUR, Robert and Lucy Ann Watson both of Gray Md. 15 Sept. 1861

BARBOUR, Lucy E. and George E. Frothingham both of Gray PUB. 5 Dec. 1861, Md. 13 Dec. 1861

BARBOUR, Fannie A. and Wilbur F. Leighton both of Gray Md. 18 Nov 1869

BARBOUR, Charles of Gray and Ella Atwood of Lisbon Md. 8 Sept 1870

BARBOUR, Emma M. of Gray and A. R. P. Witham of New Gloucester Md. 2 May 1872

BARBOUR, William L. and Emma M. Smith both of Gray Md. 4 Sept 1874

BARBOUR, Eva May and Frank C. Bohnson both of Gray Md. 25 Mar 1901 p.33

BARBOUR, Ina E. and William E. Doughty both of Gray Md. 23 Dec 1902 p.41

BARBOUR, Martha A. and William H. Webster both of Gray Md. 24 Sept 1860

BARBOUR, Robert and Lucy A. Watson both of Gray Md. 15 Sept 1861

BARBOUR, Lucy E. and George E. Frothingham both of Gray PUB. 5 Dec 1861 Md. 13 Dec 1861

BARBOUR, Martha M. and William P. Merrill both of Gray PUB. 10 May 1846

BARBOUR, Mary of Gray and William Leavitt of Portland 15 Apr 1820 p. 226

BARKER, Edward see Fletcher, Polly

BARKER, Herbert F. of Gray and Sadie R. Verrill of Durham Md. 25 Nov 1913 p.91

BARKER, Lucy E. of Gray and Peter M. Peterson of Cumberland Md. 22 Nov 1917 in West Falmouth p.107

BARKER, Philip E. of Gray and Marion E. Wescott of Poland Md. 6 Nov 1919 in Poland p.119

BARKER, Dorcas H. and Calvin S. Russell both of Gray Md. 4 Dec 1863

BARNES, Morris see Thompson, Nellie

BARNS, James and Eunice Staples both of Gray 16 Mar. 1809 p.186

BARR, Mary see Smith, Johnson

BARROWS, Annie see Libby, John M.

BARROWS, Aaron see Jones, Cynthia

BARSTOW, Percy L. of Gray and Jennie Davis of Sangerville Md. 6 June 1900 in Sangerville p.29

BARTLETT, Moses see Barber, Esther

BARTLETT, Warren S. and Helena Thompson both of Raymond Md. 19 Aug 1893 p.9

BARTON, John and Abagail Hutchinson of Raiment Town PUB. 15 July 1780; 30 July 1780

BARTON, Fred W. and Mary H. Sawyer both of Gray PUB. 14 Jan 1891, Md. 24 Jan 1891

BARTON, Ernest C. and Myra L. Frank both of Gray Md. 19 Oct 1912 p.83

BARTON, Philip W. of Gray and Viola M. Weymouth of New Gloucester Md. 21 Aug 1915 p.95

BATCHELDER, Maria and Aaron Davis both of Yarmouth 18 Jan. 1856

BATCHELDER, Amos of Gray and Clara A. Conant of Mechanic Falls PUB. 9 May 1869, Md. 16 May 1869

BAYER, Rose see Modes, Abraham

BEAN, David see Thompson, Mary

BEAN, Ebenzer of Gray and Mary Hawes of Bridgton Md. 30 Mar 1863

BEAN, Polly see Merrill, Nathaniel

BEATTY, Sarah J. and Franklin P. Morse both of Gray Md. 3 May 1881

BEERS, Mary see Dole, John

BEMIES, James B. and Matilda H. Cobb both of Gray PUB. 3 Dec 1837

BENNET, George G. and Sadie E. Hellin both of New Gloucester Md. 27 May 1897 p.21

BENNETT, William and Sally Weeks both of Gray PUB. 18 May 1817 p.210 Md. 19 June 1817 p.213

BENNETT, Hannah and Edson Buker both of Gray PUB. 25 Oct 1827 p.250

BENNETT, Howard S. and Emma S. Clark Md. 20 Nov 1875

BENNETT, Ida O. of Gray and Joseph O. Small of New Gloucester Md. 15 Jan 1894 p. 11

BENNETT, James E. Jr. and Ella S. Clark both of New Gloucester Md. 8 Nov 1914 p.93

BENNETT, James see Smith, Alice

BENNETT, Erastus B. of Gray and Melita B. Bradford of Turner Md. 16 Apr 1856

BENNETT, Sarah A. of Gray and Isaac E. Allen of Windham Pub. 24 July 1856 Md. 27 July 1856

BENNETT, Mary of Gray and Edward C. Allen of Windham PUB. 10 May 1858 Md. 15 May 1858

BENNETT, William L. of Gray and Hannah O. True of Falmouth PUB. 1 Nov 1846

BENNETT, Elizabeth A. and Henry Mayberry both of Gray PUB. 12 Aug 1849

BENSEN, Gibbs L. and Sarah A. Irish both of New Gloucester Md. 21 Apr 1889

BENSON, George see Humphrey, Hannah

BENSON, Priscilla and John Foster both of Gray PUB. 4 Mar 1832 p.269

BENSON, Eliza Ann B. and Moses B. Foster both of Gray PUB. 20 Dec 1835 p.282

BENSON, Hannah F. of Gray and George Wright of Portland Md. 16 July 1888

BENSON, Edward and Lucy Tripp both of Gray Md. 28 Sept. 1888

BENSON, Elizabeth I. of Gray and John W. May of Raymond PUB. 9 Oct 1869, Md. 17 Oct 1869

BENSON, Mathew and Catherine Doherty both of Poland Md. 20 Apr 1878

BENSON, George see Chase, Frances

BENSON, Hannah F. of Gray and Mancena Rand of Raymond Md. 8 May 1879

BENSON, Major and Maria A. Coffin both of Gray Md. 6 Jan 1883

BENSON, Mertie and Frank Dolley both of Gray Md. 12 Jan 1899 p.27

BENSON, Ethel S. and Harland H. Hodgkins both of Gray Md. 22 Oct 1905 p.51

BENSON, Mary A. of Gray and Jeremiah Edwards of Raymond Md. 21 Aug 1865

BENSON, George W. and Eunice Thurlow both of Gray PUB. 16 May 1887

BENSON, Major see Coffin, Maria

BENSON, George W. and Martha W. Tripp both of Gray PUB. 19 Nov 1843

BENSON, Jabez C. and Zilpha Foster both of Gray PUB. 7 Dec 1845

BENSON, Benjamin S. and Ann M. Libby both of Gray PUB. 22 Aug 1847

BENSON, Emeline H. and Philip C. Hodgkins both of Gray PUB. 5 Aug 1849

BENSON, George W. of Gray and Elizabeth J. Gore of New Gloucester PUB. 12 Oct 1851

BENSON, Lucy Ellen and Edwin J. May both of Gray Md. 5 Aug 1891

BENTLEY, John R. of Gray and Hopey Cobb of Portland PUB. 27 Nov 1831 p.268

BERRY, Peletiah and Hannah Twitchel both of Gray 23 Mar. 1786
    p.138
BERRY, Peletiah and Nice Starbird both of Gray 10 Nov. 1794
    p.151
BERRY, Olive and William Starbird both of Gray 27 June 1811
    p.192
BERRY, Charles of Gray and Eunice Newcomb of Gorham PUB.
    10 May 1823 p. 234
BERRY, Jerusha of Gray and Matthew Duran 3rd of Durham PUB.
    5 Apr 1829 p.260, Md. 1829 p.253 and p.262
BERRY, Hannah see Hill, Josiah
BERRY, Daniel and Louisa Haskell both of Gray PUB. 29 Sept
    1833 p.276
BERRY, Melbourne see Thompson, Laura
BERRY, Georgia A. and Charles Thayer both of Gray PUB. 29
    Sept 1872, Md. 4 Dec 1872
BERRY, Rozinna J. and David G. Tripp both of Gray Md. 14 Mar
    1873
BERRY, Roxieanna and Levi Jones both of Gray Md. 6 July 1874
BERRY, Martha H. and William W. Vinton both of Gray PUB. 14
    Sept 1876, Md. 2 Oct 1876
BERRY, Fannie J. and Mark A. Harris both of Gray PUB. 17 Dec
    1877, Md. 25 Dec 1877
BERRY, S. J. and Charles Thayer both of Gray PUB. 26 Jan 1880,
    Md. 1 Feb 1880
BERRY, George F. and Lizzie R. May both of Gray PUB. 9 May
    1881, Md. 9 June 1881
BERRY, Cora see Verrill, James
BERRY, John O. and Grace E. Barrows both of Raymond Md. 5
    Dec 1896 p.21
BERRY, George and Georgie Carpenter both of Gray Md. 28 Nov
    1903 in Dry Mills p.45
BERRY, Blanche M. of Gray and George S. Plummer of Raymond
    Md. 29 Oct 1904 p.47
BERRY, Walter see Small, Gladys May 1925 in New Gloucester
    p.147
BERRY, Florence H. of Gray and George A. Jones of Portland Md.
    15 Aug 1925 p.149

BERRY, Charles E. of Gray and Doris E. Chase of Island Pond, VT
Md. 30 Aug 1928 in Island Pond, VT p.163

BERRY, Louisa and George L. Thompson both of Gray Md. 28
Dec 1858

BERRY, Timothy see Farwell, Mary

BERRY, Rosanna J. and David G. Tripp both of Gray Md. 10 Oct
1885

BICKFORD, Sarah see Thurlow, John

BICKFORD, James I. And Sarah E. Eveleth both of New
Gloucester Md. 25 Feb 1859

BISHOP, Evelyn L. and Ralph W. Sawyer both of Gray Md. 1 Jan
1913 p.85

BISHOP, Julia H. of Gray and Samuel H. Paul of Wakefield, N.H.
Md. 26 Sept 1927 p.159

BISHOP, Evelyn Louise and Ralph Sawyer both of Gray Md. 11
Jan. 1913

BLACK, Jane see Doughty, John

BLACK, Lydia of Gray and Enoch Nason of Limington PUB. 9
May 1824 p. 236, Md. 10 June 1824 p. 239

BLACK, Olive and Edward Skillin both of Gray PUB. 20 Sept
1829p.260, Md. 20 Oct 1829 p.259

BLACK, George F. of Gray and Katie E. Spikes of Deering Md. 15
May 1888

BLACK, Josiah Jr. and Elizabeth Black both of Cumberland Md.
29 Apr 1860

BLACK, Able of Gray and Mary Crockett of Standish Md. 8 Oct
1861

BLACK, Abel and Rosilla B. Thatcher of both of Gray PUB. 9 July
1837

BLAISDELL, Abigail of Gray and Charles McDonald of New
Gloucester

BLAISDELL, Stephen see Allen, Sylvania

BLAKE, Elias and Annie Young both of Gray 28 July 1808 p.185

BLAKE, Elisha and Elizabeth Cook both of Gray PUB. 21 Nov.
1813 p.200

BLAKE, John M. and Carrie M. Smith both of Gray PUB. 13 Aug
1889, Md. 18 Aug 1889

BLAKE, Ozias G. and Matilda Hamilton both of Gray Md. 11 July
1867

BLAKE, Oliver see Low, Vesta

BLAKE, Roscoe see Gore, Maria

BLAKE, Minnie see Churchill, Demeret

BLAKE, George see Hill, Ann

BLAKE, Herbert V. and Lizzie Sawyer both of New Gloucester Md. 31 Dec 1891 at New Gloucester

BLAKE, Nellie of Gray and Fred Mason of Windham Md. 1 Mar 1894 p.11

BLAKE, Grace see Allen, Ernest H.

BLAKE, Ella G. of Gray and Alexander Farley of Lyndonville, VT. Md. 4 Apr 1900 p.27

BLAKE, Frank E. and Ella M. York both of Gray Md. 11 Apr 1901p.33

BLAKE, Ozias G. and Rebecca D. Welch both of Gray Md. 4 July 1901 p.35

BLAKE, George W. and Ella G. Dow both of Gray Md. 4 July 1901 p. 35

BLAKE, Lester C. of Yarmouth and Charlotte A. Redman of Freeport Md. 23 June 1921p.127

BLAKE, Lothrop see Higgins, Martha

BLAKE, Annie L. of Gray and William T. Perkins of Paris PUB. 23 Jan 1862 Md. 1 Feb 1862

BLAKE, Ozias of Gray and Matilda Hamilton of Portland Md. 4 Aug 1862

BLAKE, Isaac see Morse, Eunice

BLAKE, Emma R. and Alfred Campbell both of Gray PUB. 17 Mar 1865 Md. 13 Apr 1865

BLAKE, Herbert E. and Mary L. Holmes both of New Gloucester Md. 26 Nov 1885

BLAKE, Ozias G. and Abbie E. Whitney both of Gray PUB. 2 Feb 1873, Md. 8 Feb 1873 Naples

BLAKE, Minnie M. of Gray and Herbert T. Sawyer of No. Yarmouth Md. 24 June 1893 in N.H. p. 7

BLANCHARD, Eliza and Robert Ramsdell both of Gray 10 Apr. 1820 p.226

BLANCHARD, Mark and Cecile M. Leavitt both of Gray Md. 26 Mar 1924 in Portland p.141

BLANCHARD, Vernon S. of Westbrook and Lena E. Ladd of Lincoln Md. 3 June 1925 p.147

BODGE, Charles and Ermina Montgomery both of Windham Md. 18 Nov 1896 p.21

BOHNSEN, Jennie M. and Perley C. Sawyer both of Gray Md. 30 June 1906 p.55

BOHNSEN, Minnie E. and Eugene Foster both of Gray Md. 29 Apr 1908 p.65

BOHNSEN, Hazel E. of Gray and Albert E. Leighton of Hallowell Md. 22 May 1926 p.151

BOHNSEN, Inez M. of Gray and Franklin E. Hodgkins of Poland Md. 9 Apr 1928 p.161

BOHNSON, Frank C. see Barbour, Eva

BOOTHBY, William L. and Abbie Maria Haskell both of Poland Md. 22 Nov 1893 p.9

BOOTHBY, Irving S. of Saco and Florence M. Estes of New Gloucester Md. 21 Dec 1910 p.79 of York Beach Md. 28 June 1917 p.105

BOWDOIN, Ella see McDonald, Roy

BOYNTON, Bertha see Libby, George

BRACKET, Nathaniel see Humphrey, Eunice

BRACKETT, Lois see Doughty, Nathan

BRACKETT, Benjamin and Thankful Brown both of New Gloucester Md. 11 Apr 1868

BRACKETT, Geo. see Sawyer, Bessie

BRACKETT, Mary see Walker, Michael

BRADBURY, Nathaniel S. of Gray and Jane Marr of Standish PUB. 7 Nov 1830 p.264

BRADBURY, Horatio see Miller, A. May

BRADBURY, Cotton see Harris, Ella

BRADFORD, Melita see Bennett, Erastus

BRAGDON, Gilbert and Rosetta Verrill both of Gray Md. 24 June 1907 p.59

BRAGDON, Percy C. of Oxford and Margaret F. Pennington of Booth Bay Harbor Md. 23 May 1928 p.161

BRAGDON, Adeline of Gray and Chester May of New Gloucester Md. 1 Mar 1929 in New Gloucester p.167

BRAGG, Edward see Snow, Lauris

BRAYMAN, Mary of Gray and Daniel Harris of Poland PUB. 27 Sept 1829 p.260, Md. 1829 p.258

BREIEL, John P. of Cumberland and Lillian M. Holmes of
Metheun Mass. Md. 29 Sept 1915 p.95
BREWER, Ralph O. and Myrtle Verrill both of Gray Md. 21 Sept
1922 p.133
BRIANT, Elesebeth see Cummings Isaac
BROOKS, Peter W. and Rosa A. Foster both of Gray PUB. 22 Nov
1872, Md. 28 Nov 1872
BROOKS, Christiana and Sylvester L. Swan both of Gray Md. 15
Apr 1875
BROOKS, Rosezella A. and Thomas G. Whitney both of Gray Md.
25 Mar 1917 p.103
BROWN, Hannah of Gray and Thomas Crisp Jordan of
Raymondtown 10 Apr. 1803 p.175
BROWN, Olive of Gore between Raymondtown & Gray and David
Jordan of Raymondtown 15 Apr. 1802 p.172
BROWN, Peggy of Gray and Ezra Jordan of Raymond 9 Dec.
1810 p.188
BROWN, Titus O. and Sophia Furbish both of Gray PUB. 29 Dec.
1821 p.227, Md. 1821/2 p. 229
BROWN, Andrew Jr. of Gray and Sally Russ of Raymond PUB. 27
Oct. 1822 p.231
BROWN, Frances of Gray and Jebediah Burbank of Bethel PUB.
23 Dec 1827 p.250, Md. 9 Jan 1828 p.252
BROWN, Abigail H. of Gray and Amos Purington of Portland
PUB. 14 Sept 1828 p.257, Md. 1828 p.255
BROWN, Persis and D. H. Furbish both of Gray PUB. 23 Jan 1831
p.265, Md. 1 Feb 1831 p.267
BROWN, Eliza F. of Gray and Silvanus Poor of Andover PUB. 5
Jan 1834 p.277
BROWN, John see Shaw, Sarah
BROWN, George see Frank, Mary
BROWN, Alvin of Gray and Sarah F. Jordan of Raymond PUB. 25
Dec. 1861, Md. 1 Jan. 1862
BROWN, Lizzie see Dole, William
BROWN, Mary see Morrill, Matthew
BROWN, Oliver and Mary E. M. Watson both of Gray Md. 10 Oct
1869
BROWN, Elnora see Dole, Asa
BROWN, Emma see Knight, Hartley
BROWN, Charles see Dickinson, Abbie

BROWN, Dora see Morrill, Hugh

BROWN, Charles H. and Elizabeth M. Gore both of Yarmouth Md. 28 May 1894 p.13

BROWN, Ira M. and Sarah L. Gilman both of No. Yarmouth Md. 27 Jan 1895 p.15

BROWN, Arthur W. of Gray and Ethel M. Carlisle of Brewer Md. 28 June 1917 in Brewer p.107

BROWN, Alice M. of Gray and Arthur L. Hitchcock of Damriscotta Md. 18 July 1918 in Portland p.113

BROWN, Florence and Derrill O. Lamb both of Gray Md. 9 Apr 1925 p.145

BROWN, John see Shaw, Sarah

BROWN, George see Frank, Mary

BROWN, Alvin of Gray and Sarah F. Jordan of Raymond PUB. 25 Dec 1861 Md. 1 Jan 1862

BROWN, Emma of Gray and Daniel H. Chipman of Raymond Md. 21 Sept 1864

BROWN, E. J. see Small, Freda

BROWN, Deborah and William Libby 3rd both of Gray PUB. 23 Dec 1837

BROWN, Sarah A. and Dura L. Bailey both of Gray PUB. 10 Dec 1848

BROWN, Helen M. of No. Gray and James M. Kallock of Biddeford Md. 17 Aug. 1918 in Biddeford p.113

BRYANT, Jonathan of Oxford and Abigail Littlehale of Portland Md. 1830 p.262

BRYANT, Arthur see Frank, Bertha

BRYANT, Ursula L. and Moses H. Goff both of Gray PUB. 21 Sept 1863 Md. 27 Sept 1863

BUCKMAN, ? and Eliza Merrill Md. 3 May 1865

BUKER, Edson see Bennett, Hannah

BUKER, Clara of Gray and Isaac H. Lord of Norway Md. 20 May 1900 in Norway p.29

BUMPAS, Charles H. and Sarah J. Dunbar both of Oxford Md. 7 June 1913 p.87

BUNKER, Addie and Melvin Eugene Whitney both of Gray Md. 21 June 1884

BURBANK, Jebediah see Brown, Frances

BURNHAM, Mary E. and John C. Hanson both of Gray Md. 2 Jan 1921 p.125

BURNHAM, Harry see Libby, Laura

BURNHAM, Philip M. of Gray and Thelmer Melchior of Falmouth Md. 26 Jan 1929 p.165

BURNS, Bessie M. and Leroy Libby both of Gray Md. 18 Aug 1913 p.89

BURNS, Inez A. and Sewell P. Prince both of Gray Md. 2 Oct 1915 p.97

BURNS, Kenneth H. of Gray and Gladys C. Leighton of Falmouth Md. 30 July 1924 p.175

BURRILL, Albana P. and Minette M. Wells both of New Gloucester Md. 26 Dec 1894 p.13

BURROWS, Edward M. of Gray and Julia E. Frye of Cumberland Md. 27 Mar 1916 in Cumberland p.99

BURROWS, Addie J. and Wendall A. Small both of Gray PUB. 4 Aug 1887

BUTMAN, Esther of Gray and Samuel Megguier of New Gloucester 13 Oct. 1811 p.199

BUXTON, Elizabeth and John Doxey both of Gray Md. 4 July 1879

BUZZELL, Jacob see Thompson, Nancy

CAMBELL, John L. of Gray and Caroline M. Strout of Windham Md. 15 June 1929 in Westbrook p.167

CAMPBELL, Alfred of Gray and Bridget L. Young of Prince Edward Island, Canada PUB. 2 Aug 1869, Md. 6 Aug 1869

CAMPBELL, Emma R. of Gray and Thomas G. Whitney of Casco Md. 30 May 1874

CAMPBELL, Martha J. and Charles C. Knight both of Gray Md. 19 June 1897 in Windham p.23

CAMPBELL, Winnie and Thomas J. Mayberry both of Gray Md. 11 Dec 1897 p.23

CAMPBELL, Alfred see Blake, Emma

CANNELL, Minnie see Pollard, Ira

CAPEN, Mary see Van, John

CAREY, Theda of Gray and Robert M. Sykes of Auburn Md. 17 Oct 1866

CAREY, Cephas of Gray and Mary E. Farris of Oxford Md. 27 Feb 1864

CAREY, Albert A. of Gray and Lina F. Andrews of Portland PUB. 6 July 1887

CAREY, Thomas see Waterhouse, Julia

69

CARLISLE, Ethel see Brown, Arthur

CARPENTER, Frank P. and Susan E. Cobb both of New Gloucester Md. 1 Aug 1878

CARPENTER, Georgie see Berry, George

CARSWELL, John see Lane, Lucretia

CARY, Albert A. of Gray and Abby D. Strout of Raymond Md. 26 Oct 1875

CASH, Sam'l and Elizabeth Strout both of Raymondtown 20 June 1801 p.164

CASH, Orlando F. and Hannah J. Gatchall both of Raymond Md. 19 Oct 1862

CASWELL, Frances E. of Gray and Samuel F. Tufts of Standish Md. 10 June 1872

CASWELL, Edgar S. of Gray and Hattie E. Conant of Windham PUB. 30 Nov 1879, Md. 20 Dec 1879

CHADBORNE, Myra see Wing, Everett

CHADBOURNE, Sally see McKenney, Jona.

CHAMBERLAIN, Henry see Soper, Martha

CHAMBERLIN, Elizabeth see Adams, Benjamin

CHAMBERS, Benj. See Lane, Margaret

CHANDLER, Rachel of New Gloucester and Nathan Sanders of Norway 17 Jan. 1804 p.178

CHANDLER, Donald see Sweetser, Mary

CHANDLER, Mary see Grant, John

CHAPMAN, Doris see Muzzy, Marcus

CHAPMAN, Harry G. and Ethel B. Deforge both of Brunswick Md. 30 Sept. 1919 p.119

CHAPMAN, Eugene and Ailsa M. Martin both of Providence, R. I. Md. 8 Sept 1930 p.173

CHASE, Nellie see Sawyer, George

CHASE, Frances E. and George E. Benson both of Gray PUB. 30 July 1878, Md. 8 Aug 1878

CHASE, John H. and Carrie W. Stimson both of Gray PUB. 20 Oct 1890, Md. 30 Oct 1890

CHASE, Ethel M. see Skillings, Harlan R.

CHASE, Doris see Berry, Charles

CHIPMAN, Chester E. and Susie S. Thurlow both of Poland Md. 11 Nov 1890

CHIPMAN, Julia C. and Herbert L. Tripp both of Gray Md. 3 Aug 1912 in Portland p.81

CHIPMAN, Iva M. and Henry E. Sayward both of Gray Md. 13 Nov 1922 p.135

CHIPMAN, Daniel see Brown, Emma

CHIPMAN, Ernest F. and Della M. Haskell both of Gray Md. 19 Sept 1908 in No. Yarmouth p.67

CHURCHILL, Demeret S. of Gray and Minnie Blake of Raymond Md. 28 May 1877

CHURCHILL, George S. D. of Raymond and Susanne M. Penney of Brockton, Mass Md. 19 Sept 1930 p.175

CHUTE, Oliver see Plummer, Annie

CHUTE, Caroline see Eveleth, William

CHUTE, Robert see Foster, Jennie

CILLEY, Bernard see Maxwell, Catherine

CLAPP, Melissa see Quint, George

CLARK, Jacob and Mrs. Lucetta Marr both of Gray 3 May 1854

CLARK, Abigail and Jonathan Libby both of Gray 18 Sept. 1792 p.148

CLARK, Jenney and Jeams Webster both of Gray 31 Dec. 1801 p.168

CLARK, Samuel and Jane Libby both of Gray 24 Dec. 1807 p.184

CLARK, George see Libby, Wealthy

CLARK, Stephen H. and Alice A. Doughty both of Portland Md. 14 Feb 1875

CLARK, Cora J. and George B. Hodgkins both of Gray Md. 12 July 1875

CLARK, Jennie L. of Gray and George E. Loring of Boston Mass. PUB. 5 Feb 1881, Md. 14 Feb 1881

CLARK, William H. of Gray and Mary A. Hamilton of No. Yarmouth PUB. 5 Oct 1891, Md. 1 Nov 1891

CLARK, Joseph B. and Nellie F. Snow both of Gray Md. 30 Oct 1895 p.17

CLARK, Jacob and Lucetta Marr both of Gray Md. 3 May 1854

CLARK, John see Foster, Nellie

CLARK, Frank I. and Artie E. Libby both of Gray PUB. 28 Feb 1885 Md. 7 May 1885

CLAY, Prerilla see Libby, Benjamin

CLAYTON, Edward, see Thurlow, Clara

CLEAVELAND, James B. and Lucinda P. McKenna both of
     Gray PUB. 9 Feb. 1834 p.277
CLOUDMAN, Sarah see Frank, John
CLOUGH, Levi and Sarah Merrill both of Gray 1 Dec. 1820 p.221
CLOUGH, Elizabeth S. of Gray and Joshua M. Rideout of Portland
     PUB. 29 Mar 1829 p.260
CLOUGH, Levi of Gray and Martha Ash of Portland PUB 26 Sept
     1830 p.264
CLOUGH, Elbridge R. and Harriett E. Rideout both of Cumberland
     Md. 22 Nov 1875
CLOUGH, Howard B. see Whitney, Cora M.
CLOUGH, Nathan see Dutton, Paulener
CLOUGH, John see Libby, Ellen
COBB, Rebecker and Nathaniel Stevens PUB. 31 Aug 1782; 14
     Sept. 1782
COBB, Mary and David Libby both of Gray 5 June 1796   p.155
COBB, Joanna of Gray and Capt. Jonathan Cummings of Norway
     27 Feb. 1803 p.174
COBB, Benjamin and Catherine Fowler both of Gray 5 Apr. 1810
     p.188
COBB, Benjamin and Catherine Fowler both of Gray 15 Apr. 1810
     p.190
COBB, Abigail of Gray and Elisha J. Ford of Jefferson 30 June
     1811
COBB, Rebecca of Gray and Stephen Porter of North Yarmouth
     21 Jan. 1816   p.200
COBB, Benjamin and Hannah Lunt both of Gray PUB. 17 Mar.
     1822 p.228
COBB, Stephen see Fowler, Betsey
COBB, Winthrop and Marcia G Lyon both of N. Gloucester Md.
     1828 p.255
COBB, Hopey see Bentley, John
COBB, George see Ramsdell, Lucinda
COBB, Mabel F. and Luther W. Hill both of Gray Md. 9 Apr 1889
COBB, Emily C. of Gray and Leonard Flint of Westbrook PUB. 14
     Jan 1867, Md. 26 Jan 1867
COBB, Edward see Allen, Abby
COBB, Mary C. and Ephraim Tinkham both of Gray PUB. 29 June
     1868, Md. 4 July 1868

COBB, Abby A. and Hugh Smith both of Gray PUB. 25 Nov 1870, Md 1 Dec 1870

COBB, Matilda H. of Gray and Albion S. Perley of San Francisco, Cal. PUB. 11 Feb 1873, Md. 19 Feb 1873

COBB, Clara L. of Gray and Lindley M. Webb of Windham PUB. 25 Aug 1874, Md. 15 Sept 1874

COBB, Mary see Purvis, Adam

COBB, Ivory and Harriett Verrill both of New Gloucester Md. 28 Oct 1876

COBB, Sylvester B. of Gray and Mary M. Curtis of Auburn Md. 19 Apr 1880

COBB, Charles M. and Jane E. Pride both of Falmouth Md. 26 Dec 1881

COBB, Lizzie see Frank, Hersey

COBB, Mabel H. of Gray and Lewis E. Gilman of Scarboro Md. 11 June 1892

COBB, Alice G. and Fred J. Stubbs both of Gray Md. 1 June 1893 p. 7

COBB, Dwinal and Frederica Maier both of Gray Md. 26 Nov 1896 p.21

COBB, Marshall C. and Jennie R. Small both of Gray Md. 8 Dec 1901 p.37

COBB, Lillian G. and Lester D. Hall both of Gray Md. 16 May 1904 p.47

COBB, Albert see Allen, Edith

COBB, Ervena M. and Eddie B. Martin both of Gray Md. 5 May 1906 p.53

COBB, Imogene and Milton C. Frank both of Gray Md. 10 Feb 1913 p.85

COBB, Lilla M. and Harvey L. Thompson both of Gray Md. 1 Nov 1913 in Auburn p.89

COBB, Stuart S. and Bessie L. Libby both of Gray Md. 10 July 1915 in Portland p.95

COBB, Catherine A. and John A. Skilling both of Gray Md. 10 Aug 1922 in Westbrook p.133

COBB, John S. of Gray and Beatrice M. Davies of Portland Md. 27 July 1929 p.169

COBB, George see Ramsdell, Lucinda

COBB, Osburn and Christania B. Herrick both of Gray Md. 14 July
1862

COBB, William F. of Gray and Flora B. Morse of New Gloucester
PUB. 22 Mar 1886 Md. 27 Mar 1886

COBB, Matilda see Bemies, James

COBB, Ebenzer of Gray and Mary Bacon of Portland PUB. 18 Feb
1838

COBB, Almira and Joseph Ross both of Gray PUB. 3 Mar 1838

COBB, Ebenzer Col. of Gray and Hannah C. Haskell of Danville
PUB. 1841

COBB, Hope see Starbird, Henry

COFFIN, Maria see Benson, Major

COFFIN, Simeon G. and Martha May both of Gray Md. 19 Oct
1895 p.17

COFFIN, Maria and Major Benson both of Gray PUB. 12 June
1887

COLBY, Moses and Harriett E. Proctor of Portland PUB. 7 Feb
1847

COLE, Benjamin and Mary Porter both of No. Yarmouth Md. 6
Apr. 1823

COLE, Hattie M. of Gray and George W. Adams of Portland Md. 4
July 1879

COLE, Hewitt see Cummings, Jennie

COLE, Benjamin see Pennell, Susan

COLE, Ira N. of Raymond and Josephine L. Leighton of Shelburne,
N. H. Md. 22 Sept 1906 p.57

COLLEY, Hannah and Daniel Libby Junr. Both of Gray 25 May
1795 p.153

COLLEY, John of Gray and Eleanor Weymouth of Falmouth 25
Aug. 1798 p.158

COLLEY, James Junr. and Elisabeth Stowell both of Gray 19
Apr. 1801 p.165

COLLEY, Amos and Sarah Nash both of Gray 24 June 1802
p.173

COLLEY, Mary and Nathaniel Haskell both of Gray 15 Aug. 1819
p.224

COLLEY, Sarah and James C. Thompson both of Gray PUB. 31
Jan 1830 p.261, Md. 18 Feb 1830 p.258

COLLEY, Mary of Gray and John Rich of Portland PUB. 7 June
1829 p.260, Md. 5 July 1829 p.258

COLLEY, William of Albion and Esther Johnson of Portland Md.
1830 p.262

COLLEY, Hannah and John C. Tuttle both of Gray PUB. 25 July
1830 p.263

COLLEY, Benjamin and Charlotte S. Harris both of Gray PUB. 5
Dec 1830 p.264, Md. 1830 p.266

COLLEY, Richard see Lane, Eunice

COLLEY, Charles W. and Susie H. Edwards PUB. 26 Nov. 1888,
Md. 9 Dec. 1888

COLLEY, Susan A. of Gray and David Simpson of Lewiston Md.
29 Dec 1866

COLLEY, Charles H. of Gray and Addie M. Ellis of Charlestown
PUB. 19 Aug 1878, Md. 25 Aug 1878

COLLEY, John W. of Gray and Estella C. Farrar of Yarmouth Md.
17 Feb 1880

COLLEY, Hattie J. of Gray and John Fletcher Woodbury of
Waterville Md. 16 Sept 1892 p.5

COLLEY, Sturgis V. and Dora L. Morrill both of Gray Md. 2 June
1900 p.29

COLLEY, Reina A. and Fred T. Whitney both of Gray Md. 3 Nov
1915 in Buckfield p.97

COLLEY, True M. and Thirza M. Huntress both of Gray Md. 1
June 1918 p.111

COLLEY, Addie M. and Alfred Micho both of Gray Md. 27 May
1919 in Portland p.115

COLLEY, Richard and Eliza Verrill both of Gray Md. 4 Apr 1858

COLLEY, Albert T. and Mary F. Doughty both of Gray Md. 10 Oct
1864

COLLEY, Orin B. and Helen A. Hall both of Gray Md. 18 Oct
1864

COLLEY, Benjamin and Rebecca Foster both of Gray PUB. 2 Dec
1840

COLLEY, Amos Jr. and Nancy Kilbreth both of Gray PUB. 11
May 1845

COLLEY, James and Olive Stowell both of Gray PUB. 2 Nov 1845

CONANT, Clara see Batchelder, Amos

CONANT, Hattie see Caswell, Edgar

CONANT, Harry L. and Anna L. Heald both of Hebron Md. 6 Sept. 1911 p.79

CONLEY, Edward see Harris, Bell

COOK, Robert and Lydia Young both of Gray 16 Oct. 1808 p.185

COOK, Elizabeth see Blake, Elisha

COOK, Lydia of Gray and Samuel Higgins of Cape Elizabeth 28 May 1819 p.218

COOK, Sarah A. of Gray and Austin A. Fish of Lewiston Md. 30 Apr 1866

COOK, Eva M. of Gray and George S. Reed of Portland Md. 26 June 1907 p.59

COOK, Harry E. of Gray and Estella M. Johnson of Auburn Md. 20 Nov 1907 in Auburn p.61

COOMBS, George T. of Castine and Edith E. Merrill of New Gloucester Md. 28 June 1922 p.133

CORDWELL, Stephen A. and Lucinda D. Grant both of Westbrook Md. 17 Apr 1859

CORLISS, John see Skillin, Lavina

CORSON, Albert and Henrietta Mitchell both of Gray Md. 3 May 1869

CORSON, Luville H. and Alice E. Ryder both of Gray Md. 1 Jan 1895 in New Gloucester p.13

COTE, Lydia see May, William

COTE, Antoinette see Knight, Frank

COTE, Raymond see Libby, Mertie

COTTON, Carrie A. and Fred H. Sawyer both of Gray PUB. 30 June 1880, Md. 24 July 1880

COVYEOU, Elsie A. and John L. Harriman both of Gray Md. 3 July 1905 p.51

CRAGIN, Frank see Thayer, Abbie

CRAM, Frank see Deering, Carrie

CRAWFORD, John see Scully, Caroline

CREPEY, Lorenzo see Strout, Ellen

CRESSEY, Anson G. and Eunice C. Morrison both of Cumberland Md. 19 Sept 1878

CROCKER, John see Morse, Augusta

CROCKER, Jessie S. and Fred A. Cummings both of Gray Md. 1 Apr 1871

CROCKER, Harold E. and Cora A. Lufkin both of Cumberland Md. 14 May 1927 p.157

CROCKER, John see Morse, Augusta

CROCKET, Delphina see Skillin, Hiram

CROCKETT, Mary see Black, Able

CROCKETT, George L. and Abbie E. Briggs both of Cumberland Md. 31 July 1864

CROCKETT, Stative and Robert Harrington both of Gray Md. 19 July 1857

CROOKER, Mary E. and Fred H. Ireland both of Gray Md. 20 Feb 1908 p.63

CROSS, William B.S. and Isabel F. Libby both of Gray PUB. 24 Dec 1880, Md. 1 Jan 1881

CROSS, Frank H. and Sadie A. Hunt both of Gray Md. 8 Oct 1881

CROSSETT, Calvin D. and Florence E. Dow both of Portland Md. 2 Sept. 1919 p.117

CROUSE, Bessie B. and Frank C. Grover both of Gray Md. 26 Aug 1910 in Portland p.77

CROUSE, Mabel V. and Archie M. Harris both of Gray Md. 23 Nov 1912 p.83

CROWELL, Ezra and Mary Latham both of Gray PUB. 22 Aug 1841

CUMMINGS, Elisha, and Mary Dolly PUB. 26 Sept. 1778; 11 Oct. 1778 p.97

CUMMINGS, Isaac and Elesebeth Briand PUB. 2 Dec. 1780; 18 Dec. 1780

CUMMINGS, Susanna and Abraham Young PUB. 19 Apr. 1781; 4 May 1781

CUMMINGS, Ruth and David Jordan both of Gray PUB. 13 Apr. 1782; 28 Apr. 1782

CUMMINGS, Daniel and Abigail Fletcher both of Gray 2 July 1789 p.142

CUMMINGS, Amos and Betty Fletcher both of Gray 30 Oct. 1794 p.153

CUMMINGS, Jonathan see Cobb, Joanna

CUMMINGS, Joseph of Gray and Ruth Thayer of Hebron PUB. 9 Apr 1817 p.209

CUMMINGS, Abigail and Joseph York both of Gray PUB. 20 Jan. 1822 p.228, Md. 17 Mar 1822 p.229

CUMMINGS, Joanna see Barbour, Charles

CUMMINGS, William P. of Gray and Sarah Pierce of New
   Gloucester PUB. 2 May 1824 p. 236
CUMMINGS, Thirza and William Dolley Jr both of Gray PUB. 3
   Dec 1832 p.272
CUMMINGS, Abagail and Charles Libby both of Gray PUB. 8 Dec
   1833 p.276
CUMMINGS, Ira of Gray and Elizabeth Austin of Buckfield PUB.
   8 Nov 1835 p.281
CUMMINGS, Elisha and Mary Dolley Md. 26 Sept 1778
CUMMINGS, Samuel P. and Ruth I. Foster Md. 3 Dec 1865
CUMMINGS, Fred see Crocker, Jessie
CUMMINGS, Mary E. of Gray and Charles H. Small of New
   Gloucester Md. 2 Sept. 1872
CUMMINGS, Llewellyn D. and Fannie H. Libby both of Gray
   PUB. 27 Aug 1878, Md. 18 Sept 1878
CUMMINGS, Samuel W. and Emogene Swan both of Gray Md. 28
   Dec 1878
CUMMINGS, Susie S. of Gray and Lewis J. Frink of Gorham Md.
   17 Jan 1882
CUMMINGS, Fred A. and Irma G. Parker both of Gray Md. 15
   Aug 1891 at Dover N.H.
CUMMINGS, Eugene I. and Mabel Herrick both of Westbrook
   Md. 26 Mar 1892
CUMMINGS, Milo G. and Susie J. Jones both of Gray Md. 6 July
   1900 in Deering p.31
CUMMINGS, John E. and Nellie J. Grant both of Gray Md. 29
   Nov 1905 p.53
CUMMINGS, Jennie of Gray and Hewitt D. Cole of Raymond Md.
   12 June 1906 p.55
CUMMINGS, Ethel I. Of Gray and Edwin F. Pierce of Lewiston
   Md. 5 Oct 1906 p.57
CUMMINGS, Milo G. and Lucy J. Merrill both of Gray Md. 22
   June 1918 in Auburn p.111
CUMMINGS, Samuel M. and Mary McConkey both of Raymond
   Md. 24 Sept 1927 p.159
CUMMINGS, Gerald H. of Freeport and Addie E. Verrill of
   Pownal Md. 11 Oct 1930 p.173
CUMMINGS, Henry of Gray and Isabella Jordan of New
   Gloucester PUB. 10 Oct 1857 Md. 25 Oct 1857

CUMMINGS, Lizzie see Morse, Charles

CUMMINGS, Henry and Lydia E. Hallowell both of Gray PUB. 26 Feb 1841

CUNNINGHAM, James A. and --------- ------ both of No. Yarmouth Md. 29 June 1873

CURTIS, Bowery and Sarah Ramsdell both of Gray 26 Nov. 1797 p.157

CURTIS, Frank see Farwell, Olive

CURTIS, Mary see Cobb, Sylvester

CUSHING, James see Nash, Julia

CUSHING, Ella see Goff, Elias

CUSHING, Julia M. of Gray and J. W. Johnson of No. Yarmouth Md. 25 Dec 1876

CUSHING, Louis T. and Emma M. Merrill both of Gray Md. 28 Nov 1895 p.17

CUSHING, Frances L. of Gray and Frank S. Piper of Parsonsfield Md. 26 June 1926 p.153

CUSHMAN, Ara see Merrill, Esther

CUSHMAN, Nathaniel P. and Silvia Libby both of Gray 4 July 1821 p.226

CUSHMAN, Nathaniel P. and Sylvia Libby both of Gray PUB. 3 June 1821/2 p.227

CUSHMAN, Asa see Morse, Julia

DACY, Rebecca I. of Gray and Edward Knight of Pownal Md. 30 Aug 1869

DACY, Isaiah see Glines, Rebecca

DAVID, Charles and Abby G. Strout of Casco PUB. 4 Dec 1844

DAVIES, Jessie M. of Gray and Trueman H. Stone of Oxford Md. 1 Mar 1929 in Portland p.165

DAVIES, Beatrice see Cobb, John

DAVIS, Aaron see Batchelder, Maria

DAVIS, David and Sarah Hayden both of Gray 24 Sept. 1795 p.154

DAVIS, Joseph and Rebecca Merrill both of Gray 13 May 1798 p.158

DAVIS, Betsy and David Hayden both of Gray 15 Sept. 1800 p.163

DAVIS, Judath and Jebediah Hayden both of Gray 2 Oct. 1800 p.163

DAVIS, Elie and Simon Stilman Lawrence both of Gray 19 July 1818 p.218

DAVIS, Anna and Samuel Merill both of Gray PUB. 16 Jan. 1825 p.237, MD 6 Feb. 1825 p.239

DAVIS, David see Jordan, Mary

DAVIS, Etta F. and Richard E. Quint both of Gray PUB. 14 June 1889, Md. 22 June 1889

DAVIS, Eliza E. of Gray and Benjamin W. Leighton of Falmouth Md. 20 Oct 1876

DAVIS, Eliza E. of Gray and C.F. Everett of Mechanic Falls Md. 15 Oct 1883

DAVIS, Harriet see Quint, Gilman

DAVIS, Jennie see Barstow, Percy L.

DAVIS, Arthur T. and Ella Braley both of Portland Md. 30 June 1900 p.29

DAVIS, Harry of Gorham and Maude Mayberry of Windham Md. 30 Nov 1899 p.31

DAVIS, Elmer W. and Caroline D. Leighton both of Gray Md. 29 Aug 1906 p.57

DAVIS, Josephine T. and Wilbur P. Hancock both of Gray Md. 15 May 1920 p.121

DAVIS, George F. of Gray and Charlotte E. Pike of Poland Md. 5 July 1920 p.123

DAVIS, Arlene M. and George W. Edwards both of Gray Md. 27 Sept 1929 p.169

DAVIS, Aaron and Maria Batchelder both of Yarmouth Md. 18 Jan 1856

DAVIS, Joseph see Mountfort, Augusta

DAVIS, Carrie see Foster, Granville

DAVIS, Jennie see McDonald, George

DAY, Carrie M. and Charles Verrill both of Gray Md. 1 Jan 1883

DAY, Harlie see McConkey, Lena

DAY, Mary see Stowell, Luther

DAYON, Laura and Bryant A. Moors both of Gray Md. 6 Sept. 1930 in Westbrook p.173

DEERING, Carrie M. of Gray and Frank L. Cram of Gorham Md. 2 Dec 1866

DELANO, Juda and Larrabee Harris both of North Yarmouth 27 Oct. 1808   p.185

DELANO, William and Abigail C Hill both of Gray PUB. 21 Oct
1827 p.250, Md. 1827 p.251

DELANO, Mrs. Betsey of Gray and John Leighton of Falmouth
PUB. Jan 1852

DENNIS, Eleanor see Berry, Wilbur

DENNISON, Emeline see Small, John

DENNISON, Eliza G. and Joshua H. Hall both of Gray PUB. 31
Aug 1845

DICKEY, William L. and Harriett E. White both of Gray PUB. 16
Nov 1870, Md. 8 Jan 1871

DICKINSON, Sarah see Simpson, William

DICKSON, Abbie T. of Gray and Charles A. Brown of Yarmouth
Md. 8 Oct 1877

DICKSON, Mary E. and Charles F. Hill both of Gray Md. 1 Nov
1884

DILL, Alice I. of Gray and Isaac Bagnall of Lewiston Md. 17 Oct
1866

DILL, James see Doughty, Abigail

DINGLEY, Harry see Foster, Alice

DOANE, Henry J. and Blanche a. Eastman both of Mechanic Falls
Md. 16 June 1923 p.137

DOE, Charles and Peace Knight both of Windham Md. 20 Nov.
1808 p.185

DOLE, James see Leighton, Eunice

DOLE, William R. of Gray and Lizzie S. Brown of No. Haven Md.
23 Oct. 1888

DOLE, Clara A. of Gray and Albert M. Knight of Windham Md. 1
Dec. 1865

DOLE, John C. and Mrs. Matilda Doyle both of Gray Md. 6 June
1870

DOLE, Rachel see Allen, Alonzo

DOLE, John C. of Gray and Mary Beers of St. John, New
Brunswick, Canada Md. 19 Aug 1872

DOLE, Asa S. of Gray and Elnora F. Brown of N. Haven Md. 30
Oct 1874

DOLE, John T. and Annie Jordan both of Gray Md. 1 Jan 1896
p.17

DOLE, James see Leighton, Eunice

DOLE, John T. of Gray and Elizabeth Evans of Portland PUB. 24
  Dec 1885 Md. 14 Jan 1886
DOLLEY, William see Hayden, Hannah
DOLLEY, John and Betsey Mutchmore both of Gray PUB. 6 Sept.
  1818 p.215 Md. 1818 p.217
DOLLEY, George and Mary Perley both of Gray PUB. 13 Mar.
  1825 p. 242, Md. 21 Apr 1825 p.240
DOLLEY, Jeremiah H. and Catherine Tufts both of Gray PUB. 14
  Oct. 1827 p.246
DOLLEY, George and Martha Foster both of Gray PUB. 31 Jan.
  1829 p.257, Md. 1829 p.254
DOLLEY, Mary and Thomas Whitmarsh both of Gray PUB. 18
  Apr. 1830 p.263
DOLLEY, William see Cummings, Thirza
DOLLEY, Lydia and Jonas Humphrey both of Gray PUB. 13 Dec.
  1832 p.272
DOLLEY, Mary see Cummings, Elisha
DOLLEY, John see Morse, Mary
DOLLEY, Abigail of Gray and Annizibad Dolley of Falmouth
  PUB. 18 May 1866, Md. 24 June 1866
DOLLEY, Annizibad see Dolley, Abigail
DOLLEY, Daniel H. and Lucy A. Ferguson both of Gray PUB. 22
  Feb. 1869, Md. 4 Mar 1869
DOLLEY, George C. of Gray and Emma Roberts Md. 15 Dec.
  1869
DOLLEY, George and Mary S. Frank both of Gray PUB. 24 Nov.
  1870, Md. 10 Dec. 1870
DOLLEY, Helen S. of Gray and Edwin G. Moody of Needham,
  Mass. Md. 10 Aug. 1871
DOLLEY, Frank see Benson, Mertie
DOLLEY, William see Pennell, Elizabeth
DOLLEY, Lucinda of Gray and Elliott O. Robinson of Westbrook
  Md. 29 Apr. 1859
DOLLEY, John see Morse, Mary E.
DOLLEY, Hannah F. and Richard D. Harris both of Gray PUB. 4
  Sept. 1865 Md. 9 Sept. 1865
DOLLEY, Harriet T. and Charles Grant both of Gray PUB. 11 Apr.
  1841

DOLLEY, Mary E. of Gray and Prince Strout of Raymond PUB. 6
    Sept. 1846
DOLLEY, John and Mrs. Hannah Hayden both of Gray PUB. 2
    Nov. 1851
DOLLOFF, Abner and Rebecca Foster both of Gray (no date est.
    given as 1811 or 1812) p.191
DOLLOFF, Rosannah see Foster, Shephel
DOLLOFF, James M. and Sarah A. Webster both of Gray Md. 25
    Mar. 1876
DOLLOFF, Harry see Libby, Lois
DOLLY, Mary see Cummings, Elisha
DOLLY, Dorcas and Moses Twitchell PUB. 27 Nov. 1781; 12 Dec.
    1781
DOLLY, Sarah and Daniel Knight PUB. 25 Jan 1784; 8 Feb. 1784
DONALDS, Polly and Ozias Morse both of Gray Md. 24 Nov.
    1801   p.167
DONNELL, Samuel see Leighton, Ellen
DONNELLY, John R. and Myrtie A. Hodgdon both of Fairfield
    Md. 19 May 1921 p.127
DONOVAN, Daniel J. and Elizabeth A. Sawyer both of Gray Md.
    21 Sept. 1902 p.39
DOOLEY, Charles H. and Christina C. Brown both of Roslindale,
    Mass. Md. 9 Oct. 1922 p.133
DORE, Harry G. and Arleen K. McPhail both of Perry Md. 1 Sept.
    1930 p.173
DORITY, Florence see Perley, Alvin
DORMAN, Alice see Sawyer, Herbert
DOUGHTY, Hezekiah and Bathsheba Gilbert both of Gray 11 June
    1855
DOUGHTY, Martha, and Joel Stevens both of Gray PUB.3 Apr.
    1779; 18 Apr. 1779
DOUGHTY, James and Ruth Stevens both of Gray PUB. 8
    July1872 Md. 23 July 1782
DOUGHTY, Mary and Joseph Libby both of Gray 13 Mar. 1796
    p.155
DOUGHTY, Elias and Elisabeth Watson both of Gray   24 Aug.
    1801   p.167
DOUGHTY, Abigail and Charles Thaxter both of Gray 20 June
    1807   p.184

DOUGHTY, Martha and Atkinson Small both of Gray   5 June
      1808   p.185
DOUGHTY, Joshua and Jane Titcomb both of Gray 15 Dec. 1808
      p.186
DOUGHTY, John M. of Gray and Jane Black of North Yarmouth
      PUB. 7 Mar. 1813   p.200
DOUGHTY, Susan and Ezra Gibbs Jr. PUB. 4 May 1817 p.209
      Md. 19 July 1817 p.213
DOUGHTY, James Jr. and Charlotte Nason both of Gray PUB. 12
      Oct 1817 p.210 Md. 4 Dec. 1817 p.213
DOUGHTY, Hezekiah and Rachel Thompson both of Gray PUB.
      16 June 1822 p.231, Md. 18 Aug. 1822 p.230
DOUGHTY, Martha and Simon Fogg both of Gray PUB. 21 Dec.
      1823 p. 234, Md. 11 Jan. 1824 p.235
DOUGHTY, William P. and Achsah Nash both of Gray PUB. 12
      Feb 1826 p.243, Md. 1826 p.241
DOUGHTY, Edward of Gray and Mary Skillin of Cumberland
      PUB. 6 July 1826 p.245
DOUGHTY, Anne and James Leighton both of Gray PUB. 3 Dec.
      1826 p.245, Md. 1827 p.248
DOUGHTY, Eliza and Stephen Knight both of Gray PUB. 16 May
      1830 p.263, Md. 1830 p.267
DOUGHTY, Nathan of Gray and Lois Brackett of No. Yarmouth
      PUB. 31 Nov. 1833 p.276
DOUGHTY, Miriam J. of Gray and Noah Hall of Oldtown PUB.
      22 Aug 1835 p.281
DOUGHTY, Benj. F. of Gray and Mary Wilson of Cumberland
      PUB. 1836 p.282
DOUGHTY, Abagail P. of Gray and James C. Dill of Yarmouth
      Md. 13 June 1861
DOUGHTY, Fred O. of Gray and Minnie O. Ham of Windham
      Md. 28 July 1888
DOUGHTY, May E. of Gray and Joseph L. Robinson of So.
      Windham PUB. 25 Feb 1889, Md. 9 Mar. 1889
DOUGHTY, Lizzie see Low, Charles
DOUGHTY, Alvin S. and Charlotte F. Humphrey both of Gray
      PUB. 2 May 1870, Md. 8 May 1870
DOUGHTY, Olive M. and Stephen W. Stiles both of Gray Md. 5
      May 1873

DOUGHTY, Charles H. and Carrie E. Libby both of Gray Md. 30 May 1877

DOUGHTY, Esther and John Hunt both of Gray PUB. 21 Nov. 1878, Md. 28 Nov 1878

DOUGHTY, Henry C. of Gray and Addie Simmons of Lewiston Md. 24 Dec. 1878

DOUGHTY, Ellen M. and Hewett L. Megguire both of Gray Md. 31 Dec. 1879

DOUGHTY, Henry P. and Olive Strout both of Gray PUB. 16 Aug. 1880, Md. 22 Aug 1880

DOUGHTY, Alice A.H. and William Morrill Jr. both of Gray Md. 5 Dec. 1881

DOUGHTY, Daniel A. of Gray and Annie Avery of Sanford PUB. 2 Feb. 1883, Md. 6 Feb. 1883

DOUGHTY, Nathan and Addie Small both of Gray PUB. 26 Oct. 1889, Md. 9 Nov 1889

DOUGHTY, Clara H. of Gray and Oscar C. Stinchfield of New Gloucester Md. 31 July 1896 p.19

DOUGHTY, Nathan of Gray and Alice A. Hill of Bowdoin Md. 25 Aug. 1897 in Bowdoin p.23

DOUGHTY, Oscar H. of Gray and Tina H. Hamilton of No. Yarmouth Md. 16 Aug. 1901 p.35

DOUGHTY, William see Barbour, Ina

DOUGHTY, Warren P. of Gray and Elizabeth M. Perry of Rockland Md. 4 Oct 1905 p.51

DOUGHTY, Annie B. of Gray and David F. Hamilton of No. Yarmouth Md. 19 Apr. 1906 p.53

DOUGHTY, Marguerite L. and Charles H. Lawrence Jr. both of Gray Md. 19 Mar. 1913 p.85

DOUGHTY, Carroll and Lena C. Small both of Gray Md. 10 June 1913 in Portland p.87

DOUGHTY, Grace W. and Leon C. Manchester both of Gray Md. 26 Aug. 1913 p.89

DOUGHTY, Carrol of Gray and Dorothy L. Sawyer of Yarmouth Md. 27 Apr. 1921 in Falmouth p.127

DOUGHTY, Hezekiah and Bathsheba Gilbert both of Gray PUB. 11 June 1855 Md. 15 July 1855

DOUGHTY, Albert and Mary E. Simpson both of Gray Md. 16 Apr. 1859

DOUGHTY, Abigail P. of Gray and James C. Dill of Yarmouth Md. 13 June 1861

DOUGHTY, Cynthia see Allen, Charles

DOUGHTY, Mary see Colley, Albert

DOUGHTY, Rebecca F. and George Emery both of Gray Md. 1 Aug 1865

DOUGHTY,Susie A. and Lee B. Hunt both of Gray PUB. 2 Aug. 1884 Md. 8 Aug. 1884

DOUGHTY, Henry C. and Jennie W. Merrill both of Gray PUB. 6 July 1885 Md. 12 July 1885

DOUGHTY, Louie and Irving E. Small both of Gray PUB. 21 Apr. 1886 Md. 27 Apr. 1886

DOUGHTY, George R. and Celia E. Whitney both of Gray PUB. 18 June 1886 Md. 23 June 1886

DOUGHTY, Edward and Sarah Haskell both of Gray PUB. Dec. 1837

DOUGHTY, Geo. W. 2nd and Elizabeth Russell both of Gray PUB. 19 Feb. 1842

DOUGHTY, Miriam see Bailey, Alexander

DOUGHTY, Frances P. and Jeremiah Pennell both of Gray PUB. 2 Nov. 1851

DOUGLASS, Cora of Gray and Ellis Hathaway of Auburn Md. 24 Jan. 1900 p.29

DOUGLASS, Frank N. and Josephine E. Flint both of Gray Md. 30 Oct. 1901 in Falmouth p.35

DOUGLASS, William S. and Marion L. Pollard both of Gray Md. 13 June 1925 in New Gloucester p.147

DOUGLASS, Flora of Gray and E. O. May of Gorham PUB. 8 Oct. 1887

DOUGLASS, Ann see Sheldon, Rev.

DOW, William M. of Gray and Mehitable T. Libby of Gray 8 Jan. 1854

DOW, Charles see Merrill, Alice

DOW, Anna S. and William B. Prince both of Gray Md. 17 Feb. 1900 p.27

DOW, Ella see Blake, George W.

DOW, Grace P. and Fred H. Ramsdell both of Gray Md. 16 Oct. 1907 p.61

DOW, Dorothy L. and Clifford S. Libby both of Gray Md. 30 June 1913 p.87

DOW, Hettie C. and Joseph L. Webster both of Gray Md. 7 Feb. 1918 p.109

DOW, William M. Dow and Mehitable T. Libby both of Gray Md. 8 Jan. 1854 in Roxbury Mass.

DOW, William H. and Clara W. Pennell both of Gray PUB. 12 Oct. 1885 Md. 25 Oct 1885

DOXEY, John see Buxton, Elizabeth

DOYLE, Matilda see Dole, John

DRESSER, Dorothea and Charles H. Reeves both of Gray Md. 29 Aug. 1925 p.149

DRINKWATER, Rothens see Lane, Lucy

DROWN, Allen B. and Adline F. Frank both of Gray Md. 15 Aug. 1872

DUNN, Martha see Smith, William

DUNN, Walter C. and Lizzie F. Whitney both of Gray Md. 12 Nov. 1879

DUNN, Annie M. of Gray and Edward C. Leighton of Cumberland Md. 8 Nov. 1883

DUNN, Alma and Carl A. Wilson both of Gray Md. 3 Aug. 1896 in New Gloucester p.19

DUNN, Moses T. and Ellen F. Libby both of Gray Md. 9 Dec. 1909 p.75

DUNN, Hannah M. and Gilman B. Elder both of Gray Md. 26 Dec. 1863

DUNPHE, William H. and Mildred C. Lowe both of Gray Md. 14 June 1893 p. 7

DUPLISEA, Elton B. of Gray and Vannie E. Oakes of Freeport Md. 9 June 1928 p.163

DUPLISEA, Carl T. and Marguerite T. Morrill both of Gray Md. 20 June 1928 p.163

DUPLISEA, Elsie May of Gray and George E. S. Goodwin of Portland Md. 2 Sept 1920 in Portland p.123

DURAL, Peter and Joanna Rider 10 Nov. 1785 p.135

DURAN, Matthew see Berry, Jerusha

DURAN, Eliza S. and Andrew J. Marston both of Gray Md. 17 Oct. 1870

DURAN, Lydia and George B. Hodgkins both of Gray Md. 3 Oct. 1878

DURAN, Mrs. Mary S. of Gray and Sawyer Harris of New Gloucester PUB. 28 Feb. 1858 Md. 23 Mar 1858

DURGIN, Dorothy see Knight, Charles

DURGIN, John M. and Harriet R. Thayer both of Gray PUB. 29 Nov. 1839

DURIN, Elisha see Skillins, Eunice

DUTTON, Lucretia and Asa Libby Junr. both of Gray 25 Feb. 1795 p.153

DUTTON, Paulina of Gray and Charles Grant of Freeport PUB. 16 July 1826 p.245, Md. 1826 p.247

DUTTON, Thomas Jr. and Sarah McDonald both of Gray PUB. 21 Nov. 1830 p.264

DUTTON, Jane of Gray and Woodbridge Haley of Bath PUB. 15 Dec. 1833 p.276

DUTTON, Thomas W. and Emeline L. Goff both of Gray Md. 3 Sept. 1895 p.15

DUTTON, Mary A. of Gray and John M. C. Bachelder of Poland Md. 26 Aug. 1862

DUTTON, Paulener G. of Gray and Nathan Clough of Cumberland Md. 26 Aug. 1862

DUTTON, Katie M. of Gray and J. Albert Tufts of New Gloucester PUB. 9 June 1885 Md. 14 June 1885 Md. 9 Mar. 1775

DWINAL, Celia see Sweetser, Nicholas

DWINAL, Sarah see Adams, Isiah

DWYER, Alice see Gore, Jesse

DWYER, Roscoe J. and Annie A. Libby both of Gray Md. 3 May 1893 p.9

DYER, Judah and Fanny Nash both of Gray 20 Mar. 1796 p.155

DYER, Eleanor of Gray and Joshua Robinson of Durham PUB. 29 Apr. 1821, p.227, Md. 1821/2 p. 229

DYER, Sally of Gray and Daniel Leighton of Cumberland PUB. 6 Jan. 1822 p.228, Md. 1822 p. 229

DYER, Ann of Gray and Benjamin K. Scribner of Portland PUB. 3 Dec. 1832 p.272

DYER, Huldah of Gray and William Robinson of Durham PUB. 16 Feb. 1834 p.277

DYER, Abigail of Gray and John Rolf of Gorham PUB. 4 Oct. 1835 p.281

EATON, Phebe see Morse, John 3d

EATON, Charles A. and Isabell J. Prince both of Gray Md. 25 June 1874

EATON, Rupert J. and Georgia A. Spiller both of Raymond Md. 12 Sept. 1908 p.67

EATON, Will S. and Bertha M. Darling both of Auburn Md. 26 Nov. 1912 p.85

EDWARDS, Betsey and Moses Twitchell Foster both of Gray 27 Apr. 1802   p.172

EDWARDS, Sophia and Barney Phillips both of Gray PUB. 29 Feb. 1824 p. 234

EDWARDS, Susie see Colley, Charles

EDWARDS, Clista W. and Otis L. Latham both of Gray PUB. 28 Feb. 1870, Md. 15 Mar 1870

EDWARDS, Florce E. see Stimson, Harry O.

EDWARDS Lydia E. of Gray and Hewett C. Edwards of Raymond Md. 31 Dec. 1900 in Portland p. 31

EDWARDS, Hewett C. see Edwards, Hewett

EDWARDS, Juliette see Megquier, Lawson

EDWARDS, Mildred see Verrill, Harlan

EDWARDS, Clarence E. and Mary Strout both of Gray Md. 27 Mar. 1913 p.87

EDWARDS, Fred L. and Elsie E. Field both of Gray Md. 25 June 1919 p.117

EDWARDS, Flora R. and George A. Seal both of Gray Md 3 Aug. 1920 in Portland p.123

EDWARDS, Ada see Fields, Arthur

EDWARDS, Frank E. and Katherine Crockett of Poland Md 29 May 1924 p.141

EDWARDS, Channing E. and Jennie Tracy both of Poland Md 22 June 1924 p.143

EDWARDS, Jessie and Edith Field both of New Gloucester Md 14 Apr. 1928 p.161

EDWARDS, George see Davis, Arlene

EDWARDS, Jeremiah see Benson, Mary

EDWARDS, Jennie see Quint, George

ELDER, Gilman see Dunn, Hannah

ELDER, Merrill of Gray and Susan Varney of Windham PUB. 10 May 1846

ELIOTT, Mary F. and George F. Knight both of Gray Md 5 June 1871

ELLINWOOD, George A. and Josephine D. Morrill both of Gray Md. 24 Dec. 1898 p.25

ELLINWOOD, George A. Jr. of Gray and Gertrude Luckings of Bar Harbor Md. 6 Apr. 1920 in Bar Harbor p.121

ELLINWOOD, George A. Jr. of Gray and Iva F. Webb of New Gloucester Md. 9 Feb. 1929 p.165

ELLIOTT, Betsey and Nathan Foster both of Gray PUB. 28 Oct. 1832 p.272

ELLIOTT, Elizabeth see Libby, Elihu

ELLIOTT, Hannah see Hamilton, Robert

ELLIS, Addie see Colley, Charles

ELLIS, Caleb H. of Ft. Fairfield and Lois H. Ehrich of Boston, Mass. Md. 12 Aug. 1895 p.15

ELLIS, Nora see Hodgkins, Alverdo

ELWELL, William Junr. and Hannah Young both of Gray 23 Oct. 1808 p.185

ELWELL, Mary and William Strickland both of Gray 14 Oct. 1811 p.192

ELWELL, Joseph see Harmon, Mary

ELWELL, Dillia of Gray and Joseph Lowell of Standish PUB. 3 Jan. 1830 p.261, Md 1830 p.262

ELWELL, Addie see Skillin, ?

ELWELL, Charlotte see Webster, Henry

EMERSON, Ann see Foster, Samuel

EMERY, Dorcas and Edward Pray both of Gray 29 Nov. 1804 p.180

EMERY, Doris of Gray and Joseph Allen of Windham 19 Aug. 1810 p.188

EMERY, Dorcas of Gray and Joseph Allen of Windham 18 Sept. 1811 p.189

EMERY, William of Gray and Harriet Adams of Falmouth PUB. 18 Dec. 1879, Md 31 Dec 1879

EMERY, Carrie A. and Charles H. Nason both of Gray Md 2 Aug. 1900 p.31

EMERY, Daisy L. of Gray and George P. Nash of Raymond Md 4 Nov. 1930 in Westbrook p.175

EMERY, George see Doughty, Rebecca

EMERY, Jane see Wilson, Lynn

EMERY, Olive see Webster, Royal

EMERY, George W. of Gray and Carrie B. Hall of Cumberland Md
25 Mar. 1908 p.63

EMMONS, Everett E. of Portland and Gertrude L. Clark of
Caratunk Md. 7 Oct. 1922 p. 135

ESTES, Johanna and Sewall B. Prince both of Gray Md 24 Dec.
1872

ESTES, Charles E. and Ellen Cloudman both of Poland Md 17 Feb.
1878

ESTES, Ethel see Sawyer, Clarence

ESTES, Elmer L. of New Gloucester and Bessie R. Small of
Raymond Md. 28 Nov. 1907 p.63

EVANS, Elizabeth see Dole, John

EVELETH, William C. of Gray and Caroline F. Chute of Windham
Md. 20 Apr. 1876

EVERETT, C.F. see Davis, Eliza

FAREWELL, John see Stowell, Nabby

FAREWELL, Charles A. of No. Raymond and Grace Lewis of
Raymond Md. 27 May 1912 p.81

FARLEY, Alexander see Blake, Ella G.

FARNHAM, George see Sawyer, Sadie

FARNHAM, Ruth see Leonard, Ernest

FARR, John and Patience Webster both of Gray 1 June 1817
p.213

FARRAN, Annie and Andrew S. Ryder both of Gray Md 3 May
1909 p.71

FARRAR, Estella see Colley, John

FARRELL, Capt. Edward and Olive M. Libby both of Gray PUB. 6
Feb. 1842

FARRINGTON, Mary R. and Thomas Hancock both of Gray Md
14 May 1857

FARRIS, Mary see Carey, Cephas

FARWELL, Olive A. of Gray and Frank P. Curtis of Chesterville
Md. 20 June 1866

FARWELL, Samuel S. and Mary A. Leighton both of Gray Md 1
Aug. 1867

FARWELL, Arno see Strout, Martha

FARWELL, Rozilla of Gray and Raymond Sickra of Biddeford Md
2 Apr. 1875

FARWELL, Edward L. of Gray and Emma J. Mitchell of
Biddeford Md. 15 Dec. 1880

FARWELL, Amos and Ida Tripp both of Gray Md 7 Apr 1881

FARWELL, Amos A. and Lizzie F. Hodgkins both of Gray PUB.
12 May 1881, Md 21 May 1881

FARWELL, Addie E. and Ulysses G. Field both of Gray Md 14
June 1896 p.19

FARWELL, Elizabeth and Orrin Witham both of Gray Md 31 Oct.
1902 in Rochester, N. H. p.39

FARWELL, John of Gray and Nina B. Knight of Bridgton Md 2
Nov. 1907 in Bridgton p.61

FARWELL, John of Gray and Margaret Verrill of Raymond Md 13
Sept. 1862

FARWELL, Mary J. of Gray and Timothy Berry of Poland Md 19
Nov. 1862

FARWELL, Joseph H. of Gray and Olive Verrill of Poland PUB. 1
Feb. 1864 Md. 6 Feb. 1864

FAUNCE, Azel W. of Buckfield and Mary T. Gerry of New
Gloucester Md. 2 June 1917 p.105

FAUNCE, Azel see Webb, Harriet

FELCH, Eliza see Hunt, Elnathan

FENLEY, Mary see Allen, Daniel

FERGUSON, Lucy see Dolley, Daniel

FERGUSON, Nathan and Ann Humphrey both of Gray PUB. 26
Apr. 1846

FIELD, James see Low, Polly

FIELD, Minnie see Allen, Charles

FIELD, Edwin see Libby, Callie

FIELD, Ida see Allen, Josiah

FIELD, Julia see Goff, E.W.

FIELD, Fred L. and Maggie R. Sarbell both of Gray PUB. 21 Sept.
1889, Md. 29 Sept. 1889

FIELD, Schuyler C. of Gray and Lillian Swan of Greenwood Md
24 Sept. 1889

FIELD, Charles H. of Falmouth and Lizzie A. Flint of Cumberland
Md. 30 Oct. 1889

FIELD, Leola E. and Ralph A. Leslie both of Gray PUB. 20
Jan.1890, Md. 12 Mar 1890

FIELD, Ulyssis G. of Gray and Sarah L. Small of New Gloucester
   Md. 5 July 1890
FIELD, Annie of Gray and Samuel M. Mitchell of Casco PUB. 2
   Mar. 1891, Md 8 Mar 1891
FIELD, Ulysses see Farwell, Addie E.
FIELD, Edwin L. Jr. of Gray and Susan W. Strout of Cape
   Elizabeth Md. 27 Apr. 1898 in Cape Elizabeth p.25
FIELD, Ulysses G. of Gray and Margaret Webber of Cambridge,
   Mass. Md. 31 Oct. 1909
FIELD, Edward E. and Mary R. Webber both of Gray Md 20 Aug.
   1910 p.75
FIELD, Sarah see Hall, Merton
FIELD, Elsie see Edwards, Fred
FIELD, Elbridge see Skillin, Hannah
FIELD, Hattie L. of Gray and John F. Lombard of Raymond Md 25
   Sept. 1885
FIELD, Russell see Quint, Addie
FIELD, Esther see Hall, Merton
FIELDS, Almira and Jeremiah Mountford both of Gray PUB. 9
   Jan. 1819 p.216
FIELDS, George W. of Gray and Georgianna M. Whitney of Casco
   PUB. 24 Dec. 1880, Md 1 Jan. 1881
FIELDS, Arthur E. of Gray and Ada E. Edwards of Poland Md 26
   Sept. 1920 in Poland p.123
FISH, Austin see Cook, Sarah
FLANDERS, James see Fogg, Marion
FLETCHER, Abigail see Cummings, Daniel
FLETCHER, Charlotte and Jeremiah Pennell both of Gray 25 Nov.
   1802 p.173
FLETCHER, Polly of Gray and Ew'd Barker of Waterford 13 Sept.
   1804   p.178
FLING, Augusta M. and Horace O. Stimson both of Gray PUB. 1
   July 1861 Md. 6 July 1861
FLINT, Leonard see Cobb, Emily
FLINT, Josephine see Douglass, Frank
FLUENT, Caroline L. of Gray and Capt. Simeon Adams of New
   York PUB. 19 Feb. 1825 p.238, Md13 Mar. 1825 p.239

FLYE, Bernice and Trueman L. Prince both of Gray Md 25 Jan.
        1918 p.115
FOGG, Irene, see Bailey, George
FOGG, Eunice and Joseph Foster both of Gray 26 June 1796
        p.156
FOGG, Timothy and Patience Rounds both of Gray 1 Feb. 1798
        p.158
FOGG, Gena and Asa Humphrey both of Gray PUB. 2 Apr. 1818
        p.212, Md. 1818 p.217
FOGG, James of Gray and Nancy Stevens of Gardiner PUB. 1 Aug.
        1822 p. 231
FOGG, Simon see Doughty, Martha
FOGG, Louisa and Aron Humphrey both of Gray PUB. 2 Dec.
        1824 p.237,Md. 13 Dec. 1824 p. 235
FOGG, Lucinda and John Russell Jr. both of Gray PUB. 5 Sept.
        1824 p.237
FOGG, Mary of Gray and Jacob Tripp of Portland PUB. 5 Dec.
        1829 p.261, Md p.259
FOGG, Orrilla and Peltiah Harmon both of Gray PUB. 28 Mar.
        1832 p.271 Md 25 Mar 1832 p. 270 sic
FOGG, Nelson of Gray and Margaret Rounds of Buxton PUB. 24
        Sept. 1832 p.271
FOGG, Georgianna see Goff, Lucius
FOGG, Scammon and Sarah Keating both of Gray Md 1 Mar 1875
FOGG, James P. of Gray and Nettie Libby of Gorham PUB. 6 Jan.
        1881, Md 11 Jan 1881
FOGG, Etta J. of Gray and Alpheus S. Hilton of Parsonfield Md 18
        May 1881
FOGG, Adelbert see Lane, Vera
FOGG, Villa see Snow, Claude
FOGG, Marion K. of Gray and James G. Flanders of Boston, Mass.
        Md. 31 July 1926 p.153
FOGG, Ai see Foster, Miriam
FOGONE, Sebastian M. and Ethel A. Farr both of Portland Md 15
        May 1927 p.157
FOLLANSBEE, Harry see Sherwood, Louise
FORBES, Harry C. and Ida M. Conant both of Buckfield Md 17
        Jan. 1906 p.53
FORBUSH, Horace A. of Syracuse, N.Y. and Gladys J. Ryder of
        Portland Md. 4 Sept. 1916 p.101

FORD, Elisha see Cobb, Abigail

FORD, Deborah of Gray and John Webster of New Gloucester PUB. 30 Mar. 1817 p.209 Md. 1817 p.214

FORD, James and Lucy Latham both of Gray PUB. 6 Sept. 1818 p.215, Md. 1818 p.217

FORD, John B. and Abigail L. Humphrey both of Gray PUB. 25 Sept. 1825 p.243, Md 10 Nov 1825 p.241

FORTUNE, William A. and Hattie Small both of Gray Md 3 Dec. 1892 p.5

FOSS, Sumner W. and Fanny Libby both of Gray PUB. 10 Nov. 1833 p.276

FOSS, Hannah S. and Solomon B. Foster both of Gray PUB. 5 Feb. 1873, Md 5 Mar 1873

FOSS, Nancy and Daniel Mayberry both of Gray PUB. 26 Jan. 1859 Md. 1 Feb. 1859

FOSS, John see Spencer, Lydia

FOSSETT, Harold see Verrill, Lillian

FOSTER, Patience, see Goff, William

FOSTER, Jane see Bailey, Joel

FOSTER, Nathan and Meriam Hobbs both of Cummings Grant 17 May 1791 p.146

FOSTER, Joseph see Fogg, Eunice

FOSTER, Moses see Edwards, Betsey

FOSTER, Rebecca see Dolloff, Abner

FOSTER, Job of Gray and Statira Leighton of Falmouth PUB. 8 Apr. 1827 p.249

FOSTER, Martha see Dolley, George

FOSTER, Samuel J. of Gray and Ann Emerson of Poland PUB. 8 Mar. 1829 p.260

FOSTER, Rebecca and Daniel Mayberry both of Gray PUB. 5 Dec. 1830 p.264, Md 1830 p.267

FOSTER, Mary of Gray and John Hunnewell of Windham PUB. 19 Feb 1832 p.270. Md 4 Mar 1832 p.269

FOSTER, John see Benson, Priscilla

FOSTER, Nathan see Elliot, Betsey

FOSTER, Irene and John Sawyer both of Gray PUB. 31 Mar. 1833 p.275, Md. 1833 p.278

FOSTER, Betsey of Gray and Amos Legrow of Windham PUB. 29 Dec. 1833 p.277

FOSTER, Abigail of Gray and Amos Legrow of Windham PUB. 26
  Jan. 1834 p.277
FOSTER, Solomon B. of Gray and Eunice Ricker of Poland Md 4
  Nov. 1834 p.280
FOSTER, Charlotte of Gray and Noah Ricker of Poland Md 4 Nov.
  1834 p.280
FOSTER, Moses see Benson, Eliza Ann
FOSTER, Shephel of Gray and Rosannah Dolloff of Paris
  PUB. 1835 p.282
FOSTER, Silas see Bailey, Sarah
FOSTER, James H. and Almeda Archibald PUB. 14 June 1860 Md
  21 June 1860
FOSTER, Mary H. of Gray and Peter S. Whitney of Windham Md
  2 May 1888
FOSTER, Rosa P. of Gray and Edward A. Hamilton of No.
  Yarmouth Md. 21 Apr. 1866
FOSTER, Levi S. of Gray and Mary E. Higgins of No. Yarmouth
  Md. 31 Dec. 1867
FOSTER, James N. and Elizabeth D. Foster both of Gray Md 12
  Feb. 1868
FOSTER, Elizabeth see Foster, James
FOSTER, Samuel J. Jr. and Hannah J. Legrow both of Gray Md 14
  Nov. 1868
FOSTER, Delinda D. and Woodbury S. Libby both of Gray Md 18
  May 1869
FOSTER, Solomon B. and Mrs. Christina Libby both of Gray PUB.
  20 Oct. 1869, Md 21 Oct. 1869
FOSTER, Horace C. and Annie M. Frank both of Gray Md 28 Aug.
  1871
FOSTER, E. Augusta and Edward F. Libby both of Gray Md 22
  Nov. 1871
FOSTER, Rosa see Brooks, Peter
FOSTER, Solomon see Foss, Hannah
FOSTER, John R. and Eliza J. Frank both of Gray PUB. 5 Sept.
  1873, Md 24 Sept. 1873
FOSTER, Flora I. and James O. Whitney both of Gray Md 7 Oct.
  1876
FOSTER, Charles J. of Gray and Ella C. Spiller of Raymond Md
  25 Jan. 1877

FOSTER, Arthur S. and Nettie Russell both of Gray Md 17 Dec.
1878

FOSTER, Marshall and Margaret E. Rude both of Gray PUB. 27
Jan. 1883, Md 15 Feb. 1883

FOSTER, Mary R. of Gray and William E. Page of Windham PUB.
26 Oct. 1889, Md 2 Nov. 1889

FOSTER, Alice M. of Gray and Harry L. Dingley of Gorham Md
23 Jan. 1892

FOSTER, Samuel J. of Gray and Edna F. Hunnewell of Auburn Md
31 Dec. 1892 p.5

FOSTER, Jacob and Ketturah A. Young both of Gray Md 14 Aug.
1893 p. 7

FOSTER, Walter and Maude Knight both of Windham Md 28 Apr.
1894 p.11

FOSTER, Mildred E. and Ira P. Sawyer both of Gray Md 24 Nov.
1900 p.31

FOSTER, Georgie P. of Gray and Clarel H. Poore of Southport Md
25 Dec. 1900 p.31

FOSTER, George B. and Emma F. Frank both of Gray Md 25 Feb.
1905 p.49

FOSTER, Edgar and Nora E. Herick both of Gray Md 5 May 1905
p.49

FOSTER, Eugene see Bohnsen, Minnie

FOSTER, Irene S. of Gray and Irving J. Foster of Poland Md 13
June 1908 p.65

FOSTER, Irving see Foster, Irene

FOSTER, Mabel and Willis M. Goff both of Gray Md 30 June
1908 p.65

FOSTER, Luenetta W. and Fred H. Sawyer both of Gray Md 8 Oct.
1915 in New Gloucester p.97

FOSTER, Edgar of Gray and Gladys M. Morrell of Windham Md
23 Dec. 1923 p.141

FOSTER, Jennie E. of Gray and Robert D. Chute of Casco Md 10
June 1924 in Roxbury p.141

FOSTER, Patience and William Goff both of Gray Md 7 Jan. 1855

FOSTER, Jane see Bailey, Joel

FOSTER, Jonathan K. of Gray and Amelia R. Herrick of Windham
PUB. 25 May 1859 Md 19 June 1859

FOSTER, Silas see Bailey, Sarah J. H.

FOSTER, James H. and Almeda Archibald PUB. 14 June 1860 Md
    21 June 1860
FOSTER, Clara A. of Gray and Charles W. Allen of Pownal Md 20
    Sept. 1863
FOSTER, John F. and Emily J. Graffam both of Gray Md 12 June
    1865
FOSTER, Granville S. of Gray and Carrie J. Davis of New
    Gloucester Md. 20 Nov. 1884
FOSTER, Nellie of Gray and John B. Clark of Bradford Md 15 Jan.
    1885
FOSTER, Annie L. of Gray and Albert F. Merrill of Lisbon PUB.
    25 June 1887
FOSTER, Walter S. of Gray and Kedie Strout of Gray PUB. 10
    Oct. 1887
FOSTER, John and Ann H. Hodgkins both of Gray PUB. 23 Dec.
    1837
FOSTER, Joan C. and Ebenzer Hodgkins both of Gray PUB. 10
    Sept. 1840
FOSTER, Rebecca see Colley, Benjamin
FOSTER, Miriam S. of Gray and Ai S. Fogg of Raymond PUB. 17
    Sept. 1843
FOSTER, Zilpha see Benson, Jabez
FOSTER, Mahala W. and Azariah Humphrey both of Gray PUB.
    14 June 1846
FOSTER, Mary B. and Ebenzer Hodgkins both of Gray PUB. 13
    Dec. 1846
FOSTER, Mary and William H. Jackson both of Gray PUB. 20
    June 1847
FOSTER, Moses of Gray and Sarah A. Grant of Greenwood PUB.
    11 May 1851
FOSTER, Edwin P. of Gray and Clara H. Leighton of Casco PUB.
    3 Mar. 1873, Md 16 Mar 1873
FOWLER, Catherine see Cobb, Benjamin
FOWLER, Zebedee and Byer Morse both of Gray PUB. 14 Nov.
    1813   p.200
FOWLER, Isabel and Simon Webster both of Gray 25 Jan. 1819
    p.217
FOWLER, Betsey of Gray and Stephen Cobb of Poland PUB. 28
    Aug. 1825 p. 242

FOWLER, Thankful M. of Gray and C. W. Megguier of New Gloucester Md. 3 Nov. 1870

FOWLER, Thomas M. and Ann H. Leighton both of Gray PUB. 7 Nov. 1847

FOYE, Guy see Whitney, Ethel

FOYE, Harry see Small, Florence

FRANK, Margaret, see Libby, Isaac

FRANK, Josiah and Polley Small both of Gray 25 Nov. 1802 p.173

FRANK, Sally and William Whitney both of Gray 18 Apr. 1805 p.180

FRANK, Jane and Jeremiah Small both of Gray 26 Nov. 1807 p.184

FRANK, Thomas and Lucy Small both of Gray 26 Nov. 1812 p.195

FRANK, Susan of Sumner and ----- Frank of Gray PUB.10 Nov. 1817 p.210

FRANK, Alpheus and Naomi Stimson both of Gray PUB. 29 July 1821 p.227, Md 1821/2 p.229

FRANK, Jaob and John Varney both of Gray PUB 13 Mar. 1825 p.242

FRANK, Eleanor see Allen, Josiah

FRANK, Samuel see Libby, Martha

FRANK, Louisa and George Freeman both of Gray PUB. 14 Oct. 1827 p.250, Md 1827 p.251

FRANK, Lucinda of Gray and Elias H Leighton of Falmouth PUB. 6 Jan. 1828 p.250, Md 1828 p. 251

FRANK, Belinda and Nath'l F. Twombly both of Gray PUB. 17 Jan. 1830 p.261, Md 21 Mar 1830 p.259

FRANK, Belinda and Nathaniel F. Twombly both of Gray PUB. 17 Jan. 1830 p.261

FRANK, Joseph and Hariet Saunders both of Gray PUB. 1 Oct. 1832 p.272, Md 14 Oct 1832 p.274

FRANK, Isaac of Gray and Lydia Legrow of Windham PUB. 31 Dec. 1832 p.273, Md 1 Jan. 1833 p.274

FRANK, Mary A. of Gray and George W. Brown of Portland Md 20 May 1860

FRANK, George W. of Gray and Emeline P. Thurlow of No. Raymond Md. 16 June 1860

FRANK, Leantha of Gray and Daniel W. Leavitt of Raymond
PUB. 24 Sept. 1866, Md 29 Sept. 1866

FRANK, Angenora and Charles E. Nason both of Gray Md 1 May
1867

FRANK, John W. and Augusta E. Thayer both of Gray Md 13 June
1868

FRANK, Joseph W. and Mary F. Wren both of Gray PUB. 20 Nov.
1868, Md 26 Nov. 1868

FRANK, Melvin see Humphrey, Susan

FRANK, Etta and Peter B. Herrick both of Gray PUB. 2 Nov.
1869, Md 7 Nov. 1869

FRANK, Sophia of Gray and Gilbert Small of Windham Md 5 Feb.
1870

FRANK, Mary see Dolley, George

FRANK, Annie see Foster, Horace

FRANK, Almeda M. and Granville Humphrey both of Gray Md 26
Feb. 1872

FRANK, Adaline see Drown, Allen

FRANK, Eliza see Foster, John

FRANK, Ella M. and Edwin S. Skillin both of Gray PUB. 22 Aug.
1874, Md 5 Sept. 1874

FRANK, Vinton E. and Jennie W. Hall both of Gray Md 11 Dec.
1880

FRANK, Hattie E. and Charles W. Stiles both of Gray PUB. 13
Apr. 1881, Md 19 Apr. 1881

FRANK, Mary A. and George W. Thompson both of Gray PUB. 8
June 1882, Md 14 June 1882

FRANK, Alonzo G. of Gray and Lottie L. Gowin of Deering Md 8
Dec. 1883

FRANK, Hersey A. of Gray and Lizzie F. Cobb of Falmouth Md
26 Nov. 1890

FRANK, Fannie P. of Gray and Samuel C. Stuart of Windham Md
27 Feb. 1892

FRANK, Mary E. and George W. Thurlow both of Gray Md 7 May
1894 p.13

FRANK, Adrian J. of Gray and Lulu J. Hurd of Alfred Md 3 Dec.
1895 p.17

FRANK, Melvin M. and Mary E. Knight both of Gray Md 13 June
1896 p.19

FRANK, Mattie E. and Lewis Quint both of Gray Md 25 Nov.
1896 p.21

FRANK, Augustas L. and Rosie Hoey both of Gray Md 15 Oct.
1897 in Lewiston p.23

FRANK, Sadie see Allen, Eugene F.

FRANK, Wilburn H. and Ida Skillings both of Gray Md 5 Feb.
1898 p.25

FRANK, Emma see Foster, George

FRANK, Irving see Bailey, Mildred

FRANK, Walter B. of Gray and Queen B. Trenholm of Haverhill
Mass. Md. 28 June 1908 in New Gloucester p.67

FRANK, Bertha L. of Gray and Arthur B. Bryant of Weymouth,
Mass. Md. 24 Oct. 1910 p.77

FRANK, Percy A. of Gray and Elizabeth Tripp of Poland Md 14
Jan. 1912 p.81

FRANK, Myra see Barton, Ernest

FRANK, Milton see Cobb, Imogene

FRANK, Orin C. of Gray and Evelyn A. McFarland of Westbrook
Md. 7 Oct. 1926 p.155

FRANK, Annie W. and Charles J. Manchester both of Gray Md 28
Sept. 1927 p.159

FRANK, Margaret and Isaac H. Libby both of Gray PUB. 10 Dec.
1855 Md. 16 Dec. 1855

FRANK, Ardelia M. and Albert Hill both of Gray Md 21 Apr 1859

FRANK, Angelita of Gray and Howard C. Freeman of Windham
Md. 31 Oct. 1859

FRANK, Mary A. of Gray and George W. Brown of Portland Md
20 May 1860

FRANK, George W. of Gray and Emeline P. Thurlow of No.
Raymond Md. 16 June 1860

FRANK, John of Gray and Sarah E. Cloudman of Poland Md 13
June 1862

FRANK, Granville H. of Gray and Lizzie Taylor of New
Gloucester Md. 4 Nov. 1863

FRANK, David and Sophronia Hall both of Gray Pub. 18 Nov.
1864 Md. 24 Nov. 1864

FRANK, Alvin see Wentworth, Sarah

FRANK, Susie C. of Gray and John S. Libby of San Binetoles,
Calif. PUB. 9 Feb. 1885 Md. 23 Feb. 1885

FRANK, Orin L. of Gray and Eldora Sawyer of Windham PUB. 23
Feb. 1887

FRANK, Ann see King, Cyrus

FRANK, Hannah and John W. Verrill both of Gray PUB. 2 Feb.
1845

FRANK, Abigail L. of Gray and James Sawyer of Auburn PUB. 12
May 1845

FRANK, David L. and Mary Shaw both of Gray PUB. 28 Sept.
1845

FRANK, Louise and Nathaniel S. Lawrence Jr. both of Gray PUB.
25 Oct. 1846

FRANK, James E. of Gray and Sophia Mayberry of Freeport PUB.
16 May 1852

FRASIER, Susanna and Joseph Prince both of Gray   28 Aug.
1808   p.186

FREEMAN, Mary and Rufus Knight both of Gray PUB. 2 July
1824 p.236

FREEMAN, Paulina see Low, Nicholas

FREEMAN, George see Frank, Louisa

FREEMAN, Jonathan of Gray and Lucy Mitchell of Windham
PUB. 16 Aug. 1828 p.256, Md 1828 p.254

FREEMAN, George W. of Gray and Georgia A. Freeman Md Oct.
1879

FREEMAN, Warren G. and Lucy L. Freeman both of Windham
Md. 2 Sept.1905 p.51

FREEMAN, James A. and Susie L. Maxfield both of Windham Md
2 Nov. 1916 p.103

FREEMAN, Howard see Hulit, Ina

FREEMAN, Narcissa J. of Gray and Gardner D. Weeks of Standish
PUB. 11 Mar. 1856 Md. 17 Mar 1856

FREEMAN, Howard see Frank, Angelita

FRINK, Lewis see Cummings, Susie

FRISBIE, Carrie A. and Edwin T. Libby both of Gray Md 2 Aug.
1924 p.145

FRITZ, Fred see Sawyer, Annie

FROSH, Susan of Gray and Jeremiah Knight of Freeport 2 Oct.
1807   p.183

FROST, Elizabeth see Morse, William

FROTHINGHAM, George see Barbour, Lucy

FROTHINGHAM, Eliza A. and Bradbury Whitten both of Gray
PUB. 18 June 1864 Md 28 June 1864

FRYE, Julia see Burrows, Edward

FULLER, Joseph and Molly Merrill both of New Gloucester 25
Nov. 1802 p.173

FULLER, George see Pennell, Alice

FURBISH, Sophia see Brown, Titus

FURBISH, D.H. see Brown, Persis

FURBUSH, Stephen and Dorcas Nason both of Gray 20 Nov.
1800 p.163

GAMAGE, Lillian see Hancock, Wilbur

GARDNER, Martha see Lincoln, Allen

GATES, Thomas B. M. see Perley, Susan H.

GEER, Theresa S. and William G. O. Walker both of Gray Md 1
Sept. 1930 p.173

GIBBS, Henry see Nash, Charlotte

GIBBS, Ezra see Doughty, Susan

GILBERT, Bathsheba see Doughty, Hezekiah

GILBERT, Hezekiah see Doughty, Hezekiah

GILBERT, Nancy and Joseph Thompson Jr. both of Gray PUB. 21
June 1846

GILMAN, Lewis see Cobb, Mabel

GITCHELL, Able see Sweetser, Abagail

GLEASON, Margie S. and Johnson Smith both of Gray Md 4 Dec.
1884

GLINES, Charles S. and Mary E. Grant both of Gray Md 1 Jan.
1879

GLINES, Rebecca J. of Gray and Isaiah Dacy of Poland Md 12
Apr. 1863

GOFF, William Jr. and Patience Foster both of Gray 7 Jan. 1855

GOFF, William H. and Mary J. Harris both of Gray 29 Dec. 1855

GOFF, Phebe Orletta and Charles F. Harris both of Gray 29 Dec.
1855

GOFF, William and Anna Mutchemore both of Gray 28 Nov. 1799
p.160

GOFF, Barzilla and Lydia Humphrey both of Gray PUB. 18 Sept.
1825 p.242, Md 6 Oct. 1825 p.240

GOFF, Charles M. and Esther Hayden both of Gray PUB. 13 Jan.
1868, Md 5 Mar. 1868

GOFF, Cyrus and Sarah H. Rich both of Gray PUB. 27 Feb. 1868, Md. 28 Mar. 1868

GOFF, Elias F. of Gray and Ella A. Cushing of Boston, Mass. Md 14 Feb. 1870

GOFF, Barzilla H. of Gray and Ruby H. Tufts of Deering PUB. 2 Sept. 1871, Md 9 Sept. 1871

GOFF, Helen A, and Marcus W. Small both of Gray Md 9 Nov. 1871

GOFF, Alton and Ella I. Harmon both of Gray Md 3 June 1872

GOFF, Lucius S. of Gray and Georgianna B. Fogg of Gorham PUB. 26 Feb. 1873, Md 8 Mar. 1873

GOFF, Frank E. and Sarah E. Hall both of Gray PUB. 16 Sept. 1878, Md 21 Sept. 1878

GOFF, Ozias M. and Sarah A. Poole both of Gray Md 21 Oct. 1880

GOFF, E.W. of Gray and Julia A. Field of Cumberland Mills Md 2 May 1883

GOFF, Lelia F. and Walter J. Pennell both of Gray PUB. 25 Oct. 1890, Md 29 Nov. 1890

GOFF, Walter L. and Belle J. Webster both of Gray Pub. 16 June 1891, Md. 21 June 1891

GOFF, Clara P. of Gray and James L. Johnson of Portland PUB. 1 Oct. 1891, Md 29 Oct. 1891

GOFF, Herbert L. and Sybil A. Quint both of Gray Md 8 May 1892

GOFF, Winfield R. and Ida M. Allen both of Westbrook Md 13 Dec. 1893 p.9

GOFF, Melvin and Ellie J. Libby both of Gray Md 24 Sept. 1894 in Portsmouth, N.H. p.21

GOFF, Mary J. of Gray and John R. Rogers of Windham Md 16 Mar. 1899 p.25

GOFF, George L. and Villa J. Verrill both of Gray Md 14 May 1904 p.47

GOFF, Clarence E. of Gray and Nellie M. Morgan of Westbrook Md. 30 Oct. 1907 in Westbrook p.61

GOFF, Willis see Foster, Mabel

GOFF, Clara J. and Frank M. Head both of Gray Md 15 Oct. 1910 p.77

GOFF, William see Goff, Patience

GOFF, William H. and Mary J. Harris both of Gray Md 29 Dec. 1855

GOFF, Phebe O. and Charles F. Harris both of Gray PUB. 29 Dec. 1855 Md. 30 Dec. 1855

GOFF, Sarah A. of Gray and John Wilson of Gorham PUB. 21 Nov. 1859 Md. 26 Nov. 1859

GOFF, Moses see Bryant, Ursula

GOFF, Melvin and Emeline Legrow both of Gray Md 21 Oct. 1865

GOFF, Samuel of Gray and Deborah Thayer of Oxford PUB. 29 Apr. 1840

GOFF, Elias S. and Abagail B. Rowe both of Gray PUB. 4 Jan. 1841

GOFF, Lindsey of Gray and Ann Tufts of New Gloucester PUB. 15 Aug. 1841

GOFF, William and Anna Morse both of New Boston (Gray) Md. 27 May 1773

GOFF, Emeline see Dutton, Thomas

GOLDING, Harry and Luella Small both of Gray Md 20 Feb. 1908 p.63

GOLDING, Walter S. and Minnie M. Smith both of Gray Md 14 Feb. 1922 p.131

GOODING, Samuel W. and Flora B. Harris both of No. Yarmouth Md. 22 Feb. 1908 p.63

GOODWIN, George see Duplissea, Elsie

GOOLD, Hannah and William Libbey Jr. both of Gray   14 Nov. 1809   p.187

GORDON, George A. and Marcia M. Skillin both of Windham Md 25 Feb. 1891

GORE, Maria C. of Gray and Roscoe E. Blake of Lisbon PUB. 11 Oct. 1874, Md 1 Nov. 1874

GORE, Jesse of Gray and Alice M. Dwyer of Poland Md 11 Feb. 1878

GORE, Moses B. of Gray and Augusta A. Thurlow of Raymond Md. 20 Apr. 1863

GORE, George W. of Gray and Lydia Sawyer of New Gloucester PUB. 23 Apr. 1863 Md. 1 May 1863

GORE, Caroline L. of Gray and George H. Lapham of Roxbury, Mass. Md. 22 Aug. 1865

GORE, Elizabeth see Benson, George

GOSSOM, Abel see Allen, Statira

GOULD, Dorcas and John Starbird both of Gray 8 July 1798
    p.158
GOULD, Syreno of Otisfield and Hannah Merchant of New
    Gloucester Md. 1832 p.270
GOULD, Howard N. of Mt. Vernon and Cora A. Wilson of
    Falmouth Md. 12 May 1889
GOWEN, Peter see Wakefield, Nancy
GOWEN, Cora and James Verrill both of Gray Md 7 Oct. 1886
GOWIN, Lottie see Frank, Alonzo
GRAFFAM, Emily see Foster, John
GRANT, Charles see Dutton, Paulina
GRANT, Mary see Glines, Charles
GRANT, Annie E. of Gray and Rufus H. Hamilton of No.
    Yarmouth PUB. 27 Jan. 1879, Md 14 Feb. 1879
GRANT, Lafayette B. and Ella J. Chipman both of Poland Md 6
    Dec. 1892 p.5
GRANT, Gertrude see Mayberry, Willard J.
GRANT, Nellie see Cummings, John
GRANT, Sheldon S. of Portland and Winona M. Davis of
    Westbrook Md. 4 Oct. 1924 p.145
GRANT, Paulina F. of Gray and Salmon A. Wilson of Poland Md
    27 Mar. 1857
GRANT, John W. of Gray and Mary A. Chandler of Bethel Md 21
    Dec. 1859
GRANT, Alvin W. and Lillian Spencer both of Gray PUB. 28 Aug.
    1884 Md. 8 Sept. 1884
GRANT, Charles see Dolley, Harriet
GRANT, Sarah see Foster, Moses
GRANT, Charles T. and Sophronia J. Humphrey both of Gray
    PUB. 10 Aug. 1851
GRATTO, George see Mayer, Barbara
GRAY, Doris see Kent, Harold
GRAY, Algie A. and Bessie M. Robinson both of Gray Md 28
    Aug. 1926 p.155
GREELY, Hannah of Gray and Nehemiah Noyes of North
    Yarmouth 27 July 1815 p.200
GREEN, Daniel and Sarah Libby both of Gray 6 Dec. 1798
    p.157

GREEN, Emma and Meshach Humphrey both of Gray PUB. 28
Sept. 1823 p.234, Md 12 Oct. 1823 p.233

GREENE, William Warren of Gray and Lizzie A. Laurence of
Pownal PUB. 16 Feb. 1861, Md 21 Feb. 1861

GREER, Stephen E. and Helen L. Scott both of Cumberland Md 23
Apr. 1927 p.157

GROVER, Grace M. and Leon L. Small both of Gray Md 26 Feb.
1899 p.25

GROVER, Ethelyn M. of Gray and Harry Parkinson of Portsmouth,
N. H. Md 5 July 1901 in Portsmouth, N. H. p. 35

GROVER, David L. of Gray and Eva J. Libby of Portland Md 30
Apr. 1904 in Portland p.45

GROVER, Frank see Crouse, Bessie

GROVER, Vernie see Stratton, Bemis

GUNNISSON, Robert see Hatch, Sarah

HACKETT, Daisy see Quint, Archie

HADLEY, Minerva see Quint, Clarence

HADLOCK, William and Sarah Leighton both of Falmouth 5
Apr. 1801 p.164

HAINES, Thomas, see Knight, Mary

HAINES, Sallas and Louisa H. Small both of Gray Md 21 Apr.
1882

HAINES, Thomas see Knight, Mary

HAINES, John M. of Gray and Sarah Austin of Windham Md 26
Jan. 1859

HAINES, Eben see Morse, Juliett

HAINES, Sallas see Libby, Mahala

HALEY, Woodbridge see Dutton, Jane

HALL, James, see Sawyer, Lucy

HALL, William of Standish and Deliverance Stuart of Windham
28 Nov. 1804 p.178

HALL, Lot see Titcomb, Salley

HALL, Noah see Doughty, Miriam

HALL, Emma D. of Gray and Alonzo S. Sawyer of No. Yarmouth
PUB. 10 Feb. 1868, Md 27 Feb. 1868

HALL, Cushman and C. H. Libby both of Gray PUB. 10 Dec.
1870, Md 26 Dec. 1870

HALL, Edward T. of Gray and Lorana Leighton of Cumberland
PUB. 29 Mar. 1871, Md 10 Apr. 1871

HALL, Herbert B. and Emma J. Small both of Gray PUB. 2 Sept. 1872, Md 14 Sept. 1872

HALL, Sarah see Goff, Frank

HALL, Jennie see Frank, Vinton

HALL, Lester D. and Alberta F. Morrill both of Gray Md 27 Aug. 1890

HALL, Abbie S. of Gray and Andrew F. Sawyer of No. Yarmouth Md. 2 Nov. 1892 p.5

HALL, Eugene W. and Florence A. Perley both of Gray Md 1 Dec. 1892 at Yarmouth

HALL, James B. and Julia F. Hall both of Gray Md 10 Dec. 1898 in Portland p.25

HALL, Julia F. see Hall, James B.

HALL, Mary S. see Barbarick, Theophilus

HALL, Irving E. of Gray and Emily H. Kidder of Clinton Md 28 Nov. 1901 in Clinton p.35

HALL, Susie A. of Gray and Fernald D. Sawyer of Otisfield Md 23 Oct. 1902 p.39

HALL, Lester see Cobb, Lillian

HALL, Carrie see Emery, George

HALL, Alton see Sawyer, Blanche

HALL, Valentine C. of Raymond and Lonea A. Emery of Poland Md. 12 Nov. 1910 p.77

HALL, Marion see Rackley, John

HALL, Merton S. of Gray and Sarah E. Field of Falmouth Md 13 Oct. 1917 p.107

HALL, James see Sawyer, Lucy

HALL, Roscoe see Allen, Mary

HALL, Charles C. and Clara C. Knight both of Gray PUB. 26 Mar. 1857 Md. 26 Mar. 1857

HALL, Sarah see McDonald, Joseph

HALL, Helen see Colley, Orin

HALL, Sophronia see Frank, David

HALL, Cushman and Mary S. Thayer both of Gray PUB. 2 Feb. 1839

HALL, Rachel and Charles F. Webster both of Gray PUB. 11 June 1840

HALL, Joshua see Dennison, Eliza

HALL, A. A. K., of Gray and O. W. Hawkes of Minot PUB. 2 June 1850

HALL, Merton of Gray and Esther Field of Falmouth Md. 13 Oct. 1917

HALLET, Milton see Adams, Dolores

HALLOWELL, George see Osgood, May

HALLOWELL, Lydia see Cummings, Henry

HAM, Minnie see Doughty, Fred

HAMILTON, William, see Weeks, Anne

HAMILTON, Sarah and Amos Higgins both of Gray, PUB. 6 May 1821 p.227, Md 1821/2 p. 229

HAMILTON, Rufus and Mary Orne both of Gray PUB. 30 Sept. 1821 p.227, Md. 1821/2 p.229

HAMILTON, Bessie see Bailey, George

HAMILTON, Edward see Foster, Rosa

HAMILTON, Matilda see Blake, Ozias

HAMILTON, Robert of Gray and Hannah M. Elliott of New Brunswick, Canada Md. 6 Sept. 1867

HAMILTON, Rufus see Grant, Annie

HAMILTON, Florence see Knight, Willie

HAMILTON, Mary see Clark, William

HAMILTON, John M. and Annie P. Stimson both of Gray Md 11 Apr. 1892

HAMILTON, Ethel see Harris, Archie

HAMILTON, Robert see Stacy, Marjorie

HAMILTON, Matilda see Blake, Ozias

HAMILTON, Florence see Knight, Willie

HAMM, Clifton M. of Gray and Elizabeth E. Pendelton of Bangor Md. 18 Aug. 1925 in Bangor p.149

HAMMOND, Sarah A. and Albion W. Libby both of Gray Md 28 July 1860

HAMMOND, Louisa H. of Gray and William Austin of Windham Md. 11 Mar. 1861

HAMMOND, Sarah A. and Albion W. Libby both of Gray PUB. 28 July 1860 Md 5 Aug 1860

HANCOCK, Thomas see Perley, Susanna

HANCOCK, Thomas and Hattie F. Merrill both of Gray Md 22 Dec. 1873

HANCOCK, James T. and Mrs. L.A. Hill both of Gray PUB. 26
Apr. 1883, Md 27 Dec. 1883

HANCOCK, Mary of Gray and Frances Leavitt of Raymond Md 27
Nov. 1899 p.29

HANCOCK, Wilbur, see Davis, Josephine

HANCOCK, Lillian T. of Gray and Ivory P. Robinson of Raymond
Md. 10 June 1923 p.137

HANCOCK, Dorothy see Kent, Edward

HANCOCK, Wilbur P. of Gray and Lillian H. Gamage of Portland
Md. 21 June 1925 p.149

HANCOCK, Thomas see Farrington, Mary

HANEY, Ann of Gray and Joseph Pierce of New Gloucester 16
Mar. 1817 p.208

HANNAH, Robert B. and Lucy Stiles both of Gray 4 Aug. 1820
p.226

HANSCOM, Gertrude see Sawyer, Fred

HANSCOM, Leonard see Harmon, Ann

HANSON, Orville see Stiles, Susie

HANSON, John see Burnham, Mary

HANSON, Sarah see Pollard, James

HANSON, Byron L. and Frances C. Leavitt both of Gray Md 15
May 1926 in Portland p.151

HARDY, William M. of Newburyport Mass. and Persis L. Grover
of New Gloucester Md 21 June 1890

HARMON, Olive of Gray and David Huston of Falmouth PUB. 27
Apr. 1823 p. 234

HARMON, Mary of Gray and Joseph Elwell 3rd of Buxton PUB. 5
Feb. 1826 p.243

HARMON, Peltiah see Fogg, Orrilla

HARMON, Mehitable and Charles Rounds both of Gray PUB. 30
Sept. 1832 p.272, Md 25 Sept. 1832 p.274

HARMON, William of Gray and Eleanor Rounds of Buxton PUB.
2 June 1833 p.275

HARMON, Hannah and Ebenzer Manchester 30 Nov 1834 p.279

HARMON, Adeline of Gray and William Pride of Westbrook Md 9
Apr. 1867

HARMON, Charlotte of Gray and Benjamin T. Leighton of
Windham Md. 6 Oct. 1867

HARMON, Ella see Goff, Alton

HARMON, Ina A. and Elmer L. Osgood both of Gray PUB. 14
Nov. 1881, Md 24 Dec. 1881
HARMON, Elias and Eliza Morrison both of Gray Md 16 Aug.
1886
HARMON, Edward Jr. of Gray and Mehitable Patrick of Portland
PUB. 27 May 1838
HARMON, Ann of Gray and Leonard H. Hanscom of Buxton
PUB. 27 Oct. 1839
HARMON, Abigail of Gray and Samuel Trumble Jr. of Bridgton
PUB. 17 Mar. 1844 p.294
HARRIMAN, John see Covyeou, Elsie
HARRIMAN, Percy see Leavitt, Hilda
HARRINGTON, Robert see Crockett, Stative
HARRIS, Mary see Goff, William
HARRIS, Charles see Goff, Phebe
HARRIS, Moses and Charlotte Libby both of Gray 18 July 1808
p.185
HARRIS, Larrabee see Delano, Juda
HARRIS, Daniel see Brayman, Mary
HARRIS, Charlotte see Colley, Benjamin
HARRIS, Emeline and Parker S. Libby both of Gray PUB. 20 Feb.
1831 p.265, Md Mar. 1831 p.266
HARRIS, Elizabeth S. and Nathaniel S. Lawrence both of Gray
PUB. 14 Apr. 1833 p.275
HARRIS, Mary Ann and N. S. Lawrence both of Gray PUB. 22
Nov. 1835 p.281
HARRIS, Bell A. of Gray and Edward Leonard Conley of Walton,
Nova Scotia PUB. 2 Oct. 1871, Md 7 Oct. 1871
HARRIS, Mark see Berry, Fannie
HARRIS, Ella of Gray and Cotton M. Bradbury of Windham Md
10 Sept. 1879
HARRIS, Aston see Sawyer, Emma
HARRIS, Archie M. of Gray and Ethel E. Hamilton of No.
Yarmouth Md. 3 Apr. 1901 in Yarmouth p.33
HARRIS, Archie see Crouse, Mabel
HARRIS, Mary see Goff, William
HARRIS, Charles see Goff, Phebe
HARRIS, Sawyer see Duran, Mrs. Mary
HARRIS, Richard see Dolley, Hannah
HASKELL, Moses see Adams, Susan

HASKELL, Sally see Pennell, David

HASKELL, Mary see Twitchell, James

HASKELL, William see McLellan, Lydia

HASKELL, Lois see Perley, Abraham

HASKELL, Nathaniel see Colley, Mary

HASKELL, Jane of Gray and Adam Barbour Pride of Cumberland PUB. 22 Dec. 1822

HASKELL, Abigail and Robert Starbird both of Gray PUB. 22 June 1828 p.256

HASKELL, Louisa see Berry, Daniel

HASKELL, Abbie see Lovell, Millard

HASKELL, Nelker see Morrill, Annie

HASKELL, George E. of Gray and Lizzie E. Hayes of No. Yarmouth Md. 10 June 1875

HASKELL, Rev. John and Mrs. Mary Jane Starbird both of Gray PUB. 3 Dec. 1889, Md 9 Dec. 1889

HASKELL, Oliver D. and Lucinda B. Brown both of Windham Md 7 June 1905 p.49

HASKELL, Della see Chipman, Ernest

HASKELL, George E. and Anna E. Whitney both of Gray Md 7 Sept. 1914 p.93

HASKELL, Sarah see Doughty, Edward

HASKELL, Hannah see Cobb, Ebenzer

HATCH, Tho's and Abigail Pennell both of Gray 2 Sept. 1804 p.178

HATCH, Joseph see Hayden, Harriet

HATCH, Sarah of Gray and Robert Gunnison of Portland PUB. 29 May 1831 p.268

HATCH, Mary see Hutchinson, Charles

HATCH, Abigail see Adams, Benjamin

HATHAWAY, Ellis see Douglass, Cora

HAWES, Mary see Bean, Ebenzer

HAWKES, Mary see King, George

HAWKES, Isiah see Morrill, Mary

HAWKES, Don S. and Minnie J. Hubard both of New Gloucester Md. 18 Feb. 1905 p.49

HAWKES, Ida M. and Perley C. Thompson both of Gray Md 14 May 1909 in No. Yarmouth p.71

HAWKES, Lizzie see Osgood, George

HAWKES, O. W. see Hall, A. A. K.

HAYDEN, Elisha and Hannah Noble PUB. 5 Apr. 1782; 21 Apr. 1783

HAYDEN, Richard and Deidamia White both of Gray 2 Mar. 1786 p.137

HAYDEN, Jonathan and Lydia Young both of Gray 11 May 1791 p.145

HAYDEN, Hannah and William Dolley both of Gray 28 Apr. 1791 p.146

HAYDEN, Sarah see Davis David

HAYDEN, Sarah and William Small both of Gray 10 Nov. 1796 p.156

HAYDEN, Polly of Gray and Henry Tenney of Raymond 8 May 1797 p.157

HAYDEN, Joseph and Abigail Nash both of Gray 6 July 1800 p.163

HAYDEN, David see Davis, Betsy

HAYDEN, Jebediah see Davis, Judath

HAYDEN, Harriet S. and Joseph P. Hatch both of Gray PUB. 23 Mar. 1828 p.256, Md 1828 p.255

HAYDEN, Elizabeth C. of Gray and Zachariah L. Whitney of Raymond PUB. 13 Oct. 1832 p.272

HAYDEN, Clara M. and Alvin Skillin both of Gray Md 30 Aug. 1866

HAYDEN, Esther see Goff, Charles

HAYDEN, Carl W. and Geneva E. Merrill both of Gray Md 3 Jan. 1920 in Portland p.121

HAYDEN, Hannah see Dolley, John

HAYES, Lizzie see Haskell, George

HAYES, Francis see Thompson, Clara

HAYES, Ormond see Sawyer, Isabelle

HEAD, William C. and Ella A. Maier both of Gray Md 17 Apr. 1909 p.71

HEAD, Frank see Goff, Clara

HEAD, Ruth M. of Gray and Delmer A. Parker of Standish Md 4 Nov. 1915 in Windham p.97

HEATH, Verona see Morse, Lewis

HECHLER, Sarah J. and Charles E. Skillings both of Gray Md 13 Sept. 1898 p.25

HELLEN, Effie see Verrill, Ransom G.

HERRICK, Peter see Frank, Etta

HERRICK, Nora see Foster, Edgar

HERRICK, Amelia see Foster, Jonathan

HERRICK, Christania see Cobb, Osburn

HERSOM, Mary see Merrill, Ansel

HEWEY, Robert L. and Cora E. Welch both of Gray Md 31 July 1879

HICKS, Anna and Isaac Lane both of Gray 16 Dec. 1800 p.162

HIGGINS, Samuel see Cook, Lydia

HIGGINS, Amos see Hamilton, Sarah

HIGGINS, Jane and Clement Hayden Humphrey both of Gray Md 19 Nov. 1822 p.230

HIGGINS, Jane and Clement H. Humphrey both of Gray PUB. 27 Oct. 1822 p.231

HIGGINS, Samuel and Martha Lowell both of N. Yarmouth Md. 1826 p.247

HIGGINS, Arthur and Susan Perley both of Gray PUB. 14 Apr. 1833 p.275

HIGGINS, Amanda and Thomas L. Libby both of Gray Md Sept. 1866

HIGGINS, Orin S. and Henrietta Perley both of Gray Md 23 Nov. 1866

HIGGINS, Mary see Foster, Levi

HIGGINS, Martha L. and Edward A. Marr both of Gray PUB. 15 Dec. 1869, Md 21 Dec 1869

HIGGINS, Fannie of Gray and R. B. Jordan of Poland Md 26 May 1870

HIGGINS, Marion H. and James F. Newman M.D. both of Gray Md. 30 Aug. 1875

HIGGINS, Arthur M. and Annie E. Newbegin both of Gray Md 26 Sept. 1876

HIGGINS, Winnie W. and Herbert E. Sweatt both of Gray Md 24 July 1906 p.57

HIGGINS, Martha P. of Gray and Lothrop L. Blake of Lewiston PUB. 20 Nov 1856 Md 20 Nov. 1856

HIGGINS, Susan D. of Gray and Cyrus J. Perley of Pownal PUB. 18 Nov. 1862 Md. 23 Nov. 1862

HILBORN, Isaac and Hannah Kemp both of Portland Md 20 Dec. 1835 p.283

HILDRETH, Winfield Jr. and Nora Peterson both of Lewiston Md 14 Nov. 1923 p.139

HILL, Reuben of Gray and Mary Leguard of Windham 23 Sept. 1790   p.144

HILL, Jane L. and Nathaniel Vickery both of Danville 12 Mar. 1820 p.224

HILL, Abigail see Delano, William

HILL, Josiah of Gray and Hannah Berry of Portland PUB. 4 July 1830 p.263

HILL, Lucy see Morse, Horace

HILL, Luther see Cobb, Mabel

HILL, Josiah and Ann Styles both of Gray Md 2 Nov. 1870

HILL, George see Stiles, Ida

HILL, Ann of Gray and George Blake of New Gloucester Md 12 Nov. 1878

HILL, Etta see Baker, Frank

HILL, L.A. see Hancock, James

HILL, Alice A. see Doughty, Nathan

HILL, Wilbur F. and Celinda T. Nevins Md 8 May 1901 p.33

HILL, Wilbur F. and Celinda T. Hill both of Gray Md 7 Aug. 1912 p.81

HILL, Celinda see Hill, Wilbur

HILL, Arthur W. of Gray and Bernice M. Nash of Norway Md 16 Oct. 1918 in Norway p.113

HILL, Emma and James E. Leighton both of Gray Md 16 Aug. 1856

HILL, Rev. David see Stowell, Susan

HILL, Albert see Frank, Ardelia

HILL, Lucy see Morse, Horace

HILL, Charles see Dickinson, Mary

HILLMAN, Wilhemina B. and James W. Latham both of Gray Md 30 Nov. 1893 p.9

HILTON, Alpheus see Fogg, Etta

HINKLEY, Ann C. and Joseph Pierce of Danville PUB. 21 July 1844 p.294

HITCHCOCK, Arthur see Brown, Alice

HOBBS, Amos and Lucy Roberson both of Gray PUB. 20 July 1782; 5 Aug. 1782

HOBBS, Hannah and Nathan Noble both of Gray 26 Feb. 1786 p.137

HOBBS, Meriam see Foster, Nathan

HODGDON, Samuel and Sally Hunt both of Gray 24 Dec.1812 p.195

HODGKINS, Whitman see Latham, Betsey

HODGKINS, Alphonso and Synthia A. Thurlow both of Gray PUB. 1 July 1873, Md 28 July 1873

HODGKINS, George see Clark, Cora

HODGKINS, Sophronia and Abner T. Strout both of Gray PUB. 20 Oct. 1877, Md 7 Nov. 1877

HODGKINS, George see Duran, Lydia

HODGKINS, James Jr. and Cora J. Thurlow both of Gray Md 28 May 1879

HODGKINS, Lizzie see Farwell, Amos

HODGKINS, Cora B. and Charles Verrill both of Gray Md 17 June 1884

HODGKINS, Whitman and Frances B. Hodgkins both of Gray Md 21 May 1901 p.33

HODGKINS, Frances see Hodgkins, Whitman

HODGKINS, Alverdo E. of Gray and Nora B. Ellis of New Gloucester Md. 8 Nov. 1902 p.39

HODGKINS, Harland see Benson, Ethel

HODGKINS, Herman P. and Edna Lou Hatch both of New Gloucester Md. 19 June 1909 p.73

HODGKINS, Annie M. and George G. Verrill both of Gray Md 16 Nov. 1912 p.83

HODGKINS, Charles B. of No. Raymond and Gladys E. May of Poland Md. 12 May 1918 p.111

HODGKINS, Franklin see Bohnsen, Inez

HODGKINS, Jonas S. and Almeda Welch both of Gray PUB. 4 Oct. 1858 Md. 27 Oct. 1858

HODGKINS, Cora B. and Charles Verrill both of Gray Md 17 June 1884

HODGKINS, Ann see Foster, John

HODGKINS, Ebenzer see Foster, Joan

HODGKINS, Ebenzer see Foster, Mary B.

HODGKINS, Philip see Benson, Emeline

HODGKINS, Elisha and Georgia Tripp both of Gray Md 15 July 1900 p.29

HODGKINS, William S. and Margaret Smith both of Gray Md 24
   Sept. 1900 p.31
HODKINS, Molley and John Varrill both of New Gloucester 19
   June 1800 p.162
HOEY, Rosie see Frank, Augustas L.
HOLDEN, William E. and Mary A. Andrews both of Otisfield Md
   1 Jan. 1862
HOLMES, Rebecca see Young, Abraham
HOLMES, Julia see Lincoln, Rev.
HOLT, Charles L. of Gray and Charlotte L. Small of Casco Md 7
   Jan. 1865
HOPPING, Charles see Anderson, Jennie
HOUSTON, Amelia W. of Gray and Alfred Mayberry of Freeport
   PUB. 5 Jan. 1861, Md 10 Jan. 1861
HOWARD, Annie S. of Gray and Samuel A. Talbot of Portland Md
   2 Oct. 1871
HOWARD, Martha C. of Gray and Melville L. Thorndike of
   Rockland Md. 21 Dec. 1875
HOWES, Herbert R. of Gray and Ellen C. Sargent of Waterbury
   Vermont Md. 12 June 1878
HUFF, Lydia see Verrill, Herbert
HULET, Granville and Frances A. Merrill both of Gray Md 20 Jan.
   1868
HULIT, Ina M. of Gray and Howard S. Freeman of Windham Md.
   17 Oct. 1921 p.129
HULMES, James see Leavitt, Phoebe
HUMPHREY, John and Rachel Merril PUB. 21 Oct. 1780; 6 Nov.
   1780
HUMPHREY, Rebecca and Abraham Perley both of Gray 13 Aug.
   1801 p.165
HUMPHREY, Hannah and Samuel Andrews Nash both of Gray 20
   Feb. 1802 p.168
HUMPHREY, Hannah of Gray and George Benson of New
   Vineyard 1811 p.192
HUMPHREY, John 3rd and Sarah Young both of Gray PUB. 13
   June 1813 p.200
HUMPHREY, Phebe and Charles Latham both of Gray 4 Nov.
   1814 p.201

HUMPHREY, Eunice of Gray and Nathaniel Bracket of New
    Gloucester   8 Jan. 1815 p.201
HUMPHREY, Sally and Isaac Libby both of Gray PUB. 11 Feb.
    1816 p.205
HUMPHREY, Sally and Isaac Libby both of Gray 16 Mar. 1817
    p.208
HUMPHREY, Asa see Fogg, Gena
HUMPHREY, Anna of Gray and David Kemp of Gorham PUB.
    20 Oct. 1819 p.220, Md. 21 Oct. 1819 p.224
HUMPHREY, Hannah and Stephen Winter both of Gray PUB. 20
    June 1820 p.222, Md. 18 May 1820 p.226
HUMPHREY, John and Ruth Lord both of Gray PUB. 14 Oct. 1821
    p.227, Md. 31 Oct. 1821 p.229
HUMPHREY, Clement see Higgins, Jane
HUMPHREY, Meshach see Green, Emma
HUMPHREY, Aron see Fogg, Louisa
HUMPHREY, Martha of Gray and Jonathan Kemp of Gorham
    PUB. 1 May 1825 p.242, Md 26 May 1825 p.240
HUMPHREY, Lydia see Goff, Barzilla
HUMPHREY, Abigail see Ford, John
HUMPHREY, Charity M. of Gray and John Wescott of Gorham
    PUB. 2 July 1832 p.271
HUMPHREY, Jonas see Dolley, Lydia
HUMPHREY, Rebecca and Hiram Jordan both of Gray PUB. 3
    Nov. 1833 p.276
HUMPHREY, M. Lizzie of Gray and Jacob B. Morrill of Windham
    Md. 30 Mar. 1867
HUMPHREY, Susan A. of Gray and Melvin P. Frank of Portland
    Md. 5 Oct. 1869
HUMPHREY, Charlotte see Doughty, Alvin
HUMPHREY, Granville see Frank, Almeda
HUMPHREY, Delphina N. of Gray and Jacob A. Morrell of
    Windham Md. 23 June 1872
HUMPHREY, James C. and Lizzie M. Spencer both of Gray PUB.
    23 Nov. 1877, Md 1 Dec. 1877
HUMPHREY, Ellen J. and Eugene H. Lowe both of Gray Md 24
    Dec. 1900 p.31
HUMPHREY, George G. and Xena E. Verrill both of Gray Md 26
    Nov. 1902 p.39

HUMPHREY, Mildred H. and Oren E. Richards both of Gray Md
20 Oct. 1915 p.97

HUMPHREY, Gerald R. and Harriett L. Russell both of Gray Md
14 Nov. 1923 in Mechanic Falls p.139

HUMPHREY, Howard L. and Doris May Roberts both of Gray Md
29 Aug. 1928 p.163

HUMPHREY, Addie F. of Gray and William L. Noyes of No.
Yarmouth PUB. 29 Sept. 1864 Md. 24 Dec. 1864

HUMPHREY, John W. and Angie Sampson both of Gray PUB 7
Nov. 1864 Md. 24 Dec. 1864

HUMPHREY, Aaron and Caroline Low both of Gray PUB. 13 Jan.
1841

HUMPHREY, M. W. and Capt. T. H. Weymouth both of Gray
PUB. 14 Nov. 1842

HUMPHREY, Henry P. and Augusta M. Weston both of Gray
PUB. 22 Dec. 1844

HUMPHREY, Ira and Cynthia J. Morrison of Cumberland PUB. 16
Feb. 1845

HUMPHREY, Hiram of Gray and Aurelia Whitney of Cumberland
PUB. 30 Nov. 1845

HUMPHREY, Ann see Ferguson, Nathan

HUMPHREY, Azariah see Foster, Mahala

HUMPHREY, Sophronia see Grant, Charles

HUMPHREY, James and Mary Twitchell both of New Boston
(Gray) Md. 28 July 1774

HUNNEWELL, John see Foster, Mary

HUNNEWELL, Edna see Foster, Samuel

HUNT, David Junr. and Hannah Morrill both of Gray 6 Mar. 1797
p.157

HUNT, David Junr. and Sarah Miller both of Gray 20 Nov. 1800
p.163

HUNT, Moses and Sarah Staples both of Gray 1 May 1803 p.174

HUNT, Moses of Gray and Betsey Roberts of Windham PUB. 4
May 1816 p.205

HUNT, David and Sarah Miller both of Gray 21 Feb. 1818 p.213

HUNT, Hannah and Benjamin Weeks both of Gray 3 Dec. 1818
p.218

HUNT, Columbus and Mary Shaw both of Windham Md 14 Dec.
1834 p.279

HUNT, Samuel and Emeline Skillin both of Gray Md 31 Dec. 1860

HUNT, Lee B. and Clara B. Vinton both of Gray PUB. 1 Aug. 1889, Md 21 Aug. 1889

HUNT, Charles and Phebe E. Leslie both of Gray Md 8 Jan. 1869

HUNT, George and Cynthia P. Smith both of Gray Md 13 June 1869

HUNT, Mary E. and Augustus T. Thompson both of Gray Md 2 June 1870

HUNT, Holman and Sarah M. Tripp both of Gray Md 25 Oct. 1874

HUNT, John see Doughty, Esther

HUNT, Emma W. and Charles T. Pennell both of Gray Md 18 Mar. 1879

HUNT, Sadie see Cross, Frank

HUNT, Delbert L. of Gray and Jennie E. Spiller of Raymond PUB. 23 Sept. 1889, Md 9 Oct. 1889

HUNT, Fred L. of Gray and Arvilla S. Knight of Windham PUB. 16 Dec. 1889, Md 1 Jan. 1890

HUNT, Henry L. of Gray and Blanche A. Smith of Deering Md 26 Sept. 1895 in Woodfords p.17

HUNT, George of Gray and Fannie S. Way of Portland Md 3 Nov. 1904 in Portland p.47

HUNT, Henry L. and Laura C. Mountfort both of Gray Md 16 Dec. 1911 p.79

HUNT, Arline M. and Dana M. Russell both of Gray Md 31 Aug.1916 p.101

HUNT, Paul F. of Lewiston and Bertha F. Pennington of Auburn Md. 16 June 1928 p.163

HUNT, Hiram P. of Gray and Hattie N. Tucker of Boston, Mass. Md. 5 Dec. 1859

HUNT, Samuel and Emeline Skillin both of Gray Md 31 Dec 1860

HUNT, Lee see Doughty, Susie

HUNT, James H. and Julia E. Merrill both of Gray PUB. 13 Oct. 1885 Md. 21 Oct. 1885

HUNT, Abigail of Gray and Benjamin Hunt of Windham PUB. 12 Mar. 1837

HUNT, Benjamin see Hunt, Abigail

HUNT, Sarah of Gray and Thomas W. O'Brien of Cornish PUB. 18 Feb. 1838

HUNT, Elnathan of Gray and Eliza J. Felch of Gorham PUB. 9 Sept. 1838

HUNTRESS, Thirza see Colley, True

HURD, Lulu see Frank, Adrian

HUSTON, William and Susan Skillins both of Gray PUB. 18 June 1818 Md. 1818 p.217

HUSTON, Hannah see Smith, Benjamin

HUSTON, David see Harmon, Olive

HUSTON, Sarah S. and Samuel T. Skillin both of Gray Md 21 Jan. 1866

HUSTON, Fanny and David --------- both of Gray Md 14 Mar. 1866

HUSTON, Melissa E. of Gray and Joseph E. Purrington of Windham Md. 24 Sept. 1866

HUSTON, Josephine E. and John M. Legrow both of Gray Md 4 Dec. 1868

HUSTON, Augustas H. of Gray and Dora E. Shaw of Standish Md 31 May 1879

HUSTON, Nancy see Thompson, Joseph Jr.

HUSTON, Joseph F. and Alice M. Knight both of Gray PUB. 14 Feb. 1891, Md 25 Feb. 1891

HUSTON, John P. N. of Gray and Addie B. Legrow of Windham Md. 25 June 1902 p.37

HUSTON, Edwin E. and Maude E. Libby both of Gray Md 17 Feb. 1906 p.53

HUSTON, Alice M. of Gray and George B. Strout of Westbrook Md. 4 May 1929 p.167

HUSTON, Stephen see Adams, Helen

HUSTON, Joseph Jr. of Gray and Frances C. Long of Portland Md 22 Mar. 1856

HUSTON, Elizabeth R. of Gray and Benjamin Porter of Freeport Md. 9 May 1857

HUSTON, Susan see Small, Joseph

HUSTON, Elijah and Lucy Libby both of Gray PUB. 7 Apr. 1839

HUSTON, Hannah of Gray and John Needham Jr. of Bethel PUB. 4 Nov. 1852

HUTCHINS, Abigail see Libby, Benjamin

HUTCHINS, Benjamin see Morse, Leonisa

HUTCHINS, Philina W. of Gray and Richard Plummer Jr. of Sandwich, N.H. PUB. 20 Feb. 1831 p.265

HUTCHINSON, Frederic, see Libby Elizabeth

HUTCHINSON, Abagail see Barton, John

HUTCHINSON, Stephen see Ross, Susan

HUTCHINSON, Frederic see Libby, Elizabeth

HUTCHINSON, Charles of Gray and Mary I. Hatch of Bath Md 30
Dec. 1864

INGALLS, Melville see Stimson, Abbie

INGERSOL, George W. of Falmouth and Ella A. Hulit of
Cumberland Md. 22 June 1884

INGERSOL, George W. of Falmouth and Ella A. Hulit of
Cumberland Md. 22 June 1884

IRELAND, Fred see Crooker, Mary

IRISH, William see Prince, Georgianna

IRISH, Albert N. and Ula L. Mayberry both of Windham Md 1
June 1907 p.59

IRVING, Annie and Stanley H. Witham both of Gray Md 25 Jan.
1921 p.125

JACK, Andrew see Lane, Sally

JACKSON, Emily see Martin, Henry

JACKSON, Fannie see Verrill, George

JACKSON, William see Foster, Mary

JENKS, Betty and Jeremiah Twitchell both of Gray, 14 Sept. 1791
p.145

JEWETT, Jacob see Merrill, Sarah

JEWETT, Ralph of No. Yarmouth and Lora Provenchey of New
Gloucester Md. 5 Feb. 1910 p.75

JOHNSON, J. W. see Cushing, Julia

JOHNSON, James see Goff, Clara

JOHNSON, Estella see Cook, Harry

JOHNSON, Clara see Ramsdell, Fred

JOHNSON, Joseph see Pennell, Mrs. Charlotte

JONES, Mary see Whitney, Amos

JONES, Levi see Berry, Roxieanna

JONES, Susie J. see Cummings, Milo

JONES, Charles L. of Gray and Bertha Morrill of Casco Md 7
Aug. 1902 p.37

JONES, Harland M. and Mabel R. True both of New Gloucester
Md. 10 Nov. 1908 p.67

JONES, George see Berry, Florence

JONES, Cynthia J. of Gray and Aaron V. Barrows of Raymond Md
10 Aug. 1865

JONES, Ann see Merrill, Nathaniel

JONES, Lillian M. of Gray and Wenlock Sanborn of No. Sebago Md. 6 Nov. 1909 p.73

JORDAN, David see Cummings, Ruth

JORDAN, Solomon and Lidia Russell both of Gray PUB. 6 July 1782; 2- July 1782

JORDAN, David and Temperance Russell both of Gray 17 Aug. 1785 p. 136

JORDAN, Thomas see Brown, Hannah

JORDAN, David see Brown, Olive

JORDAN, Ezra see Brown, Peggy

JORDAN, Calvin and Betsey Weeks both of Gray 30 Dec. 1810 p.188

JORDAN, Calvin and Betsey Weeks both of Gray 20 Jan. 1811 p.189

JORDAN, Ezekiel and Susan Libby both of Gray 13 July 1817 p.207

JORDAN, Mary of Gray and David Davis of Bangor PUB. 2 Oct. 1825 p.243

JORDAN, George T. of Gray and Sarah Thomas of Westbrook PUB. 23 Nov. 1828 p.257

JORDAN, Hiram see Humphrey, Rebecca

JORDAN, James M. and Emma M. Brown both of Raymond Md 20 May 1861

JORDAN, Sarah see Brown, Alvin

JORDAN, R. B. see Higgins, Fannie

JORDAN, Isaac R. and Susie B. Field Md 24 June 1874

JORDAN, Enos see Skillin, Evelyn

JORDAN, George see Quint, Fannie

JORDAN, Annie see Dole, John T.

JORDAN, Ella L. and David N. Thurlow both of Gray Md 13 Nov. 1913 p.89

JORDAN, Harold E. of So. Portland and Margaret E. Ward of New Bedford, Mass. Md 14 Aug. 1928 p.163

JORDAN, John H. of Raymond and Margaret A. Stinchfield of New Gloucester Md. 29 Aug. 1857

JORDAN, Isabella see Cummings, Henry

JORDAN, James M. and Emma M. Brown both of Raymond Md 20 May 1861

JORDAN, Sarah see Brown, Alvin

JORDAN, Charles W. and Eugeanna L. Merrill Md 4 Aug. 1865

JURY, Charles H. and Carrie M. Stubbs both of Gray PUB. 10 June 1871, Md. 17 Aug. 1871

KALLOCK, James see Brown, Helen

KEATING, Sarah see Fogg, Scammon

KEMP, Mary and Levi Knight both of Gorham 13 Sept. 1804 p.178

KEMP, David see Humphrey, Anna

KEMP, Jonathan see Humphrey, Martha

KENNARD, Harry W. and Faustina M. Maines both of Windham Md. 10 June 1908 p.65

KENT, Edward W. and Dorothy H. Hancock both of Gray Md 2 Nov. 1923 in Portland p.139

KENT, Harold E. of Gray and Doris E. Gray of No. Deer Isle Md 26 Apr. 1924 in Portland p.141

KIDDER, Charles E. and Anna J. Morse both of Gray Md 11 Nov. 1882

KIDDER, Emily see Hall, Irving

KIDDER, Benjamin F. of Gray and Mrs. Mary M. Morrison of Cumberland PUB. 5 Nov. 1887

KILBORN, Eliza and Joseph B Motley both of Windham Md. 1828 p.255

KILBRETH, Nancy see Colley, Amos Jr.

KIMBALL, Ernest see Sawyer, Mildred

KIMBALL, Lester I. and Mildred R. C. Latham both of Gray Md 6 Nov. 1926 p.155

KING, Edvardus and Eleanor Pennell both of Gray PUB. 13 Aug. 1826 p. 245

KING, George M of Gray and Mary Hawkes of Windham PUB. 20 May 1827 p.249

KING, Hiram B. of Gray and Ellen E. Record of Oxford Md 17 July 1860

KING, Dora E. of Gray and Andrew J. Parsons of York Md 1 June 1861

KING, Hiram B. of Gray and Ellen E. Record of Oxford Md 17 July 1860

KING, Dora E. of Gray and Andrew J. Parsons of York Md 1 June 1861

KING, Thomas and Clarissa J. Sawyer both of Gray PUB. 5 Sept. 1884 Md. 6 Sept. 1884

KING, Cyrus K. and Ann M. Frank PUB. 23 June 1844 p.294

KNAPP, David E. and Florence H. McNulty both of Gray Md 27 Oct. 1930 p.175

KNIGHT, Mary S. of Gray and Thomas I. Haines of Windham 1 Oct. 1854

KNIGHT, Adeline. see Libby, William

KNIGHT, Charles O. of Gray and Abbie J. Maxwell of Windham 24 Sept. 1855

KNIGHT, Daniel see Dolly, Sarah

KNIGHT, Levi see Kemp, Mary

KNIGHT, Jeremiah see Frosh, Susan

KNIGHT, Peace see Doe, Charles

KNIGHT, Rufus see Freeman, Mary

KNIGHT, Stephen see Doughty, Eliza

KNIGHT, Sarah see Morse, Thomas

KNIGHT, Albert see Dole, Clara

KNIGHT, John of Gray and Mary S. Shaw of Standish Md 21 Dec. 1867

KNIGHT, Emily G. of Gray and Francis M. Wilkins of St. Albans PUB. 22 May 1868, Md 31 May 1868

KNIGHT, Edward see Dacy, Rebecca

KNIGHT, George see Eliott, Mary

KNIGHT, Hartley W. of Gray and Emma J. Brown of Sebago PUB. 5 July 1877, Md 16 July 1877

KNIGHT, Lizzie E. and Charles H. Lawrence both of Gray Md 18 Dec. 1877

KNIGHT, Charles E. and Mary F. Strout both of Gray PUB. 29 Sept. 1883, Md 20 Oct. 1883

KNIGHT, Arvilla see Hunt, Fred

KNIGHT, Lillian S. and Edward M. Small both of Gray Md 23 Dec. 1889

KNIGHT, Alice see Huston, Joseph

KNIGHT, Mary see Frank, Melvin M.

KNIGHT, Charles C. see Campbell, Martha

KNIGHT, Fred A. and Fannie E. Pritham both of Gray Md 24 Aug. 1898 p.25

KNIGHT, Grace E. and Frank H. McQuarrie both of Gray Md 16 May 1900 p.29

KNIGHT, Nina see Farwell, John

KNIGHT, Frank E. of Gray and Antoinette A. Cote of Lewiston Md. 17 Apr. 1909 p.71

KNIGHT, Charles E. of Gray and Dorothy Durgin of Casco Md 1 Dec. 1923 p.139

KNIGHT, Clara see Hall, Charles

KNIGHT, Elizabeth A. and John Maxwell both of Gray PUB. 14 Feb. 1858 Md. 28 Feb 1858

KNIGHT, Harriett see Allen, Andrew

KNIGHT, Lovina M. of Gray and Lucius P. Libby of Windham Md 4 Mar. 1884

KNIGHT, Willie A. of Gray and Florence C. Hamilton of No. Yarmouth PUB. 23 June 1884 Md 1 July 1884

KNIGHT, Reuben and Hannah Starbird both of Gray PUB. 14 Nov. 1841

KNIGHT, Lovina M. of Gray and Lucius P. Libby of Windham Md 4 Mar. 1884

KNIGHT, Willie A. of Gray and Florence C. Hamilton of No. Yarmouth PUB. 23 June 1884, Md 1 July 1884

KNIGHT, Mary S. of Gray and Thomas I. Haines of Windham Md 1 Oct. 1854

KNIGHT, Adeline B. and William Libby PUB 13 May 1855, Md 11 June 1855

KNIGHT, Charles O. of Gray and Abbie J. Maxwell of Windham PUB. 24 Sept. 1855 Md. 30 Sept. 1855

KNIGHTLY, Walter T. see Leavitt, Annie A.

KNOWLTON, Frances E. of Gray and Martin Robinson of No. Yarmouth Md. 4 July 1879

LaBARRON, James of Shepherds Field and Jennie Russel of No. Four. 11 Aug. 1791 p.146

LAMAN, Sidney E. and Cora M. Rand both of Portland Md 24 June 1888

LAMB, John see Stiles, Elizabeth

LAMB, Derrill see Brown, Florence

LAMBERT, Lois see Loring, Josiah

LANE, Isaac see Hicks, Anna

LANE, Sally H. of Gray and Andrew Jack of Topsham PUB. Nov. 1820 p. 223 Md. 18 Jan. 1821 p.225

LANE, Eliza of Gray and Nathaniel Merrill Jr. of Cumberland
PUB. 12 Jan. 1823 p.232

LANE, Lucy of Gray and Capt. Rothens Drinkwater of Darien
Georgia PUB. 9 Oct. 1825 p.243, Md 1825 p.241

LANE, Cyrene of Gray and Nathan Wight of Otisfield PUB. 18
Apr. 1830 p.263, Md 1830 p.267

LANE, Dorcas of Gray and Charles L. Loring of N. Yarmouth
PUB. 19 Mar. 1833 p.273

LANE, Eunice H. of Gray and Capt. Richard Colley of Falmouth
PUB. 1 Nov. 1835 p.281

LANE, Margaret T. of Gray and Benj. B. Chambers of Otisfield
PUB. 29 Nov. 1835 p.281

LANE, Charles M. of Gray and Frances A. Young of Paris Md 5
June 1867

LANE, Frances E. of Gray and Lyman B. True of Pownal PUB. 28
May 1868, Md 7 June 1868

LANE, Vera E. of Gray and Adelbert W. Fogg of Pownal Md 20
Nov. 1905 p.51

LANE, Lucretia of Gray and John P. Carswell of Pownal Md 29
Sept. 1862

LAPHAM, George see Gore, Caroline

LARABEE, Susan A. and Frank A. Morgan M.D. both of Gray Md
19 June 1873

LARRABEE, James W. of Limington and Katherine L. Dort of
Woolwich Md. 7 Sept. 1893 p.9

LARRABEE, George see Skillings, Myrta

LARRABEE, Albert see Verrill, Ruth

LATHAM, George and Sarah Mathews both of Gray 14 May 1789
p.142

LATHAM, George of Gray and Polly Saunders of New Gloucester
30 Jun. 1811 p.190

LATHAM, Galen and Betsy Soper both of Gray 29 Feb. 1816
p.200

LATHAM, Charles see Humphrey, Phebe

LATHAM, Lucy see Ford, James

LATHAM, Woodard and Statira Small PUB. 22 May 1819 p.219

LATHAM, Eliab of Gray and Sarah Tufts of Phillips PUB. 22 Sept.
1822 p.231

LATHAM, Jane of Gray and Morris Libby of Raymond PUB. 19
Sept. 1824 p.237

LATHAM, Charlotte of Gray and John Small of Raymond PUB. 13
    Feb. 1825 p.237
LATHAM, Elvira of Gray and James Small of Raymond PUB. 21
    Sept. 1828 p.257, Md 1828 p.253
LATHAM, Nath'l see Mountfort, Betsey
LATHAM, Charles see Lawrence, Abigail
LATHAM, Betsey M. of Gray and Whitman Hodgkins of
    Raymond PUB. 7 May 1888, Md 13 May 1888
LATHAM, Sarah M. of Gray and James McGowan of Portland
    PUB. 11 Oct. 1888, Md 13 Nov. 1888
LATHAM, Otis see Edwards, Clista
LATHAM, David B. and Sarah M. ----- both of Gray Md 6
    Mar.1871
LATHAM, Clarence V. and Lizzie E. Small both of Raymond Md
    17 Feb. 1891
LATHAM, James see Hillman, Wilhemina
LATHAM, Betsey M. and Charles A. Philbrook both of Gray Md 7
    July 1895 p.15
LATHAM, Fred W. of Gray and Mary A. Velioure of Portland Md
    1 June 1918 p.111
LATHAM, Mildred see Kimball, Lester
LATHAM, Charles see Bailey, Mary
LATHAM, Abigail and Capt. Edward Thayer both of Gray PUB.
    20 May 1856 Md 20 May 1856
LATHAM, Jabez M. of Gray and Elizabeth Usher of Limington
    PUB. 1841
LATHAM, Mary see Crowell, Ezra
LAURENCE, Lizzie see Greene, William
LAWRENCE, Sally and Moses Libby both of Gray 28 May 1809
    p.187
LAWRENCE, Ephraim Jr. and Fanney Small both of Gray 24 Oct.
    1816 p.207
LAWRENCE, Ann and Robert Small both of Gray 24 Apr. 1817
    p.208
LAWRENCE, Ann and Robert Small both of Gray PUB. 30 Mar.
    1817 p.209
LAWRENCE, Simon see Davis, Elie
LAWRENCE, Mary and Theophilus Stimson both of Gray PUB.
    26 Feb. 1826 p.243
LAWRENCE, Nath'l see Harris, Elizabeth

LAWRENCE, N. S. see Harris, Mary Ann

LAWRENCE, Abigail of Gray and Charles Latham of Raymond Md. 1836 p.283

LAWRENCE, Frank see Sawyer, Lucinda

LAWRENCE, Charles see Knight, Lizzie

LAWRENCE, Cora see Adams, Fred

LAWRENCE, Charles see Doughty, Marguerite

LAWRENCE, Elmer see Osgood, Nellie

LAWRENCE, Perley W. and Helen H. Merrill both of Gray Md 31 Oct. 1917 in Portland p.107

LAWRENCE, Mary F. and Isaac Libby both of Gray PUB. 1 Dec. 1856 Md. 1 Dec. 1856

LAWRENCE, Frank see Sawyer, Lucinda P.

LAWRENCE, Amanda M. and Hugh Smith both of Gray Md 23 Nov. 1865

LAWRENCE, John and Sarah E. Starbird both of Gray PUB. 27 Aug. 1837

LAWRENCE, Nathaniel see Frank, Louise

LAWRENCE, David and Amanda M. Whitney both of Gray PUB. 2 Apr. 1848

LEACH, Zechariah and Betty Simanton of Raymington PUB. 26 Feb. 1792 p.127

LEACH, Bela E. of Gray and Cora E. Wells of Gorham Md 13 July 1892

LEACH, Jennie and George W. Snow both of Gray Md 22 Jan. 1896 in Deering p.17

LEACH, Victor see Merrill, Annie

LEACH, Victor W. and Hortense H. Lowe both of Gray Md 28 June 1930 in Cumberland p.171

LEAVITT, William see Barbour, Mary

LEAVITT, Seth and Ann Libby both of Gray PUB. 30 Aug. 1835 p.281, Md 22 Sept. 1835 p.283

LEAVITT, Daniel see Frank, Leantha

LEAVITT, Phoebe C. of Gray and James Hulmes of Casco Md 13 June 1894 p.13

LEAVITT, Annie A. of Gray and Walter T. Knightly of Paris Md 11 Aug. 1897 in W. Poland p.23

LEAVITT, Elsie L. and Edward W. Parker both of Gray Md 27 May 1899 in New Gloucester p.27

LEAVITT, Frances see Hancock, Mary

LEAVITT, Clarence W. and Henrietta E. Pritham both of Freeport Md. 21 Apr. 1917 p.105

LEAVITT, Hilda J. of Gray and Percy G. Harriman of Windham Md. 5 June 1918 p.111

LEAVITT, Neal A. of New Vineyard and Nellie M. Miller of Wilton Md. 17 June 1922 p.133

LEAVITT, Frances see Hanson, Byron

LEAVITT, Kathryn S. and Guy O. Prince both of Gray Md 19 June 1926 p.153

LEAVITT, Keith L. and Marguerite F. Webster both of Gray Md 20 Oct. 1930 p.175

LEGROW, Lydia see Frank, Isaac

LEGROW, Amos see Foster, Betsey

LEGROW, Amos see Foster, Abigail

LEGROW, ? And Lucinda McDonald Md 1865

LEGROW, Hannah see Foster, Samuel

LEGROW, John see Huston, Josephine

LEGROW, Rufus see Libby, Fannie

LEGROW, Addie see Huston, John

LEGROW, Emeline see Goff, Melvin

LEGUARD, Mary see Hill, Reuben

LEIGHTON, Sarah see Hadlock, William

LEIGHTON, Lovey and Nicholas Low both of Gray 31 Mar. 1803 p.174

LEIGHTON, Daniel see Dyer, Sally

LEIGHTON, James see Doughty, Anne

LEIGHTON, Statira see Foster, Job

LEIGHTON, Elias see Frank, Lucinda

LEIGHTON, Dorchus see Libby, Ebenzer

LEIGHTON, Robert of Cumberland and Cynthia Morse of N. Gloucester Md. June 1832 p.270

LEIGHTON, Eunice G. of Gray and James S. Dole of Westbrook Md. 3 Jan. 1860

LEIGHTON, James E. and Judith M. Shaw both of Gray Md 9 Jan. 1860

LEIGHTON, Mary see Farwell, Samuel

LEIGHTON, Benjamin see Harmon, Charlotte

LEIGHTON, Wilbur see Barbour, Fannie

LEIGHTON, Lorana see Hall, Edward

LEIGHTON, Joshua D. of Gray and Carrie W. Loring of Pownal Md. 10 June 1871

LEIGHTON, Arabell see Mountfort, Sewall

LEIGHTON, Joseph B. and Lizzie L. Carter both of Falmouth Md 28 Feb. 1872

LEIGHTON, Clara see Foster, Edwin

LEIGHTON, Benjamin see Davis, Eliza

LEIGHTON, Robert see Whitney, Ellen

LEIGHTON, Harriet see Mountfort, Albert

LEIGHTON, Walter F. and Hattie E. Osgood both of Gray Md 26 June 1880

LEIGHTON, Herbert see Mountfort, Julia

LEIGHTON, Edward see Dunn, Annie

LEIGHTON, Walter F. of Gray and Flora A. Philbrick of Troy Md 28 Apr. 1897 in West Troy p.21

LEIGHTON, Walter F. and Sadie Murch both of Gray Md 31 Mar. 1900 p.27

LEIGHTON, Caroline see Davis, Elmer

LEIGHTON, Melvin of Windham and Edna J. Rogers of So. Paris Md. 19 Nov. 1919 p.119

LEIGHTON, Walter E. of Gray and Stella M. Leighton of No. Yarmouth Md. 14 Dec. 1919 in No. Yarmouth p.121

LEIGHTON, Stella see Leighton, Walter

LEIGHTON, Gladys see Burns, Kenneth

LEIGHTON, Albert see Bohnsen, Hazel

LEIGHTON, Marion E. and William H. Small both of Gray Md 27 Aug. 1930 in So. Paris p.171

LEIGHTON, James see Hill, Emma

LEIGHTON, Louisa B. of Gray and Andrew G. Loring of Pownal PUB. 8 Nov. 1857 Md. 3 Dec. 1857

LEIGHTON, Ann M. and William H. Low both of Gray Md 9 Feb. 1859

LEIGHTON, Eunice G. of Gray and James S. Dole of Westbrook Md. 3 Jan. 1860

LEIGHTON, James E. and Judith M. Shaw both of Gray Md 9 Jan. 1860

LEIGHTON, Henrietta C. and Lewis A. Simpson both of Gray Md 11 Nov. 1863

LEIGHTON, Ellen M. of Gray and Samuel C. Donnell of Falmouth Md. 6 July 1865

LEIGHTON, Annie see Whitney, Lewis

LEIGHTON, Carrie B. and Edward Peck both of Gray Md 28 Nov. 1886

LEIGHTON, Joann see Thompson, William

LEIGHTON, Ann see Fowler, Thomas

LEIGHTON, John see Delano, Mrs. Betsey

LEONARD, Ernest W. of Gray and Ruth L. Farnham of New Gloucester Md. 25 Feb. 1928 in New Gloucester p.161

LEONARD, Joseph A. of Gray and Susan H. Moores of Springfield Md. 12 July in Bangor p.167

LESLIE, Phebe see Hunt, Charles

LESLIE, Mrs. Sarah and Albert Pennell both of Gray Md 9 Sept. 1878

LESLIE, Ralph see Field, Leola

LESLIE, Whitman and Aggie L. Allen Md – Sept. 1865

LESSLY, George of Gray and Olive Fowler of New Gloucester PUB. 17 Jun. 1780; 3 July 1780

LIBBEY, William see Goold, Hannah

LIBBY, Mehitable T. of Gray and William Dow of Gray 8 Jan, 1854

LIBBY, Elizabeth of Gray and Frederic A. Hutchinson of Portland 6 Sept. 1854

LIBBY, William and Adeline B. Knight both of Gray 13 May 1855

LIBBY, Elihu and Elizabeth M. Elliott both of Windham 30 Sept. 1855

LIBBY, Isaac H. and Margaret Frank both of Gray 10 Dec. 1855

LIBBY, Joel and Mehetable Nash both of Gray 4 Dec. 1785 p. 136

LIBBY, William and Jane McCaffery both of Gray 5 Dec. 1785 p. 136

LIBBY, Joseph and Mary Young both of Gray 1 Mar. 1789 p.142

LIBBY, Nancy of Gray and Parker Sawyer of New Gloucester 17 Nov. 1791 p.145

LIBBY, Jonathan see Clark, Abigail

LIBBY, Asa see Dutton, Lucretia

LIBBY, Daniel see Colley, Hannah

LIBBY, Dorcas and Isaac Nason both of Gray 11 Aug.
1795 p.153

LIBBY, Hannah and Samuel Nash both of Gray 4 Feb. 1796
p.155

LIBBY, Joseph see Doughty, Mary

LIBBY, David see Cobb, Mary

LIBBY, Seth and Elizabeth Welch both of Raymondtown 6 Sept.
1797 p.157

LIBBY, Sarah see Green, Daniel

LIBBY, Sarah and Samuel Young both of Gray 11 Jan. 1801
p.167

LIBBY, Mary of Gray and Charles Thaxter of Windham 11 Nov.
1804 p.180

LIBBY, Jane see Clark, Samuel

LIBBY, Charlotte see Harris, Moses

LIBBY, Moses see Lawrence, Sally

LIBBY, Andrew and Susan Small both of Gray 13 July 1809 p.187

LIBBY, Benjamin Jr. of Gray and Periilla Clay of Gorham PUB. 3
Apr. 1816 p.205

LIBBY, Eunice and James Weymouth PUB. 13 Apr. 1816 p.205
Md. 3 July 1816 p.207

LIBBY, Jebediah Cobb and Hannah Prince both of Gray PUB. 27
Apr. 1816 p.205 Md. 5 Sept. 1816 p.207

LIBBY, Isaac see Humphrey, Sally

LIBBY, Susan see Jordan, Ezekiel

LIBBY, Christiana and John Small both of Gray PUB. 22 May
1818 p.216, Md. 16 May 1819 p.224

LIBBY, Anna and Curtis Stiles both of Gray PUB. 11 July 1819
p.219 Md. 11 July 1819 p.224

LIBBY, Isaac and Comfort Weymouth both of Gray 5 Aug. 1819
p.224

LIBBY, Ebenzer of North Yarmouth and Sarah S. Nason of
Freeport 30 Nov. 1820 p.225

LIBBY, Silvia see Cushman, Nathaniel

LIBBY, Paulina W. and Solomon N. Ramsdell both of Gray PUB.
9 Feb. 1822 p.228, Md 1822 p.235

LIBBY, Joseph Jr. of Gray and Mary Simonton of Portland PUB.
30 Aug. 1823 p. 234

LIBBY, Morris see Latham, Jane

LIBBY, Benjamin of Gray and Abigail Hutchins of Minot PUB. 13
Mar. 1825 p.242

LIBBY, Joseph see Ramsdell, Hannah

LIBBY, Benjamin of Gray and Martha Starbird of Greene PUB. 26
Feb. 1826 p.244

LIBBY, Esther P. and Peter M. Ramsdell both of Gray PUB. 28
May 1826 p.245

LIBBY, George and Maryann Stimson both of Gray PUB. 8 Oct.
1826 p.245, MD 1827 p.248

LIBBY, David Jr. and Martha Weymouth both of Gray PUB. 10
Dec. 1826 p.246, Md 1827 p.247

LIBBY, Martha and Samuel Frank both of Gray PUB. 24 Dec.
1826 p.246

LIBBY, Andrew 3rd of Gray and Huldah Manchester of Windham
PUB. 20 Apr. 1828 p.256, Md 1828 p.253

LIBBY, Ebenzer C. of Gray and Dorchus Leighton of Falmouth
PUB. 22 June 1828 p.256

LIBBY, Hannah see Purkis, John

LIBBY, Lucy and Alvin Skillin both of Gray PUB. 13 Sept. 1829
p.260

LIBBY, Willard and Huldah Stiles both of Gray PUB. 25 July 1830
p.263

LIBBY, William Jr. of Gray and Patience H. Staples of Windham
PUB. 26 Sept. 1830 p.264

LIBBY, Sally and John Muchmore both of Gray PUB. 17 Oct.
1830 p.264, Md 1830 p.266

LIBBY, Eliza and Nathaniel Small both of Gray PUB. 9 Jan.
1831 p.265

LIBBY, Almer H. and Rebecca C. Libby both of Gray PUB. 18
Mar. 1831 p.268

LIBBY, Rebecca see Libby, Almer

LIBBY, Stephen see Low, Mary

LIBBY, Ebenzer C. of Gray and Hannah Elliot of Windham PUB.
29 Sept. 1833 p.276, Md 31 Oct. 1833 p.279

LIBBY, Fanny see Foss, Sumner

LIBBY, Charles see Cummings, Abagail

LIBBY, Simon see Morse, Rebecca

LIBBY, Ann see Leavitt, Seth

LIBBY, Jebediah of Gray and Mary Pierce of New Gloucester Md
1836 p.283

LIBBY, Albion see Hammond, Sarah

LIBBY, Julia E. and James A. Woodbury both of Gray Md 7 Dec. 1888

LIBBY, Eliza J. and Joseph H. Ramsdell both of Gray PUB. 20 Feb. 1866, Md 4 Mar. 1866

LIBBY, Ellen and Benjamin F. Skillings both of Gray PUB. 18 June 1866, Md 24 June 1866

LIBBY, Callie A. of Gray and Edwin L. Field PUB. 26 Aug. 1866 Md. 1 Sept. 1866

LIBBY, Thomas see Higgins, Amanda

LIBBY, Wealthy M. of Gray and George D. Clark of Portland Md 12 June 1867

LIBBY, Jebediah and Hattie W. Parsons both of Gray Md 21 Dec. 1868

LIBBY, Woodbury see Foster, Delinda

LIBBY, Sarah E. of Gray and Isaac G. Waters of Boston Md 5 July 1869

LIBBY, Christina see Foster, Solomon

LIBBY, C. H. see Hall, Cushman

LIBBY, John H. and Fannie T. Stiles both of Gray Md 25 Apr. 1871

LIBBY, Frank A. of Gorham and Sadie A. Knight of Naples Md. 11 June 1871

LIBBY, Susie J. of Gray and John B. Nash of Windham Md 8 Nov. 1871

LIBBY, Edward see Foster, E. Augusta

LIBBY, John M. of Gray and Victoria S. Foss of Bradley Md 28 Feb. 1872

LIBBY, George see Allen, Evelyn

LIBBY, Ellen F. of Gray and Andrew Libby of Standish Md 16 Feb. 1877

LIBBY, Andrew see Libby, Ellen

LIBBY, Carrie see Doughty, Charles

LIBBY, James P. and Nettie F. Small both of Gray Md 6 Mar. 1878

LIBBY, Fannie see Cummings, Llewellyn

LIBBY, George and Emma S. Stiles both of Gray Md 17 Mar. 1879

LIBBY, Fannie F. of Gray and Rufus Legrow of Cumberland PUB. 29 Sept. 1879, Md 8 Oct. 1879

LIBBY, Isabell see Cross, William

LIBBY, Nettie see Fogg, James

LIBBY, James E. and Nellie G. White both of Gray Md 18 Dec.
1882

LIBBY, Jennie E. and Howard D. Verrill both of Gray Md 22 Nov.
1883

LIBBY, Lucius see Knight, Lovina

LIBBY, Ida F. and Orin F. Whitney both of Gray PUB. 8 Mar.
1884, Md 15 Mar. 1884

LIBBY, Herbert C. and Fannie A. Thayer both of Gray PUB. 23
Mar. 1891, Md 31 Mar. 1891

LIBBY, Kate H. and Harry Merrill both of Gray Md 23 June 1892

LIBBY, Mabel E. and William H. Small both of Gray Md 19 Apr.
1893 p. 7

LIBBY, Annie see Dwyer, Roscoe

LIBBY, Jebediah of Gray and Elizabeth McCollister of Rumford
Md. 9 May 1893 p.9

LIBBY, Simon and H. Augusta Stiles both of Gray Md 1 Dec. 1894
p.13

LIBBY, Albert see Pennell, Jennie

LIBBY, Herbert M. of Gray and Mary A. Ready of Rumford Falls
Md. 13 June 1896 p.19

LIBBY, Ellie J. see Goff, Melvin

LIBBY, John M. of Gray and Annie Barrows of Raymond Md 12
Mar. 1899 p.25

LIBBY, Harry L. and Marion S. Merrill both of Gray Md 22 July
1901 p.35

LIBBY, Charles A. and Edith G. Thompson both of Gray Md 27
Sept. 1902 p.39

LIBBY, Minnie M. and Wendall A. Small both of Gray Md 31
Dec. 1902 p.41

LIBBY, Alice see Richards, Fred

LIBBY, Eva see Grover, David

LIBBY, Eva B. and Herbert C. Morrell both of Gray Md 27 Oct.
1904 p.47

LIBBY, Linda M. and Augustas W. Maier both of Gray Md 6 Jan.
1906 p.53

LIBBY, Maude see Huston, Edwin

LIBBY, William M. and Grace E. Libby both of Portland Md 19
May 1906 p.55

LIBBY, Clarence A. and Mabel A. Hunt both of Portland Md 1
Aug. 1906 p.57
LIBBY, Lois B. of Gray and Harry A. Dolloff of No. Yarmouth Md
22 May 1908 p.65
LIBBY, Ellen see Dunn, Moses
LIBBY, Clifford see Dow, Dorothy
LIBBY, Leroy see Burns, Bessie
LIBBY, Roy L. of No. Yarmouth and Wilmer F. Conley of New
Gloucester Md. 21 Nov. 1914 p.93
LIBBY, Bessie see Cobb, Stuart
LIBBY, Mertie of Gray and Raymond M. Cote of Brookfield, N.H.
Md. 21 Mar. 1916 in Ossipee, N.H. p.99
LIBBY, Florence H. of Gray and Charles H. Nelson of New
Gloucester Md. 16 Mar. 1921 in Portland p.127
LIBBY, Edwin see Frisbie, Carrie
LIBBY, George E. of Gray and Bertha A. Boynton of East Lynn,
Mass. Md. 23 Aug. 1926 in Lynn, Mass p.155
LIBBY, Laura E. of Gray and Harry E. Burnham of Portland Md
10 Dec. 1927 p.159
LIBBY, Joseph L. of Cumberland Mills and Ruth E. Lund of
Portland Md. 8 July 1929 p.169
LIBBY, Mehitable see Dow. William
LIBBY, Elizabeth of Gray and Frederic A. Hutchinson of Portland
Md. 6 Sept. 1854
LIBBY, William see Knight, Adeline
LIBBY, Elijah and Elizabeth M. Elliott both of Windham Md 30
Sept. 1855
LIBBY, Isaac see Frank, Margaret
LIBBY, Isaac see Lawrence, Mary
LIBBY, Betsey R. of Gray and George F. Thurlow of Poland Md
23 May 1857
LIBBY, Stephen see Stiles, Elizabeth
LIBBY, Mary A. of Gray and Valentine C. Hall of Casco PUB. 18
Apr. 1859 Md. 1 May 1859
LIBBY, Albion see Hammond, Sarah
LIBBY, Fernald see Skillin, Lucy E.
LIBBY, Lucius see Knight, Lovina
LIBBY, Ida F. and Orin Whitney both of Gray PUB. 8 Mar. 1884
Md. 15 Mar. 1884
LIBBY, John see Frank, Susie

137

LIBBY, Artie see Clark, Frank

LIBBY, Ellen F. of Gray and William P. Woodbury of Raymond
PUB. 9 May 1887

LIBBY, Harriet E. and Levi G. Small both of Gray PUB. 1 Sept.
1887

LIBBY, William 3rd see Brown, Deborah

LIBBY, Jonathan of Gray and Matilda S. Bacon of No. Yarmouth
PUB. 8 Dec. 1838

LIBBY, Lucy see Huston, Elijah

LIBBY, Ellen of Gray and John K. Clough of Meredith, N.H. PUB.
14 Apr. 1839

LIBBY, Olive see Farrell, Capt. Edward

LIBBY, Mahala of Gray and Sallas Haines of Windham PUB. 3
Apr. 1842

LIBBY, Calvin see Purkis, Eliza

LIBBY, Ann see Benson, Benjamin

LINCOLN, Rev. Allen of Gray and Martha Gardner of Woburn,
Mass. Md. 8 Apr. 1856

LINCOLN, Rev. Allen of Gray and Julia A. Holmes of Auburn
PUB. 1 Aug. 1847

LOAN, Daniel C. of Auburn and Annie L. Churchill of Minot Md 1
Sept. 1889

LOMBARD, Marshall of Boston Mass. And Rhoda L. Tobie of
Windham Md. 26 Jan. 1860

LOMBARD, John see Field, Hattie

LONG, Frances see Huston, Joseph Jr.

LORD, Ruth see Humphrey, John

LORD, Lydia see Bachelder, Amos

LORD, Isaac H. and Lillian Mason both of Gray Md 20 Sept. 1914
p.93

LORD, Nathan see Verrill, Lucy

LORD, Isaac H. see Buker, Clara

LORING, Isaac and Mary Staples Md 1826 p.247

LORING, Charles see Lane, Dorcas

LORING, Josiah S. of Gray and Lois M. Lambert of Westbrook
Md. 7 Jan. 1867

LORING, Carrie see Leighton, Joshua

LORING, George see Clark, Jennie

LORING, Percy see Whitney, Carrie

LORING, Ina W. of Gray and Harold W. Norton of Falmouth Md
    24 June 1917 p.105
LORING, Andrew see Leighton, Louisa
LORING, Mrs. Ann C. and Benjamin Mitchell both of Gray Md 21
    May 1863
LORING, Elbridge see Staples, Eliza
LOTHROP, Eaton see Sweetser, Alice
LOVELL, Millard F. of Gray and Abbie F. Haskell of No.
    Yarmouth Md. 8 May 1888
LOW, Nicholas and Abigail Miller both of Gray 29 Nov. 1792
    p.148
LOW, Levi see Soper, Polly
LOW, Nicholas see Leighton, Lovey
LOW, John and Mary Merrill both of Gray 29 Nov. 1804   p.180
LOW, William of Gray and Almira Wilson of Falmouth 21 Oct.
    1810 p.188
LOW, Polly of Gray and James Field of North Yarmouth PUB. 16
    Aug. 1817 p.210
LOW, Nicholas of Gray and Paulina Freeman of Minot PUB. 5
    Sept. 1824 p.237
LOW, Hannah see Perley, George
LOW, Mary of Gray and Stephen Libby of Gorham PUB. 13 Nov.
    1831 p.268
LOW, Charles F. of Gray and Lizzie Doughty of Cumberland Md 9
    Nov. 1869
LOW, Sarah see Ramsey, Ezra
LOW, Horace H. of Gray and Ida M. Parker of Lewiston Md 24
    Jan. 1871
LOW, Vesta A. of Gray and Oliver F. Blake of New Gloucester Md
    6 Mar. 1871
LOW, Ausgustas of Gray and Mary E. Mahoney of Yarmouth Md
    29 May 1871
LOW, Florence see Sawyer, Frank
LOW, William see Leighton, Ann
LOW, Winfield S. and Nellie V. Welch both of Gray Md 25 Oct.
    1862
LOW, Willard of Gray and Abba A. Babb of Windham Md 9 July
    1865
LOW, Caroline see Humphrey, Aaron

LOWE, Mildred see Dunphe, William

LOWE, Christopher S. and Blanche Meguier both of Gray Md 3
    Dec. in New Gloucester p.23

LOWE, Eugene see Humphrey, Ellen

LOWE, Eugene H. and Wilmer Adele Snow both of Gray Md 17
    Sept. 1921 p.129

LOWE, Hortense see Leach, Victor

LOWELL, Martha see Higgins, Samuel

LOWELL, Joseph see Elwell, Dillia

LOWELL, Mary E. and Elmer Strout both of Gray Md 25 Jan.
    1919 p.115

LUCAS, Mehitable see Soper, Asa

LUCKINGS, William P. and Velma Smith both of Gray Md 4 Oct.
    1919 in Lewiston p.119

LUCKINGS, Gertrude see Ellinwood, George Jr.

LUFKIN, Nathaniel and Lucy Serjant both of North Yarmouth 20
    Feb. 1810 p.189

LUNT, Hannah see Cobb, Benjamin

LUNT, Benjamin and Mary C. Tobie both of New Gloucester Md
    24 Oct. 1860

LUNT, Neal D. of Gray and Addie S. Wakefield of Deering Md 25
    Apr. 1882

LUNT, Benjamin and Mary C. Tobie both of New Gloucester Md
    24 Oct. 1860

LYON, Eunice and Joseph Tubbs both of Gray 15 Mar. 1787
    p.138

LYON, Marcia see Cobb, Winthrop

MABURY, Daniel see Nash, Betsy

MACE, Alice M. and George Willis Thompson both of Gray PUB.
    11 Apr. 1891, Md 3 May 1891

MacLEOD, Tena see Story, Horace

MAHONEY, Mary see Low, Augustas

MAIER, Frederica see Cobb, Dwinal

MAIER, Christina B. and Fred A. Tinkham both of Gray Md 4 Oct.
    1902 p.39

MAIER, Augustas see Libby, Linda

MAIER, Ella see Head, William

MAIER, Ethel M. and William B. Prince both of Gray Md 1 Feb.
    1913 p.85

MAINS, Elizabeth of Gray and Joseph Neal of Monmouth PUB.
19 Mar. 1820 p.222

MAINS, Perley see Witham, Frank

MAINS, Benjamin and Mrs. Emma C. Manchester both of
Windham Md. 18 Nov. 1885

MALEY, Thomas J. and Arline V. Larby both of Portland Md 30
Nov. 1930 p.177

MANCHESTER, Leon see Doughty, Grace

MANCHESTER, Charles see Frank, Annie

MANN, Mildred and John M. Sawyer both of Gray Md 18 July
1925 in Kittery p.149

MANNING, Eliza J. of Gray and Charles D. Rider of New
Gloucester Md. 17 Apr. 1867

MANNING, Mary E. and Charles T. Mayberry both of Gray PUB.
9 Jan. 1869, Md 14 Jan. 1869

MARINER, Sarah see Stiles, Caleb

MARR, Lucetta, see Clark, Jacob

MARR, Jane see Bradbury, Nath'l

MARR, Edward see Higgins, Martha

MARR, William L. and Amy F. Hamilton both of Portland Md 5
Oct. 1929 p.169

MARR, Lucetta see Clark, Jacob

MARSDEN, Horace C. of Gray and Wilma A. Morrill of
Westbrook Md. 24 Apr. 1918 in Westbrook p.109

MARSTON, Simeon and Susan F. Morse both of Gray PUB. 21
Oct. 1827 p.250, Md 1827 p.251

MARSTON, Andrew see Duran, Eliza

MARSTON, Andrew J. and Deborah A. Woodsom both of Gray
PUB. 1 Dec. 1883, Md 6 Dec. 1883

MARSTON, Frank C. and Geneva Morrill both of New Gloucester
Md. 21 Dec. 1892

MARSTON, John H. and Sarah M. Libby both of Windham Md 1
Dec. 1894 p. 13

MARSTON, Lenord G. of No. Yarmouth and Jennie L. Riggs of
New Gloucester Md. 1 June 1911 p.79

MARTIN, Henry of Gray and Emily A. Jackson of Raymond Md
13 Dec. 1879

MARTIN, Eddie see Cobb, Ervena

MARTIN, Harry E. and Helen M. Sweetser both of Gray Md 26
Sept. 1923 p.139

MARTON, Herbert see Skillin, Etta

MASON, Edward M. of Raymond and Mabel C. Dingley of Casco Md. 4Feb. 1894 p.11

MASON, Fred see Blake, Nellie

MASON, Lillian see Lord, Isaac

MATHWES, Sarah see Latham, George

MAXELL, Esther of Gray and Jacob Maxell of Windham PUB. 15 Aug. 1824 p.237, Md 2 Sept. 1824 p.239

MAXELL, Jacob see Maxell, Esther

MAZELL, Irene and Jeremiah Pennell both of Gray PUB. 24 Sept. 1832 p.271

MAXFIELD, Sumner C. and Mahala Purington both of Windham Md. 15 July 1860

MAXWELL, Abbie see Knight, Charles

MAXWELL, Ebenezer and Jane Webster both of Gray   25 Sept. 1814 p.201

MAXWELL, Ebenezer and Esther Pennell both of Gray 15 Apr. 1817 p.208

MAXWELL, Mary Jane and Woodbury Stimson both of Gray Md 21 Aug. 1834 p.279

MAXWELL, George W. and Vergie W. Morrill both of Gray Md 4 June 1919 p.117

MAXWELL, Catherine J. of Gray and Bernard S. Cilley of Portland Md. 31 Dec. 1920 p.125

MAXWELL, Abbie see Knight, Charles

MAXWELL, John see Knight, Elizabeth

MAXWELL, Frank E. of Gray and Cora B. Allen of Windham PUB. 13 Oct. 1885 Md. 21 Oct. 1885

MAY, Jeremiah and Sarah Verrill both of Gray PUB. 24 Mar. 1822 p.228, Md. 16 Apr. 1822 p.230

MAY, John and Hannah Verrill both of Gray PUB. 3 Apr. 1825 p.242

MAY, William of Gray and Lydia Ann Cote of Saco PUB 10 Dec. 1825 p.243

MAY, John see Benson, Elizabeth

MAY, Lizzie see Berry, George

MAY, Alica A. and Stephen R. Thurlow both of Gray PUB. 5 Aug. 1882, Md 12 Aug. 1882

MAY, Charles see Strout, Ada

MAY, Edwin see Benson, Lucy

MAY, Martha see Coffin, Simeon

MAY, Isabella and Ephraim P. C. Strout both of Gray Md 18 Aug. 1900 p.31

MAY, Jeremiah and Mary F. Hinckley both of New Gloucester Md 16 Sept. 1909 p.73

MAY, Jesse P. of New Gloucester and Hattie Verrill of Raymond Md. 5 May 1919 p.115

MAY, Hiram G. and Lillian M. Parent both of New Gloucester Md 11 Dec. 1920 p.125

MAY, Stephen and Julia McCollister both of Gray Md 23 June 1921 p.127

MAY, Chester see Bragdon, Adeline

MAY, Stephen and Bernice Trumble both of Gray Md 18 May 1929 p.167

MAY, Jeremiah of Gray and Hannah R. Mitchell of Portland Md 8 May 1858

MAY, Jeremiah Jr. and Ellen L. Tripp both of Gray PUB. 31 July 1859 Md. 10 Aug. 1859

MAY, Jeremiah of Gray and Anna F. Plaice of Scarborough PUB. 26 Jan. 1863 Md. 16 Mar. 1863

MAY, E. O. see Douglass, Flora

MAYALL, Margaret and James Radcliff both of Gray 28 Jan. 1811 p.189

MAYALL, Joney of Gray and Mary Sanborn of Standish PUB. 24 Jan. 1813 p.200

MAYBERRY, William of Gray and Jane Mayberry of Gorham PUB. 7 Oct. 1827 p.249

MAYBERRY, Jane see Mayberry, William

MAYBERRY, Daniel see Foster, Rebecca

MAYBERRY, Alfred see ?melia, Houston

MAYBERRY, Charles see Manning, Mary

MAYBERRY, Mary see Sawyer, George

MAYBERRY, Frederick E. and Ida E. Stanford both of Gray PUB. 3 Dec. 1881, Md 25 Dec. 1881

MAYBERRY, Alice S. and Charles L. Thompson both of Gray Md 22 Oct. 1882

MAYBERRY, Herbert and Susie M. Tenney both of Gray Md 18 Dec. 1893 p.11

MAYBERRY, Edith W. and Charles G. Sawyer both of Gray Md
25 Nov. 1896 p.21
MAYBERRY, Willard J. of Gray and Gertrude A. Grant of Poland
Md. 17 July 1897 in So. Poland p.23
MAYBERRY, Thomas J. see Campbell, Winnie
MAYBERRY, Frederick E. and Orpha W. Cloudman both of Gray
Md. 31 May 1919 p.117
MAYBERRY, Daniel see Foss, Nancy
MAYBERRY, Alfred see Houston, Amelia
MAYBERRY, Randall see Walker, Mary
MAYBERRY, Mark see Shaw, Jane
MAYBERRY, Henry see Bennett, Elizabeth
MAYBERRY, Sophia see Frank, James E.
MAYBERRY, Orland H. of Gray and Mildred B. Mead of Portland
Md. 17 June 1918 in Portland p.113
MAYBURY, Helen M. and Albert Skillin both of Gray Md 27
Dec. 1857
MAYER, Barbara of Gray and George Gratto of Portland Md 10
May 1925 in Windham p.147
MAYO, Thomas and Betsy Titcomb both of Gray 17 Mar. 1811
p.190
McCAFFERY, Jane see Libby, William
McCALMON, Edwin H. and Grace R. Wilcox both of Gray Md 18
June 1921 p.127
McCALMON, Edwin H. of Gray and Susie R. Ayer of Portland
Md. 30 June 1926 p.153
McCOLLISTER, Elizabeth see Libby, Jebediah
McCOLLISTER, Julia see May, Stephen
McCONKEY, Mary J. and Mathew C. Morrill both of Gray PUB. 5
Jan. 1873, Md 11 Jan. 1873
McCONKEY, William H. and Fannie D. Pennell both of Gray
PUB. 29 Apr. 1878, Md 8 May 1878
McCONKEY, John R. of Gray and Bertha E. Tripp of New
Gloucester Md. 26 Oct. 1897 in Wilsons Springs p.23
McCONKEY, Lena M. of Gray and Harlie M. Day of Gorham Md
28 Nov. 1901 p.37
McCONKEY, Elizabeth see Bailey, Roy
McCONKEY, Thriza R. of Gray and Herbert M. Waterman of New
Gloucester Md. 14 Dec. 1920 in New Gloucester p.125

144

McCONKEY, Dana G. of Gray and Leona Taylor of Falmouth Md 14 June 1924 p.143

McDANIELS, Susanna and William Morse both of Gray 15 Dec. 1796 p.156

McDONALD, Charles see Blaisdell, Abigail

McDONALD, Sarah see Dutton, Thomas

McDONALD, Charles J. of Gray and Dora S. Pierce of New Gloucester Md. 19 Dec. 1870

McDONALD, Roy C. of Gray and Ella W. Bowdoin of Lisbon Md 27 Nov. 1918 in Topsham p.115

McDONALD, Joseph of Gray and Sarah A. Hall of Falmouth PUB. 30 Dec. 1858 Md. 20 Jan. 1859

McDONALD, William see VanBuskirk, Genie

McDONALD, George T. of Gray and Jennie M. Davis of Danville Md. 1 Dec. 1886

McELROY, Josephine see Way, Henry

McFARLAND, Evelyn see Frank, Orin

McGOWAN, James see Latham, Sarah

McGOWEN, Eliza see Verrill, Charles

McGOWEN, Eva E. and John E. Verrill both of Gray Md 4 Mar. 1912 p.81

McGUILE, Mary see Thompson, Royal

McINNIS, Hector W. and Martha P. Skillings both of Gray Md 17 Sept. 1913 in Portland p.89

McINTIRE, Joseph see Sawyer, Clarissa

McINTIRE, Wilson W. and Alice L. Parsons both of Gray Md 23 July 1875

McINTOSH, Mary A. and Albert J. Morrill both of Gray PUB. 29 Dec. 1890, Md 4 Jan. 1891

McINTOSH, Margaret see Whitney, Earl

McKENNA, Lucinda see Cleaveland, James

McKENNEY, Jona. of Gray and Sally Chadbourne of Biddeford PUB. 17 Nov. 1838

McLELLAN, Lydia of Gray and William Haskell of New Gloucester PUB. 3 Oct. 1813 p.200

McLONG, Louise see Pollard, Russell

McNULTY, Florence see Knapp, David

McQUARRIE, Frank H. see Knight, Grace

MEAD, Mildred see Mayberry, Orland

MEGGUIER, Samuel see Butman, Esther

MEGGUIER, Rachel see Weeks, Benjamin

MEGGUIER, C. W. see Fowler, Thankful

MEGGUIER, Mary see Webster, Simon

MEGGUIER, Salley see Small, George

MEGGUIER, Hewett see Doughty, Ellen

MEGGUIER, Hewitt I. and Lois E. Megguier both of Gray PUB.
    15 Jan. 1891, Md 25 Jan. 1891

MEGGUIER, Lois see Megguire, Hewitt

MEGQUIER, Lawson L. of Gray and Juliette Edwards of New
    Gloucester Md. 7 June 1905 p.49

MEGUIER, Blanche see Lowe, Christopher S.

MELCHIOR, Thelmer see Burnham, Philip

MERRILL, Rachel see Humphrey, John

MERRILL, Joseph see Barber, Mariam

MERRILL, Abigail and Levi Morse both of Gray 19 Mar. 1786
    p.137

MERRILL, Abel and Phebe Perley both of Gray 18 Feb. 1790
    p.144

MERRILL, Rebecca see Davis, Joseph

MERRILL, Molly see Fuller, Joseph

MERRILL, Rich'd and Dorcas Stuart of Windham 21 Aug. 1804
    p.178

MERRILL, Joshua and Hannah Stuart both of Windham 10 Sept.
    1804 p.178

MERRILL, Mary see Low, John

MERRILL, Sarah of Gray and Jacob Jewett of No. 4, 6th Range 7
    Oct. 1810 p.188

MERRILL, Nathan and Abigail Symonds both of Gray 25 Oct.
    1812 p.196

MERRILL, Mary and Whitely Webster both of Gray 1 Sept. 1816
    p.207

MERRILL, Esther of Gray and Ara Cushman of Minot 12 Jan.
    1817 p.208

MERRILL, Rebecca and Whitley Webster both of Gray PUB. 24
    June 1818 p.215, Md. 10 Sept. 1818 p.218

MERRILL, Sarah see Clough, Levi

MERRILL, Nathaniel see Lane Eliza

MERRILL, Mary see Weymouth, Timothy

MERRILL, Mary and Joel Stevens both of New Gloucester Md 21 Aug. 1827 p.252

MERRILL, Ruth of Gray and Mary Myrick of Portland PUB. 23 Mar. 1828 p.256

MERRILL, Alice S. and Charles L. Dow both of Gray Md 23 Aug. 1888

MERRILL, Julia of Gray and William L. Russell of Cumberland Md. 10 Dec. 1888

MERRILL, Fred C. and Offie J. Verrill both of Gray PUB. 17 Dec. 1888, Md. 25 Dec. 188

MERRILL, True M. and Hattie E. Rhino both of New Gloucester Md. 2 Feb 1889

MERRILL, Frank and Abbie E. Verrill both of New Gloucester Md 29 June 1889

MERRILL, Frances see Hulet, Granville

MERRILL, D. Maria of Gray and Denslow A. Pease of Conn. Md 2 Mar. 1868

MERRILL, Hattie see Hancock, Thomas

MERRILL, Ansel W. of Gray and Mary Hersom of Concord New Hampshire Md. 29 Jan. 1890

MERRILL, Harry see Libby, Kate

MERRILL, Emma see Cushing, Louis

MERRILL, Marion see Libby, Harry

MERRILL, Frank G. and Lena P. Stevens both of Gray Md 27 Apr. 1910 p.75

MERRILL, George D. and Ruby R. Wilson both of Gray Md 15 Oct. 1916 p.101

MERRILL, Annie F. of Gray and Victor W. Leach of New Gloucester Md. 10 Oct. 1917 in New Gloucester p.107

MERRILL, Helen see Lawrence, Perley

MERRILL, Lucy see Cummings, Milo

MERRILL, Geneva see Hayden, Carl

MERRILL, Robert of Gray and Mrs. Sarah Merrill of Portland Md 18 Mar. 1857

MERRILL, Sarah see Merrill, Robert

MERRILL, George F. of Gray and Emeline Merrill of Falmouth Md. 21 June 1857

MERRILL, Emeline see Merrill, George

MERRILL, Harriett E. of Gray and Joseph Merrill of West Minot Md. 15 June 1858

MERRILL, Joseph see Merrill, Harriet
MERRILL, Abbie see Ramsdell, Seth
MERRILL, Eliza see Buckman, ?
MERRILL, Jennie see Doughty, Henry
MERRILL, Julia see Hunt, James
MERRILL, Benjamin W. and Harriet K. Morgan both of New
    Gloucester Md. 15 May 1886
MERRILL, Albert see Foster, Annie
MERRILL, George E. of Gray and Mary E. Merrill of Falmouth
    PUB. 17 Oct. 1887
MERRILL, Mary see Merrill, George
MERRILL, Elizabeth and Moses Plummer both of Gray PUB. 9
    Nov. 1839
MERRILL, Nathaniel and Polly Bean of Conway, N.H. PUB. 6
    Oct. 1844
MERRILL, William see Barbour, Martha
MERRILL, Nathaniel of Gray and Mrs. Ann Jones of Lewiston
    PUB. 1 Sept. 1850
MERRILL, William L. of Gray and Lizzie F. Tufts of New
    Gloucester PUB. 24 June 1886 Md 1 July 1886
MERROW, Eliza and Samuel Rowe both of Gray PUB. 7 Jan. 1839
MERROW, Noah and Mary A. Rowe both of Gray PUB. 3 May
    1840
MICHO, Alfred see Colley, Addie
MILLER, Abigail see Low, Nicholas
MILLER, Sarah see Hunt, David
MILLER, Abigail and Gideon Ramsdell both of Gray 28 Nov.
    1804 p.179
MILLER, Sarah see Hunt, David
MILLER, Moses of Gray and Rhoda Shaw of Minot PUB. 22 June
    1823 p.234
MILLER, A. May of Gray and Horatio N. Bradbury Jr. of Buxton
    PUB. 12 Nov. 1878, Md 19 Nov. 1878
MILLS, Emily see Andrews, Elbert
MITCHELL, Lucy see Freeman, Jonathan
MITCHELL, Elizabeth see Skillins, Joseph
MITCHELL, Henrietta see Corson, Albert
MITCHELL, Emma see Farwell, Edward
MITCHELL, Samuel see Field, Annie

MITCHELL, Annie S. and Albert J. Small both of Gray Md 12
May 1900 in Westbrook p.29

MITCHELL, Hannah see May, Jeremiah

MITCHELL, Hezekiah see Morse, Martha

MITCHELL, Benjamin see Loring, Mrs. Ann

MITCHELL, Elmer and Arvilla Haynes both of Lewiston Md 13
Sept. 1884

MODES, Abraham of Gray and Rose Bayer of Boston, Mass Md 5
Mar. 1917 in Boston, Mass p.105

MONK, Paul A. and Dorothy Loring both of Auburn Md 28 Aug.
1930 p.173

MONTE, Mary see Smith, John

MOODY, Daniel see Small, Lucy

MOODY, Frank D. and Margie Fogg both of Windham Md 13
June 1871

MOODY, Edwin see Dolley, Helen

MOORE, William see Stimson, Mary

MOORE, Jane see Webster, James

MOORE, Wm. see Weymouth, Eunice

MOORES, Susan see Leonard, Joseph

MOORS, Bryant see Dayon, Laura

MOREY, Ada see Plummer, Lindley

MOREY, Ella see Warren, William

MORGAN, Elizabeth see Barbour, Robert

MORGAN, William H. and Lucy J. Hulet both of New Gloucester
Md. 18 June 1871

MORGAN, Frank see Larabee, Susan

MORGAN, Nellie see Goff, Clarence

MORGAN, Pitman see Rolfe, Abigail

MORRELL, Jacob see Humphrey, Delphina

MORRELL, Herbert see Libby, Eva

MORRELL, Ruth see Morrill, John

MORRELL, Gladys see Foster, Edgar

MORRELL, Silvia S. of Gray and Alvin Armstrong of Winthrop
PUB. 15 Sept. 1838

MORRILL, Hannah see Hunt, David Junr.

MORRILL, Susanna and Samuel Watson both of Gray 9 Nov.
1798   p.157

MORRILL, Matthew C. of Gray and Mary Brown of Raymond
PUB. 4 Jan. 1867, Md 13 Jan. 1867

149

MORRILL, Jacob see Humphrey, M. Lizzie

MORRILL, Annie of Gray and Nelker D. Haskell of Poland Md 5 Aug. 1873

MORRILL, Mathew see McConkey, Mary

MORRILL, Asa P. and Lydia A. Morrill both of Gray Md 8 Nov. 1875

MORRILL, Lydia see Morrill, Asa

MORRILL, William see Doughty, Alice

MORRILL, Alberta see Hall, Lester

MORRILL, Albert see McIntosh, Mary

MORRILL, Asa P. and Eunice H. Powers both of Gray Md 14 Oct. 1892 p.5

MORRILL, Roland and Sadie G. Spiller both of Raymond Md 12 Nov. 1892 p.5

MORRILL, Hugh P. of Gray and Dora L. Brown of Raymond Md 6 Feb. 1894 p.11

MORRILL, Mary B. of Gray and Isiah Hawkes of Westbrook, Md Westbrook 9 Mar. 1894 p.11

MORRILL, George R. and Grace E. Webster both of Gray Md 9 June 1894 p.13

MORRILL, Randall B. see Whitney, Bertha

MORRILL, Josephine D. see Ellinwood, George A.

MORRILL, Dora L. see Colley, Sturgis

MORRILL, John W. see Anderson, Bessie

MORRILL, Bertha see Jones, Charles

MORRILL, Wilma see Marsden, Horace

MORRILL, Gardner M. and Annie A. Osgood both of Gray Md 14 May 1918 in Biddeford p.111

MORRILL, Vergie see Mazwell, George

MORRILL, John A. and Ruth E. Morrell both of Gray Md 15 June 1923 in Augusta p.137

MORRILL, Marguerite see Duplisea, Carl

MORRILL, Flora see Quint, Frank

MORRISON, Eliza see Harmon, Elias

MORRISON, Mary see Kidder, Benjamin

MORRISON, Cynthia see Humphrey, Ira

MORSE, Julia W. of Gray, and Asa Cushman Jr. of Minot 21 June 1853

MORSE, Augusta F. of Gray and John M. Crocker of Portland 18
   Aug. 1855
MORSE, Jane O. of Gray and Sumner C. Murch of Portland 3 Nov.
   1855
MORSE, Sarah see Weeks, Joseph
MORSE, Levi see Merrill, Abigail
MORSE, William see McDaniels, Susanna
MORSE, Ozias see Donalds, Polly
MORSE, David of Gray and Polly Rider of Yarmouth 22 Nov.
   1801 p.168
MORSE, Abigail of Gray and Samuel Rider of North Yarmouth 5
   Dec. 1801 p.168
MORSE, Rebecca of Gray and Ebenr. Simonton of Raymondtown
   19 Jan.1804 p.177
MORSE, Ozias and Polly Ross both of Gray 5 Jan. 1812 p.199
MORSE, Byer see Fowler, Zebedee
MORSE, Levi Jr. of Gray and Eliza S. Tenney of Poland PUB. 13
   Dec. 1817 p.210
MORSE, Mary and Isaac Weeks both of Gray PUB. July 1818 p.
   216
MORSE, John 3d of Gray and Phebe Eaton of Portland PUB. 30
   Apr. 1818 p.219
MORSE, Benjamin and Margaret Sherman both of Gray PUB. 2
   Sept. 1819 p.220
MORSE, William of Gray and Elizabeth Frost of New Gloucester
   PUB. 20 Jan. 1820 p.220, Md. 16 Feb. 1820 p.221
MORSE, Benjamin of Gray and Lucy Rodgers of Windham PUB.
   22 Dec. 1822 p.232
MORSE, Patty and John Russell both of Gray PUB. 11 July 1824
   p.236, Md. 15 Aug. 1824 p.239
MORSE, John 3rd of Gray and Betsey Redding of Falmouth PUB.
   5 Mar. 1826 p.244
MORSE, Thomas of Gray and Sally M. Sawyer of New Gloucester
   PUB. 22 Apr. 1827 p.249
MORSE, Joseph Jr. of Gray and Sarah C. Small of Falmouth PUB.
   20 May 1827 p.249
MORSE, Susan see Marston, Simeon
MORSE, Reuben Jr. and Charlotte Sawyer both of Gray PUB. 23
   Mar. 1828 p.256, Md 1828 p.254

MORSE, Leonisa R. of Gray and Benjamin Hutchins of Minot
PUB. 1 Mar. 1829 p.257

MORSE, Judith M. and Robert D. Shaw both of Gray PUB. 9 May
1830 p.263

MORSE, Happiah of Gray and Edward Allen Jr. of Cumberland
Md. 1830 p.267

MORSE, Thomas E. of Gray and Sarah Knight of Pownal PUB. 17
Sept. 1832 p.271

MORSE, Rebecca Ann of Gray and Simon Libby of Oxford Md
1834 p.280

MORSE, Mary E. of Gray and John M. Dolley of Portland Md 7
Oct. 1861

MORSE, Horace L. of Gray and Lucy A. Hill of Wilton Md 3 Dec.
1861

MORSE, Annie M. and Parker Sawyer both of Gray PUB. 24 Aug.
1866, Md 29 Aug. 1866

MORSE, William H. of Gray and Hattie W. Nason of Auburn Md 9
Jan. 1867

MORSE, Emily S. of Gray and Thomas F. Rose of Guilford Md 30
May 1870

MORSE, Ellen see Small, John

MORSE, Margaret A. and Thomas Skillin both of Gray Md 16 Oct.
1876

MORSE, Lewis M. of Gray and Verona W. Heath of Auburn PUB.
23 July 1877, Md 29 Aug. 1877

MORSE, Franklin see Beatty, Sarah

MORSE, Anna see Kidder, Charles

MORSE, Elsie B. and George M. Stevens both of Gray Md 8 July
1905 p.51

MORSE, Julia W. of Gray and Asa Cushman Jr. of Minot Md 21
June 1853

MORSE, Augusta F. of Gray and John M. Crocker of Portland
PUB. 18 Aug. 1855 Md. 19 Aug. 1855

MORSE, Jane O. of Gray and Sumner C. Murch of Portland PUB.
3 Nov. 1855 Md. 4 Nov. 1855

MORSE, Thomas E. and Mary E. Staples both of Gray Md 21 Feb.
1858

MORSE, Juliett of Gray and Eben M. Haines of Windham PUB. 19
Apr. 1859 Md. 24 Apr 1859

MORSE, Delia P. of Gray and Horace M. Wight of Poland PUB. 6
June 1859 Md. 19 June 1859

MORSE, Martha P. of Gray and Hezekiah B. Mitchell of Yarmouth
Md. 19 Dec. 1859

MORSE, Mary E. of Gray and John M. Dolley of Portland Md 7
Oct. 1861

MORSE, Horace L. of Gray and Lucy A. Hill of Wilton Md 3 Dec.
1861

MORSE, William R. of Gray and Mary J. Parker of Portland Md 6
Feb. 1862

MORSE, Charles M. of Gray and Lizzie S. Cummings of New
Gloucester Md. 20 Oct. 1862

MORSE, Eunice M. of Gray and Isaac Blake of New Gloucester
PUB. 10 June 1864 Md 22 June 1864

MORSE, Mary see Bailey, George

MORSE, Charles see Newbegin, Jennie

MORSE, Flora see Cobb, William

MORSE, Joshua R. and Louella A. Sawyer both of Gray PUB. 23
Feb. 1887

MORSE, Margaret see Allen, Alfred

MORSE, Mary S. and Daniel Nash both of Gray PUB. 9 May 1840

MORSE, Frederick P. of Gray and Martha Prince of No. Yarmouth
PUB. 3 Apr. 1842

MORSE, Sarah of Gray and Nahum A. Poole of Minot PUB. 28
Feb. 1847

MORSE, Cyrus K. of Gray and Caroline W. Wells of New
Gloucester PUB. 12 Oct. 1851

MORSE, Anna see Goff, William

MORTON, William see Prince, Mary

MORTON, Irving D. and Louisa H. Plummer both of Raymond Md
5 Apr. 1890

MORTON, Ansel G. of Naples and Ola G. Field of Falmouth Md 8
Feb. 1913 p.85

MORTON, William see Prince, Mary

MORTON, Thomas and Harriet J. Brown both of Raymond Md 20
Jan. 1885

MOTLEY, Joseph see Kilborn, Eliza

MOULTON, Henry M. of Cumberland and Ina M. Wilson of
Falmouth Md. 9 Sept. 1888

MOUNTFORD, Jeremiah see Fields, Almira

MOUNTFORD, Lucy of Gray and James Whitney of Cumberland PUB. 15 Feb. 1823 p.232

MOUNTFORD, John Jr. of Gray and Elmira M. Whitney of Cumberland PUB. 19 Mar. 1848

MOUNTFORT, Priscilla of Gray and Joseph Thompson of North Yarmouth 1 Jan. 1817 p.208

MOUNTFORT, Elias of Gray and Nancy Sweetser of Cumberland PUB. 27 Dec. 1829 p.261

MOUNTFORT, Greenleaf of Gray and Hannah T. Allen of Poland PUB. 17 Apr. 1831 p.268

MOUNTFORT, Mary D. of Gray and Samuel Skillin of Cumberland PUB. 4 Sept. 1831 p.268

MOUNTFORT, Betsey of Gray and Nathaniel B. Latham of N. Yarmouth Md. 15 Jan. 1832 p.269

MOUNTFORT, Joshua and Rachel S. Washburn both of Falmouth PUB. 4 Nov. 1860, Md 11 Nov. 1860

MOUNTFORT, Sewall of Gray and Arabell S. Leighton of Cumberland PUB. 2 Sept. 1871, Md 19 Sept. 1871

MOUNTFORT, Albert of Gray and Harriet E. Leighton of Cumberland Md. 25 Apr. 1878

MOUNTFORT, Julia A. of Gray and Herbert R. Leighton of Cumberland Md. 22 Feb. 1883

MOUNTFORT, Joseph O. and Emma F. Whitney both of Gray PUB. 7 Feb. 1890, Md 22 Feb. 1890

MOUNTFORT, Laura see Hunt, Henry

MOUNTFORT, Laura G. of Gray and Winfield S. Snow of New Gloucester Md. 1 Jan. 1918 in New Gloucester p. 109

MOUNTFORT, Augusta of Gray and Joseph E. Davis of Falmouth Md. 15 Mar. 1856

MOUNTFORT, Joshua and Rachel S. Washburn both of Falmouth PUB. 4 Nov. 1860 Md. 11 Nov. 1860

MOUNTFORT, Hollis R. and Roxanna A. Leighton both of Cumberland Md. 26 Dec. 1863

MOUNTFORT, Louise E. of Gray and George H. Prince of New Gloucester Md. 2 July 1881

MOXCOY, Joseph see Allen, Sylvia

MUCHMORE, John see Libby, Sally

MULCUM, Margaret see Verrill, Ami

MURCH, Sumner see Morse, Jane

MURCH, Sadie see Leighton, Walter F.

MURCH, Sumner see Morse, Jane

MUSHRALL, Joseph W. and Mary J. Skillin both of Gray PUB. 31 July 1876, Md 7 Aug. 1876

MUTCHEMORE, Ana see Goff, William

MUTCHEMORE, Betsey see Dolley, John

MUZZY, Marcus M. of Gray and Doris B. Chapman of No. Yarmouth Md. 2 Oct. 1916 in No. Yarmouth p.101

MYRICK, Mary see Merrill, Joseph

NASH, Mehetable see Nash, Joel

NASH, Eunice (Annie) and Joseph Pennell both of Gray 25 June 1789 p.142

NASH, Elijah of Gray and Mary Small of Raimington PUB. 29 Jan. 1792 p.127

NASH, George and Sarah Nash both of Gray PUB. 10 Feb. 1792 p.127

NASH, Samuel see Libby, Hannah

NASH, Fanny see Dyer, Judah

NASH, Abigail see Hayden, Joseph

NASH, Sarah and Joseph Small both of Gray 20 Apr. 1800 p.162

NASH, Samuel see Humphrey, Hannah

NASH, Sarah see Colley, Amos

NASH, Betsy of Gray and Daniel Mabury of Raymondtown 29 May 1803 p.176

NASH, Deborah see Allen, Elisha

NASH, Rebecca and Thomas Pennell both of Gray 25 Nov. 1810 p.188

NASH, Rebecca and Thomas Pennell both of Gray 27 Dec. 1810 p.189

NASH, Frances and William Thayer both of Gray PUB. 18 Apr. 1824 p. 236, Md 10 June 1824 p.239

NASH, Achsah see Doughty, William

NASH, Daniel and Perthena Smith both of Gray PUB. 18 Sept. 1831 p.268

NASH, Hannah and Charles Smith both of Gray PUB. 30 Apr. 1833 p.275, Md 16 May 1833 p.278

NASH, Adaline of Gray and Albert G. Robinson of Paris PUB. 15 Sept. 1833 p.275

NASH, Mary E. of Gray and Ashman H. Taylor M.D. of
   Shelbourne Falls, Mass Md 4 Oct. 1866
NASH, Julia M. of Gray and James H. Cushing of No. Yarmouth
   Md. 21 Sept. 1869
NASH, Esmeralda of Gray and Alonzo A. Thompson of Natick
   Mass. Md. 27 Sept. 1871
NASH, John see Libby, Susie
NASH, Bernice see Hill, Arthur
NASH, George see Emery, Daisy
NASH, Charlotte of Gray and Henry B. Gibbs of Porter PUB. 16
   June 1839
NASH, Daniel see Morse, Mary
NASON, Isaac and Sarah Wilson PUB. 18 Jan. 1784; 2 Feb. 1784
NASON, Tabitha and Isaac Royal both of Gray 8 Dec. 1786 p.138
NASON, Isaac see Libby, Dorcas
NASON, Dorcas see Furbush, Stephen
NASON, Samuel see Small, Dolley
NASON, Charlotte see Doughty, James
NASON, Sarah see Libby, Ebenzer
NASON, Enoch see Black, Lydia
NASON, Hattie see Morse, William
NASON, Charles see Frank Angenora
NASON, Charles H. see Emery, Carrie
NASON, Thomas S. and Fanny L. Mitchell both of No. Windham
   Md. 18 Oct. 1916 p.101
NEAL, Joseph see Mains Elizabeth
NEEDHAM, John see Huston, Hannah
NELSON, George B. of New Gloucester and Louella Greely of
   Pownal Md. 29 Sept. 1888
NELSON, Charles see Libby, Florence
NEVINS, Celinda see Hill, Wilbur
NEWBEGIN, Annie see Higgins, Arthur
NEWBEGIN, James H. and Florence A. Podbury both of Hyde
   Park, Mass Md. 24 May 1909 p.71
NEWBEGIN, Jennie l. of Gray and Charles M. Morse of Topeka,
   Kansas PUB. 10 Feb. 1886 Md. 22 Feb. 1886
NEWCOMB, Eunice see Berry, Charles
NEWCOMB, Howard E. and Ada M. Mayberry both of Windham
   Md. 21 Oct. 1891

NEWMAN, James see Higgins, Marion
NICKERSON, George B. Jr. and Elizabeth M. Witham both of
    Gray Md. 8 Sept. 1908 in Portland p.67
NOBLE, Hannah see Hayden, Elisha
NOBLE, Nathan see Hobbs, Hannah
NORTON, Harold see Loring, Ina
NOYES, Nehemiah see Greely, Hannah
NOYES, William see Humphrey, Addie
OAKES, Vannie see Duplisea, Elton
OAKMAN, Isaac see Soper, Peggey
O'BRIEN, Rodney J. of Bingham and Louise J. Cummings of
    Portland Md. 15 Nov. 1930 p.175
O'BRIEN, Thomas see Hunt, Sarah
ORNE, David and Polly Webster both of Gray 17 Nov. 1791 p.145
ORNE, Sally and William Purvis both of Gray 14 Dec. 1815 p.200
ORNE, Mary see Hamilton, Rufus
OSGOOD, Emma and Daniel H. Twombly both of Gray Md 2 Mar.
    1870
OSGOOD, Frank E. and Alice C. Shaw both of Gray PUB. 5
    July1876, Md. 10 July 1876
OSGOOD, Hattie see Leighton, Walter
OSGOOD, Elmer see Harmon, Ina
OSGOOD, May W. of Gray and George H. Hallowell of Portland
    Md. 4 Feb. 1893 p.7
OSGOOD, Nellie B. of Gray and Elmer F. Lawrence of Portland
    Md. 28 June 1913 p.87
OSGOOD, Annie see Morrill, Gardner
OSGOOD, William C. of Gray and Laura M. Soule of Plaster
    Rock, N.B. Md 14 Oct. 1922 p.135
OSGOOD, George W. of Gray and Lizzie E. Hawkes of No.
    Yarmouth Md. 26 June 1886
OXNARD, Emma see Thayer, Henry
PAGE, William see Foster, Mary
PAGE, Walter A. of Windham and Mary A. Leavitt of Raymond
    Md. 16 June 1892
PARKER, Ida see Low, Horace
PARKER, William S. and Sarah H. Steele both of Boston, Mass.
    Md. 5 Aug. 1873
PARKER, Irma see Cummings, Fred

PARKER, Charles A. and Minnie Knight both of Raymond Md 26
    Nov. 1891
PARKER, Edward W. see Leavitt, Elsie L.
PARKER, Delmer see Head, Ruth
PARKER, Mary see Morse, Willliam
PARKINSON, Harry see Grover, Ethelyn
PARREN, George see Small, Isa
PARSONS, Andrew see King, Dora
PARSONS, Hattie see Libby, Jebediah
PARSONS, Alice see McIntire, Wilson
PARSONS, Andrew see King, Dora
PATRICK, Mehitable see Harmon, Edward Jr.
PAUL, Samuel see Bishop, Julia
PEASE, Denslow see Merrill, D.
PECK, James see Sweetser, Kathryn
PECK, Edward see Leighton, Carrie
PENDELTON, Elizabeth see Hamm, Clifton
PENNELL, Joseph see Nash Eunice (Annie)
PENNELL, Jeremiah see Fletcher, Charlotte
PENNELL, Joseph and Betsey Stow both of Gray 27 Jan. 1803
    p.174
PENNELL, Abigail see Hatch, Thomas
PENNELL, Rachel and William Thompson both of Gray 30 Sept.
    1804 p.180
PENNELL, Thomas see Nash, Rebecca
PENNELL, James and Betsy Pray both of Gray 29 Aug. 1811
    p.192
PENNELL, Phinias Jr. and Suky Ramsdell both of Gray 27 Apr.
    1812   p.193
PENNELL, David of Gray and Sally Haskell of N. Gloucester 16
    Feb. 1812 p.199
PENNELL, Moses see Phillips, Mary
PENNELL, Esyher see Maxwell, Ebenzer
PENNELL, Mary and Samuel Young both of Gray PUB. 9 Aug.
    1817 p.209 Md. 28 Aug. 1817 p.213
PENNELL, Eleanor see King, Edvardus
PENNELL, Dixey S. and Abigail Small both of Gray Md 29 Jan.
    1832 p.269
PENNELL, Jeremiah see Maxell, Irene

PENNELL, Henry and Mary Susan Weston both of Gray PUB. 19
Nov. 1832 p.272
PENNELL, Fannie see McConkey, William
PENNELL, Albert see Leslie, Sarah
PENNELL, Charles see Hunt, Emma
PENNELL, Walter see Goff, Lelia
PENNELL, Jennie L. of Gray and Albert A. Libby of Windham Md
11 Sept. 1895 p.15
PENNELL, George F. of Gray and Mabel J. Ross of No. Yarmouth
Md. 1 Jan. 1896 in Yarmouth p.17
PENNELL, Edgar L. of Gray and Annie E. Watson of Caribou Md
3 Oct. 1901 p.35
PENNELL, Elizabeth S. of Gray and William F. Dolley of
Yarmouth PUB. 6 Nov. 1856 Md. 8 Nov. 1856
PENNELL, Clara see Dow, William
PENNELL, Alice A. of Gray and George R. Fuller of Tremont Md
18 Sept. 1886
PENNELL, Susan of Gray and Benjamin Cole of No. Yarmouth
PUB. 18 July 1840
PENNELL, Mrs. Charlotte of Gray and Joseph Johnson of New
Gloucester PUB. 6 Mar. 1842
PENNELL, Luther of Gray and Susan Smith of Portland PUB. 30
Nov. 1845
PENNELL, Jeremiah see Doughty, Frances
PENNELL, Samuel and Priscilla Thompson both of Gray   15 Oct.
1797 p.157
PENNEY, Herbert D. and Ella L. Witham both of New Gloucester
Md. 29 Mar. 1890
PERKINS, Amy see Quint, Percy
PERKINS, William see Blake, Annie
PERLEY, Phebe see Merrill, Abel
PERLEY, Susanna of Gray and Thomas Hancock of Otisfield 19
Mar. 1801   p.165
PERLEY, Abraham see Humphrey, Rebecca
PERLEY, Mary see Dolley, George
PERLEY, George of Gray and Hannah H. Low of N. Yarmouth
PUB. 5 Aug. 1827 p.249
PERLEY, Paulina and Nath'l Rounds both of Gray PUB. 19 Apr.
1829 p.260, Md 10 May 1829 p.259

PERLEY, Susan see Higgins, Arthur

PERLEY, Melinda and John F. Sawyer both of Gray PUB. 10 Nov. 1833 p.276

PERLEY, Joseph H. and Jane Sweetser both of Gray Md 31 Oct. 1834 p.280

PERLEY, Frederic A. and Mary A. S. Blanchard both of Cumberland Md. 25 Dec. 1860

PERLEY, Howard see Sawyer, Elnora

PERLEY, Henrietta see Higgins, Orin

PERLEY, Roscoe of Gray and Fannie L. Porter of No. Yarmouth Md. 23 Nov. 1866

PERLEY, Cephus W. of Gray and Sarah A. Johnson of No. Yarmouth Md. 25 Sept. 1868

PERLEY, Albion see Cobb, Matilda

PERLEY, Mary see Sawyer, William

PERLEY, Alvin H. of Gray and Florence A. Dority of Charlestown Md. 6 Nov. 1879

PERLEY, Sarah A. of Gray and Samuel H. Sweetser of No. Yarmouth Md. 5 Apr. 1890

PERLEY, Florence see Hall, Eugene

PERLEY, Susan H. of Gray and Thomas B. M. Gates of New York City Md. 28 Dec. 1897 p.23

PERLEY, Sumner see Witham, Ada

PERLEY, Frederic A. and Mary A. S. Blanchard both of Cumberland Md. 25 Dec. 1860

PERLEY, Cyrus see Higgins, Susan

PERLEY, Abraham of Gray and Lois Haskell of New Gloucester PUB. 25 Dec. 1817 p.210 Md. 22 Jan. 1818 p.211

PERRY, Elizabeth see Doughty, Warren

PETERSON, Peter see Barker, Lucy

PETERSON, Lizzie see Sayward, Earl

PETERSON, Jens and Clara L. Hamilton both of Portland Md 3 Oct. 1925 p.151

PETERSON, Raymond see Wing, Louise

PETERSON, Martha see Sawyer, Thorndike

PHILBRICK, Flora A. see Leighton, Walter F.

PHILBROOK, Charles see Latham, Betsey

PHILBROOKS, George W. and Ada V. Small both of Gray Md 8 Nov. 1893 p.9

PHILLIPS, Mary of Gray and Moses Pennell Jr. of New Gloucester
    PUB. 6 June 1813 p.200
PHILLIPS, Barney see Edwards, Sophia
PIERCE, Joseph see Haney, Ann
PIERCE, Sarah see Cummings, William
PIERCE, Mary see Libby, Jebediah
PIERCE, Dora see McDonald, Charles
PIERCE, Edwin see Cummings, Ethel
PIERCE, Cornelia see Plummer, Moses
PIERCE, Joseph see Hinkley, Ann
PIKE, Charlotte see Davis, George
PIPER, Frank see Cushing, Frances
PLACE, Asa see Van Buskirk, Lizzie
PLAICE, Anna see May, Jeremiah
PLUMMER, Elish and Jenney West both of Raymondtown 25
    June 1799 p.160
PLUMMER, Sarah see Young, Daniel
PLUMMER, Hannah see Young, Nathaniel
PLUMMER, Richard see Hutchins, Philina
PLUMMER, Annie of Gray and Oliver Chute of Raymond PUB.
    29 July 1875, Md 8 Aug. 1875
PLUMMER, Lindley of Gray and Ada Morey of Raymond Md 26
    Mar. 1879
PLUMMER, Rozilla of Gray and Alvin C. Shaw of Standish Md 8
    Feb. 1880
PLUMMER, Henry and Lydia J. Verrill both of Gray PUB. 2 Apr.
    1881, Md 17 Apr. 1881
PLUMMER, Georgia A. and Joseph M. Sawyer both of Gray Md 6
    June 1881
PLUMMER, George see Berry, Blanche
PLUMMER, Moses of Gray and Cornelia Pierce of Pownal Md 24
    Jan. 1858
PLUMMER, Cyrus H. of Gray and Hannah C. Redlon of Casco Md
    31 Jan. 1858
PLUMMER, Hannah see Bangs, Edwin
PLUMMER, Moses see Merrill, Elizabeth
POLLARD, Ira C. of Gray and Lillian M. Varney of Windham Md
    5 Feb. 1918 p.109

POLLARD, James W. B. of Gray and Sarah F. Hanson of Topsham Md. 1 Feb. 1924 in Portland p.141

POLLARD, Ira C. of Gray and Minnie E. Cannell of Windham Md 10 May 1924 p.141

POLLARD, Russell W. and Bertha G. Twombly both of Gray Md 13 June 1925 p.147

POLLARD, Marion see Douglass, William

POLLARD, Russell W. of Gray and Louise E. McLong of Portland Md. 28 Apr. 1930 in Portland p.171

POOLE, Sarah, Goff, Ozias

POOLE, Nahum see Morse, Sarah

POOR, Silvanus see Brown, Eliza

POORE, Clarel see Foster, Georgie

PORTER, Nehemiah see Barber, Joanna

PORTER, Stephen see Cobb, Rebecca

PORTER, Joanna of North Yarmouth and William Stearns of Paris 29 June 1817 p.214

PORTER, Lydia and David Tukey both of North Yarmouth 2 Oct. 1817 p.214

PORTER, Mary see Cole, Benjamin

PORTER, Fannie see Perley, Roscoe

PORTER, Elmer see Sawyer, Cora A.

PORTER, William see Verrill, Jennie

PORTER, Byron T. and Roberta Strout both of Gray Md 21 Dec. 1918 p.115

PORTER, Ralph C. of Portland and Blanche E. Greenlief of Westbrook Md. 28 July 1923 p.139

PORTER, Benjamin see Huston, Elizabeth

POWERS, Eunice see Morrill, Asa

PRATT, Louisa see Small, David

PRAY, Edward see Emery, Dorcas

PRAY, Edmond of Gray and Rebecca White of Gorham 22 July 1810 p.188

PRAY, Betsy see Pennell, James

PRIDE, Adam see Haskell, Jane

PRIDE, Alexander and Mary E. Stevens both of Gray Md 20 May 1861

PRIDE, William see Harmon, Adeline

PRINCE, Mary B. of Gray and William Morton of Gorham 21 Sept. 1855

PRINCE, Joseph see Frasier, Susannah

PRINCE, Hannah see Libby, Jebediah

PRINCE, Bela and Salome Styles both of Gray PUB. 15 Nov. 1829 p.260, Md 1829 p.262

PRINCE, Georgianna of Gray and William H. Irish of Windham Md. 22 July 1866

PRINCE, Sewall see Estes, Johanna

PRINCE, Isabell see Eaton, Charles

PRINCE, George see Mountfort, Louise

PRINCE, William B. see Dow, Anna S.

PRINCE, Sewall B. and Edward W. Skillin both of Gray Md 18 Aug. 1906 p.55

PRINCE, William see Maier, Ethel

PRINCE, Sewell see Burns, Inez

PRINCE, Mildred see Thompson, Bertrand

PRINCE, Trueman see Flye, Bernice

PRINCE, Guy see Leavitt, Kathryn

PRINCE, Mary B. of Gray and William Morton of Gorham Md 21 Sept. 1855

PRINCE, Phebe E. of Gray and Greenleaf Sawyer of No. Yarmouth PUB. 22 Apr. 1858 Md. 2 May 1858

PRINCE, Martha see Morse, Frederick

PRITHAM, Samuel see Stiles, Alice

PRITHAM, Fannie E. see Knight, Fred A.

PROCTOR, Jennie see Allen, John

PROCTOR, Harriett see Colby, Moses

PROVENCHY, Henry of New Gloucester and Rosanna Gilbert of Lewiston Md. 9 Oct. 1909 p.73

PURINGTON, Amos see Brown, Abigail

PURKIS, John of Gray and Hannah Libby of Gorham PUB. 2 Nov. 1828 p.257

PURKIS, Eliza A. of Gray and Calvin E. Libby of Bethel PUB. 12 Mar. 1843

PURRINGTON, Joseph see Huston, Melissa

PURVES, William of Gray and Mrs. Nancy Russ of Paris

PURVIS, Betsy and Daniel Young both of Gray 10 Dec. 1815 p.200

PURVIS, William see Orne, Sally

PURVIS, Susanna and Abraham Young both of Gray PUB. 20 July
    1817 p.209 Md. Aug. 21 p.213

PURVIS, Adam of Gray and Mary C. Cobb of Falmouth Md 28
    Mar. 1876

PURVIS, Adam and Rebecca Sawyer both of Gray PUB. 28 Oct.
    1840

PURVIS, Ellen see Webster, James

QUINT, Richard see Davis, Etta

QUINT, Lucy J. and Freeland M. Small both of Gray Md 27 June
    1872

QUINT, Sybil see Goff, Herbert

QUINT, Fannie L. of Gray and George W. Jordan of Brunswick
    Md. 27 May 1893 p. 7

QUINT, Gilman G. of Gray and Hariet A. Davis of Raymond Md
    Raymond 28 Nov. 1894 p.13

QUINT, Lewis see Frank, Mattie E.

QUINT, George W. of Gray and Melissa E. Clapp of Chelsea,
    Mass. Md. 1 May 1902 in W. Poland p.37

QUINT, Earl C. of Gray and Margaret L. Spear of Poland Md 4
    May 1910 in So. Poland p.75

QUINT, Archie H. of Gray and Daisy M. Hackett of New
    Gloucester Md. 2 Mar. 1916 in Portland p.97

QUINT, Earl C. of Gray and Susie S. Spiller of Raymond Md 9
    Jan. 1926 p.151

QUINT, Percy S. of Gray and Amy L. Perkins of So. Portland Md
    28 Sept. 1929 in So. Portland p.169

QUINT, Clarence M. of Gray and Minerva L. Hadley of New
    Gloucester Md. 24 Oct. 1930 in New Gloucester p.175

QUINT, George W. of Gray and Jennie H. Edwards of Lewiston
    PUB. 22 Jan. 1885 Md. 31 Jan. 1885

QUINT, Addie M. of Gray and Russell M. Field of Gorham Md 26
    July 1886

QUINT, Frank A. of Gray and Flora Morrill of Raymond Md 12
    Nov. 1886

RACKLEY, Mary C. and Ruben Sawyer both of Gray Md 11 June
    1916 in So. Bridgton p.99

RACKLEY, John E. of Gray and Marion G. Hall of Topsham Md
    21 Oct. 1916 in Portland p.101

RADCLIFF, James see Mayall, Margaret

RAMSDELL, Sarah see Curtis, Bowery

RAMSDELL, Molly and Samuel Skillings both of Gray 10 Apr. 1800 p.163

RAMSDELL, Gideon see Miller, Abigail

RAMSDELL, Suky see Pennell, Phinias

RAMSDELL, Robert see Blanchard, Eliza

RAMSDELL, Solomon see Libby, Paulina

RAMSDELL, Sally and Joseph Wilson both of Gray Md 4 July 1822 p. 235

RAMSDELL, Hannah of Gray and Joseph Libby of Poland PUB. 1 May 1825 p. 242

RAMSDELL, Peter see Libby, Esther

RAMSDELL, Lucinda A. of Gray and George F. Cobb of New Gloucester PUB. 24 Dec. 1860, Md 1 Jan. 1861

RAMSDELL, Joseph see Libby, Eliza

RAMSDELL, Ella F. and Wilbert I. Whitney both of Gray Md 8 June 1902 p.37

RAMSDELL, Fred see Dow, Grace

RAMSDELL, Fred H. of gray and Clara P. Johnson of Portland Md 2 June 1926 p.153

RAMSDELL, Hannah E. and Charles C. Thompson both of Gray PUB. 29 Oct. 1859 Md. 6 Nov. 1859

RAMSDELL, Lucinda A. of Gray and George F. Cobb of New Gloucester PUB. 24 Dec. 1860 Md. 1 Jan. 1861

RAMSDELL, Seth of Gray and Abbie I. Merrill of Cumberland Md 9 Aug. 1864

RAMSEY, Ezra of Gray and Sarah A. Low of Cumberland PUB. 5 Jan. 1871, Md 10 Jan. 1871

RAND, Mancena see Benson, Hannah

RAND, John and Alice L. Thompson both of Gray Md 28 June 1930 p.171

READY, Mary see Libby, Herbert M.

RECORD, Ellen see King, Hiram

REDDING, Betsey see Morse, John

REDLON, Nellie see Stevens, John

REDLON, Hannah see Plummer, Cyrus

REED, George see Cook, Eva

REED, Ralph F. and Margaret S. Thompson both of Gilman Vt. Md. 18 June 1924 p.143

REED, Charles see Skillin, Deborah

REEVES, Charles see Dresser, Dorothea

REMICK, Royal C. and Mary A. McKinney PUB. 30 July 1837

RICH, John see Colley, Mary

RICH, Royal F. and Jennie Stowell Md 20 Jan 1866

RICH, Sarah see Goff, Cyrus

RICH, George W. of Gray and Angie W. Bailey of New Gloucester
     Md. 17 June 1862

RICHARDS, John and Lillian Spencer both of Gray Md 26 Jan.
     1897 p.21

RICHARDS, Harry E. of No Yarmouth and Harriett E. Leighton of
     Pownal Md. 19 Nov. 1902 p.39

RICHARDS, Fred L. of No Yarmouth and Carrie E. Leighton of
     Pownal Md. 19 Nov. 1902 p.39

RICHARDS, Fred J. of Gray and Alice E. Libby of Machiasport
     Md. 25 Nov. 1903 in Machias p.45

RICHARDS, Oren see Humphrey, Mildred

RICHARDS, Orin E. and Hester E. Wallace both of Gray Md 24
     Feb. 1930 in New Gloucester p.171

RICKER, Eunice see Foster, Solomon

RICKER, Noah see Foster, Charlotte

RIDEOUT, Joshua see Clough, Elizabeth

RIDER, Joanna see Dural, Peter

RIDER, Polly see Morse, David

RIDER, Samuel see Morse, Abigail

RIDER, Charles see Manning, Eliza

ROBBINS, Delia see Stimson, Russel

ROBERSON, Lucy see Hobbs, Amos

ROBERTS, Betsey see Hunt, Moses

ROBERTS, Emma see Dolley, George

ROBERTS, Marion E. of Gray and Maurice E. Russell of
     Westbrook Md. 1 Sept. 1924 p.145

ROBERTS, Doris see Humphrey, Howard

ROBINSON, Joshua see Dyer, Eleanor

ROBINSON, Albert see Nash, Adaline

ROBINSON, William see Dyer, Huldah

ROBINSON, Joseph see Doughty, May

ROBINSON, Martin see Knowlton, Frances

ROBINSON, Bessie see Verrill, Clark

ROBINSON, Ivory see Hancock, Lillian

ROBINSON, Bessie see Gray, Algie

ROBINSON, Elliott see Dolley, Lucinda

RODGERS, Lucy see Morse, Benjamin

ROGERS, Frank O. and Dora Shaw both of Windham Md 5 Oct. 1890

ROGERS, William H. and Jennie F. Royal both of Windham Md 1 July 1891

ROGERS, John R. see Goff, Mary J.

ROLF, John see Dyer, Abigail

ROLFE, Abigail of Gray and Pitman Morgan of No. Yarmouth PUB. 9 Apr 1840

ROSE, Thomas see Morse, Emily

ROSS, Polly see Morse, Ozias

ROSS, Susan of Gray and Stephen Hutchinson of North Yarmouth PUB. 30 Sept. 1817 p.210 Md. 27 Nov. 1817 p. 211

ROSS, Mabel see Pennell, George F.

ROSS, Joseph see Cobb, Almira

ROUNDS, Patience see Fogg, Timothy

ROUNDS, Samuel see Austen, Elizabeth

ROUNDS, Nathaniel see Perley, Paulina

ROUNDS, Margaret see Fogg, Nelson

ROUNDS, Charles see Harmon, Mehitable

ROUNDS, Eleanor see Harmon, William

ROWE, Angie see Verrill, Merritt

ROWE, Samuel see Merrow, Eliza

ROWE, Mary see Merrow, Noah

ROWE, Abagail see Rowe, Elias

ROYAL, Isaac see Nason, Tabitha

RUDE, Margaret see Foster, Marshall

RUSS, Sally see Brown, Andrew Jr.

RUSS, Mrs. Nancy see Purves, William

RUSSELL, Lidia see Jordan, Solomon

RUSSELL, Temperance see Jordan, David

RUSSELL, Jennie see LaBarron, James

RUSELL, Mary and Ebenezear Stowell both of Gray 19 Jan. 1801 p.167

RUSSELL, John and Hannah Weeks both of Gray 28 Mar. 1812 p.199

RUSELL, John see Morse, Patty

RUSSELL, John Jr. see Fogg, Lucinda

RUSSELL, Charles and Susanna Shaw both of Gray PUB. 16 July
    1826 p.245

RUSSELL, William see Merrill, Julia

RUSSELL, Nettie see Foster, Arthur

RUSSELL, Lucinda see Verril, Wardsworth

RUSSELL, Dana see Hunt, Arline

RUSSELL, Harriett see Humphrey, Gerald

RUSSELL, Maurice see Roberts, Marion

RUSSELL, Major J. of Gray and Sarah M. Sampson of Norway
    PUB. 15 Apr. 1856 Md. 23 Apr. 1856

RUSSELL, Mary S. of Gray and John H. Ward of Gorham Md 20
    June 1862

RUSSELL, Calvin see Barker, Dorcas

RUSSELL, Elizabeth see Doughty, Geo. 2nd

RYDER, William see Spencer, Harriet

RYDER, Lizzie see Adams, Will

RYDER, Alice see Corson, Luville

RYDER, Andrew see Farran, Annie

RYERSON, Costella see Wing, Frederick

SAMPSON, Sarah see Russell, Major

SAMPSON, Angie see Humphrey, John

SAMUELS, Robert A. of Utica, N.Y. and Marjorie Gowen of
    Springvale Md. 2 May 1925 p.147

SANBORN, Mary see Mayall, Joney

SANBORN, Orren see Skillin, Amelia

SANBORN, Wenlock see Jones, Lillian

SANBORN, Charles A. and Agnes V. Flagg both of Buckfield Md
    24 Nov. 1910 p.77

SANDERS, Jonathan see Weeks, Susanna

SANDERS, Nathan see Chandler, Rachel

SARBELL, Maggie see Field, Fred

SARGENT, Ellen see Howes, Herbert

SARGENT, Herbert see Armitage, Fannie

SAUL, Eliza H. and Joshua S. Snow both of Gray PUB. 23 Aug.
    1861, Md 3 Sept. 1861

SAUNDERS, Polly see Latham, George

SAUNDERS, Hariet see Frank, Joseph

SAVAGE, Robert W. of Casco and Ada A. Wilson of New
    Gloucester Md. 4 Oct. 1893 p.9

SAWYER, Lucy C. of Gray and James Hall of Cohassett, Mass. 1 June 1855

SAWYER, Parker see Libby, Nancy

SAWYER, Clarissa of Gray and Joseph McIntire of New Gloucester PUB. 25 Apr. 1824 p.236

SAWYER, Sally see Morse, Thomas

SAWYER, Charlotte see Morse, Reuben

SAWYER, John see Foster, Irene

SAWYER, John see Perley, Melinda

SAWYER, Lucinda P. of Gray and Frank Lawrence of Portland Md 25 June 1861

SAWYER, George F. of Gray and Nellie E. Chase of S. Framingham, Mass. Md 6 Aug. 1888

SAWYER, Joseph C. and Louise M. Harmon both of Raymond Md 9 Sept. 1888

SAWYER, John M. and Elnora Sawyer both of Gray PUB. 21 Dec. 1888, Md. 25 Dec. 1888

SAWYER, Elnora see Sawyer, John

SAWYER, Elnora of Gray and Howard S. Perley of No. Yarmouth PUB. 8 Jan. 1889, Md 16 Jan. 1889

SAWYER, Parker see Morse, Annie

SAWYER, John D. and Clara A. Thayer both of Gray PUB. 27 Jan. 1867 Md. 18 Apr. 1867

SAWYER, Alonzo see Hall, Emma

SAWYER, William of Gray and Mary L. Perley of No. Yarmouth Md. 26 Apr. 1873

SAWYER, Frank of Gray and Florence M. Low of No. Yarmouth PUB. 25 July 1876, Md 3 Aug. 1876

SAWYER, Fred see Cotton, Carrie

SAWYER, George F. of Gray and Mary Mayberry of Windham PUB. 14 Aug. 1880, Md 22 Aug. 1880

SAWYER, Emma of Gray and Aston Harris of New Gloucester PUB. 27 Nov. 1880, Md 12 Dec. 1880

SAWYER, Joseph see Plummer, Georgia

SAWYER, Mary see Barton, Fred

SAWYER, Herbert J. of Gray and Alice E. Dorman of Dixmont Md. 7 July 1891

SAWYER, Andrew see Hall, Abbie

SAWYER, Herbert see Blake, Minnie

SAWYER, Charles G. see Mayberry, Edith W.

SAWYER, Ira P. see Foster, Mildred

SAWYER, Cora A. of Gray and Elmer I. Porter of No. Yarmouth Md. 6 June 1901 in So. Portland p.35

SAWYER, Charles G. and Josephine Sawyer both of Gray Md 27 Nov. 1901 p.37

SAWYER, Josephine see Sawyer, Charles

SAWYER, Clarence E. of Gray and Ethel M. Estes of New Gloucester Md. 5 July 1902 p.37

SAWYER, Elizabeth see Donovan, Daniel

SAWYER, Fernald see Hall, Susie

SAWYER, Joseph P. and Emma M. Tweedie both of Gray Md 18 Nov. 1903 in No. Yarmouth p.45

SAWYER, Sadie B. of Gray and George E. Farnham of New Gloucester Md. 16 Nov. 1904 p.47

SAWYER, Perley see Bohnsen, Jennie

SAWYER, Bessie of Gray and Geo. T. Brackett of Portland Md 24 July 1907 p.59

SAWYER, Hannibal W. and Lucy A. Whitney both of Gray Md 27 Nov. 1907 p.61

SAWYER, Blanche of Gray and Alton L. Hall of Lisbon Falls Md 23 May 1908 in Bowdoin p.65

SAWYER, Hattie H. and Roy F. Webb both of Gray Md 21 Oct. 1908 p.67

SAWYER, Charles see Allen, Ella

SAWYER, Ralph see Bishop, Evelyn

SAWYER, Velma H. of Gray and Raymond D. Sears of Raymond Md. 4 June 1913 p.87

SAWYER, Fred see Foster, Luenetta

SAWYER, Ruben see Rackley, Mary

SAWYER, Mildred E. of Gray and Ernest M. Kimball of Bridgton Md. 8 Apr. 1917 in No. Yarmouth p.103

SAWYER, Eva N. of West Gray and Roland E. Whitney of Standish Md. 24 July 1918 in Freeport p.113

SAWYER, Dorothy see Doughty, Carrol

SAWYER, Bernard L. of Gray and Grace L. Anderson of Portland Md. 22 Apr. 1922 p.131

SAWYER, John see Mann, Mildred

SAWYER, Arthur M. and Eleanor F. Witham both of Gray Md 2 July 1927 p.157

SAWYER, Isabelle K. of Gray and Ormond D. Hayes of No. Yarmouth Md. 20 Sept. 1927 p.159

SAWYER, Fred I. Of Gray and Gertrude L. Hanscom of Portland Md. 29 Nov. 1930 p.177

SAWYER, Lucy C. of Gray and James Hall of Cohassett, Mass Md 1 June 1855

SAWYER, Sarah see Webster, Simon

SAWYER, Greenleaf see Prince Phebe

SAWYER, Lucinda P. of Gray and Frank Lawrence of Portland Md 25 June 1861

SAWYER, Lydia see Gore, George

SAWYER, Albert W. and Clarice O. Small both of Gray PUB. 10 Oct. 1863 Md. 15 Oct. 1863

SAWYER, Clarissa see King, Thomas

SAWYER, Horatio M. and Addie C. Staples both of Gray Md 28 Oct. 1884

SAWYER, Carrie S. and Walter S. Small both of Gray PUB. 23 Feb. 1885 Md. 10 Mar. 1885 Feb. 1886 Md. 23 Feb. 1886

SAWYER, Eldora see Frank, Orin

SAWYER, Annie M. of Gray and Fred W. Fritz of Yarmouth PUB. 15 Dec. 1887

SAWYER, Thorndike of Gray and Martha B. Peterson of Portland PUB. 6 May 1838

SAWYER, Rebecca see Purvis, Adam

SAWYER, James see Frank, Abigail

SAWYER, Ralph see Bishop, Evelyn

SAYWARD, Charles see Verrill, Rosetta

SAYWARD, Wilbur see Alley, Alice

SAYWARD, Earl of Gray and Lizzie J. Peterson of Windham Md 29 Nov.1917 in Windham p.109

SAYWARD, Kate of Gray and Walter C. Varney of Windham Md 8 Nov. 1919 in Westbrook p.119

SAYWARD, Carroll E. of Gray and Beatrice A. Varney of Windham

SAYWARD, Henry see Chipman, Iva

SAYWARD, Carroll E. and Bertha A. Webster both of Gray Md 26 Aug. 1927 p.157

SCHAFFER, Carl R. and Ethel L. Allen both of So. Paris Md 16 Mar. 1929 p.167

SCRIBNER, Benjamin see Dyer, Ann

SCULLY, Caroline P. of Gray John W. Crawford of Kenduskeag
Md. 14 May 1930 in Portland p.171

SEAL, George see Edwards, Flora

SEARS, Raymond, see Sawyer, Velma

SEGARS, Clyde see Snow, Velma

SENTER, Charles P. and Millie M. Libby both of Windham Md 19
Aug. 1890

SERJANT, Lucy see Lufkin, Nathaniel

SHACKFORD, Charles W. and Laura J. Brown both of New
Gloucester Md. 9 Feb. 1889

SHARP, Arthur see Witham, Hattie

SHAW, Rhoda see Miller, Moses

SHAW, Susanna see Russell, Charles

SHAW, Robert see Morse, Judith

SHAW, Judith see Leighton, James

SHAW, Sarah of Gray and John S. Brown of Raymond Md 16 Apr.
1860

SHAW, Mary see Knight, John

SHAW, Willie P. and Augusta A. Smith both of Gray Md 20 Apr.
1877

SHAW, Nicholas and Jane Young both of Gray PUB. 17 Dec.
1878, Md 14 Jan. 1879 at Windham

SHAW, Dora see Huston, Augustas

SHAW, Alvin see Plummer, Rozilla

SHAW, Lizzie see Baldwin, Charles A.

SHAW, Florence M. of Gray and Charles A. Welch of Yarmouth
Md. 10 Dec. 1913 in Yarmouth p.91

SHAW, Judith see Leighton, James

SHAW, Sarah A. of Gray and John S. Brown of Raymond PUB. 16
Apr. 1860 Md. 23 Apr 1860

SHAW, Jane of Gray and Mark C. Mayberry of Windham PUB. 1
June 1840

SHAW, Mary see Frank, David

SHELDON, Rev. N.W. Sheldon of Gray and Ann Douglass of
Portland PUB. 4 Sept. 1842

SHERMAN, Margaret, see Morse, Benjamin

SHERWOOD, Louise of Gray and Harry Follansbee of Enfield,
N.H. Md. 18 June 1923 in Enfield, N.H.

SICKRA, Raymond see Farwell, Rozilla

SIMANTON, Betty see Leach, Zechariah

SIMMONS, Addie see Doughty, Henry

SIMONTON, Ebenr. see Morse, Rebecca

SIMONTON, Mary see Libby, Joseph

SIMONTON, Hardy l. of Yarmouth and Effie F. Whitney of Portland Md. 8 Sept. 1909 p.73

SIMPSON, David see Colley, Susan

SIMPSON, William R. of Gray and Mrs. Sarah A. Dickinson of Portland Md. 24 Oct. 1869

SIMPSON, Etta C. and Howard S. Stubbs both of Gray PUB. 11 Mar. 1870, Md 19 Mar. 1870

SIMPSON, Mary see Doughty, Albert

SIMPSON, Lewis see Leighton, Henrietta

SKILLIN, Eunice of Windham, and Andrew Smith of Gorham 4 Mar. 1854

SKILLIN, James see Adams, Caroline

SKILLIN, Mary see Doughty, Edward

SKILLIN, Edward see Black, Olive

SKILLIN, Alvin see Libby, Lucy

SKILLIN, Samuel see Mountfort, Mary

SKILLIN, Emeline see Hunt, Samuel

SKILLIN, Samuel see Huston, Sarah

SKILLIN, Alvin see Hayden, Clara

SKILLIN, Hiram of Gray and Delphina E. Crocket of Scarappa PUB. 28 Sept. 1871, Md 5 Oct. 1871

SKILLIN, George see Allen, Katie

SKILLIN, Almeda see Adams, Charles

SKILLIN, Amelia F. of Gray and Orren C. Sanborn of Portland PUB. 4 May 1873, Md 24 May 1873

SKILLIN, Edwin see Frank, Ella

SKILLIN, Evelyn L. of Gray and Enos L. Jordan of Cape Elizabeth Md. 7 June 1875

SKILLIN, Alice P. of Gray and Henry F. Thompson of Deering Md 7 June 1875

SKILLIN, Israel see Smith, Carrie

SKILLIN, Mary see Mushrall, Joseph

SKILLIN, Thomas see Morse, Margaret

SKILLIN, ? of Gray and Addie F. Elwell of Buxton Md 14 Jan. 1880

SKILLIN, Etta L. of Gray and Herbert P. Marton of Windham Md
    29 Dec. 1895p.17
SKILLIN, Edward see Prince, Sewall
SKILLIN, Albert see Maybury, Helen
SKILLIN, Hannah E. of Gray and Elbridge Field of Falmouth
    PUB. 19 Apr. 1858 Md. 19 Apr. 1858
SKILLIN, Sophia A. and John Smith both of Gray Md 5 Jan. 1859
SKILLIN, Emeline see Hunt, Samuel
SKILLIN, Deborah F. of Gray and Charles R. Reed of Westbrook
    Md. 17 Jan. 1864
SKILLIN, Lucy E. of Gray and Fernald Libby of Portland Md 4
    Jan. 1865
SKILLIN, Mary A. of Gray and Josiah Skillin of Garland PUB. 16
    Sept. 1837
SKILLIN, Josiah see Skillin, Mary
SKILLIN, Lavina K. and John Corliss of No. Yarmouth PUB. 4
    Dec. 1844
SKILLING, Eleanor of Gray and Leland N. Wentworth of
    Westbrook Md. 13 May 1922 in Westbrook p.131
SKILLING, John see Cobb, Catherine
SKILLINGS, Joseph and Sally Skillings both of Gray 26 Nov.
    1801 p.166
SKILLINGS, Sally see Skillings, Joseph
SKILLINGS, Samuel see Ramsdell, Molly
SKILLINGS, Myrta C. of Gray and George H. Larrabee of
    Bridgton Md. 15 Aug. 1895 p.15
SKILLINGS, Ida see Frank, Wilburn H.
SKILLINGS, Charles E. see Hechler, Sarah J.
SKILLINGS, Harlan R. of Gray and Ethel M. Chase of Auburn Md
    2 May in Auburn p.29
SKILLINGS, Martha see McInnis, Hector
SKILLINS, Sabrina see Adams, Joshua
SKILLINS, Susan see Huston, William
SKILLINS, Eunice of Gray and Elisha S. Durin of Cumberland
    Md. 28 Aug. 1834 p.278
SKILLINS, Joseph of Gray and Elizabeth A. Mitchell of Raymond
    PUB. 3 Jan. 1836 p.282
SMALL, Lucy of Gray and Daniel Moody of Scarborough PUB. 11
    Nov. 1780; 27 Nov. 1780
SMALL, Mary and Joel Stevens both of Gray 29 Dec. 1785 p. 136

SMALL, Mary see Nash, Elijah
SMALL, George see Nash, Sarah
SMALL, William see Hayden, Sarah
SMALL, Joseph see Nash, Sarah
SMALL, Polley see Frank, Josiah
SMALL, Jeremiah see Frank, Jane
SMALL, Atkinson see Doughty, Martha
SMALL, Susan see Libby, Andrew
SMALL, Mary and Sidney Thaxter both of Gray 14 June 1812
     p.195
SMALL, Lucy see Frank, Thomas
SMALL, Sally see Austin, Minion
SMALL, Dolley of Gray and Samuel Nason of Minot 22 Jan. 1815
     p.201
SMALL, Fanney see Lawrence, Ephraim
SMALL, Robert see Lawrence, Ann
SMALL, George Jr. of Gray and Salley Megguire of New
     Gloucester PUB. 30 Mar. 1817 p.209
SMALL, Robert see Lawrence, Ann
SMALL, John see Libby, Christiana
SMALL, Statira see Latham, Woodard
SMALL, Hannah of Gray and David Small of Minot PUB. 16 Feb.
     1820 p.220 Md. 30 Apr. 1820 p.226
SMALL, David see Small, Hannah
SMALL, Apha of Gray and Robert Starbird of Poland PUB. 30
     Nov. 1820 p.223
SMALL, John see Latham, Charlotte
SMALL, Sarah see Morse, Joseph
SMALL, Anne of Gray and John Small of Raymond PUB. 10 Feb.
     1828 p.250, Md 1828 p.251
SMALL, John see Small, Anne
SMALL, James see Latham, Elvira
SMALL, Nathaniel see Libby, Eliza
SMALL, Abigail see Pennell, Dixey
SMALL, Belinda of Gray and William Small of New Gloucester
     PUB. 31 Dec. 1832 p.272
SMALL, William see Small, Belinda
SMALL, Ebenzer and Mary D. Welch both of Gray PUB. 5 May
     1833 p.275, Md 18 July 1833 p.279

SMALL, Stephen R. and Margaret E. Morrell both of Raymond Md
    18 Aug. 1861

SMALL, Benjamin S. and Adriene Huston both of New Gloucester
    Md. 29 Nov. 1888

SMALL, Gilbert see Frank, Sophia

SMALL, Marcus see Goff, Helen

SMALL, Freeland see Quint, Lucy

SMALL, Emma see Hall, Herbert

SMALL, Charles see Cummings, Mary

SMALL, John W. and Nellie F. Weymouth both of Gray PUB. 25
    Apr. 1873, Md 30 Apr. 1873

SMALL, John L. of Gray and Ellen M. Morse of Groveland Mass.
    Md. 9 Oct. 1874

SMALL, Nettie see Libby, James

SMALL, Sarah H. and Charles F. Webster both of Gray PUB. 14
    June 1878, Md 26 June 1878

SMALL, Mamie see Stimson, Hiram

SMALL, Louisa see Haines, Sallas

SMALL, John and Angeline Wright both of Auburn Md 12 Jan.
    1884

SMALL, Addie see Doughty, Nathan

SMALL, Edward see Knight, Lillian

SMALL, Sarah see Field, Ulyssis

SMALL, Richard Jr. and Abbie T. Small both of Raymond Md
    May 1891

SMALL, William N. and Georgie A. Small both of Raymond Md
    26 Nov. 1891

SMALL, Hattie see Fortune, William

SMALL, William see Libby, Mabel

SMALL, Ada see Philbrooks, George

SMALL, Joseph see Bennett, Ida

SMALL, Leon L. see Grover, Grace M.

SMALL, Albert J. see Mitchell, Annie S.

SMALL, Jennie see Cobb, Marshall

SMALL, Wendall see Libby, Minnie

SMALL, Luella see Golding, Harry

SMALL, Gladys M. of Gray and Walter R. Berry of New
    Gloucester Md. 9 Oct. 1912 p.83

SMALL, Lena see Doughty, Carroll

SMALL, Isa E. of Gray and George H. Parren of Franklin Mass. Md. 5 Mar. 1914 p.91

SMALL, Florence A. of Gray and Harry H. Foye of Portland Md 30 Aug. 1919 p.117

SMALL, William see Leighton, Marion

SMALL, Almer H. and Mary J. Webster both of Gray PUB. 6 Mar. 1858 Md. 24 Mar. 1858

SMALL, Angette see Allen, Alvin

SMALL, Stephen R. and Margaret E. Morrell both of Raymond Md 18 Aug. 1861

SMALL, Martha H. and Calvin W. Young both of Gray Md 13 Oct. 1826

SMALL, Clarice see Sawyer, Albert

SMALL, Charlotte see Holt, Charles

SMALL, John and Angeline Wright both of Auburn Md 12 Jan. 1884

SMALL, Walter see Sawyer, Carrie

SMALL, Freda W. of Gray and E. J. Brown of Grafton Md 7 Oct. 1885

SMALL, James M. of Casco and Lizzie M. Small of New Gloucester Md. 24 Dec. 1885

SMALL, Gertie see Sawyer, Fred

SMALL, Irving see Doughty, Louie

SMALL, Wendall see Burrows, Addie

SMALL, Levi see Libby, Harriet

SMALL, Joseph of Gray and Susan Huston of Windham PUB. 16 Sept. 1837

SMALL, John G. of Gray and Emeline Dennison of Freeport PUB. 30 June 1839

SMALL, David Jr. and Louisa Pratt PUB. 28 Apr 1844 p.294

SMALL, Ai M. of Gray and Julia A. Whitney of Cumberland PUB. 8 Oct. 1848

SMITH, Andrew, see Skillin, Eunice

SMITH, Benjamin of Gray and Hannah Huston of Falmouth PUB. 10 Nov. 1820 p.223

SMITH, William of Gray and Martha Dunn of Gorham PUB. 3 Oct. 1830 p.264

SMITH, Perthena see Nash, Daniel

SMITH, Hannah see Adams, Silas

SMITH, Charles see Nash, Hannah

SMITH, Carrie see Blake, John

SMITH, Cynthia see Hunt, George

SMITH, Hugh see Cobb, Abby

SMITH, Mariner L. and Addie H. Berry both of Portland Md 30 May 1871

SMITH, Emma see Barbour, William

SMITH, Carrie B. of Gray and Israel A. Skillin of Yarmouth PUB. 19 June 1876, Md 29 June 1876

SMITH, Augusta see Shaw, Willie

SMITH, James E. of Gray and Thankful B. Whitney of No. Yarmouth PUB. 24 July 1890, Md 16 Aug. 1890

SMITH, Blanche see Hunt, Henry

SMITH, Charles C. and Annie Thurlow both of Gray Md 23 Apr. 1896 p.19

SMITH, Margaret see Hodgkins, William S.

SMITH, Ralph W. and Evelyn P. Libby both of Westbrook Md 6 Oct. 1902 p.39

SMITH, William and Myrtle M. Files both of Raymond Md 5 Dec.1914 p.93

SMITH, Velma see Luckings, William

SMITH, Alice M. of Gray and James E. Bennett Jr. of New Gloucester Md. 29 Nov. 1919 p.119

SMITH, Gerald see Thurlow, Adaline

SMITH, Minnie see Golding, Walter

SMITH, Fred S. and Ida M. Perkins both of Windham Md 20 May 1922 p.131

SMITH, Sumner H. and Alice M. Copp both of New Gloucester Md. 17 May 1928 p.161

SMITH, Gladys see Strout, Clifford

SMITH, Andrew of Gorham and Eunice Skillin of Windham Md 4 Mar. 1854

SMITH, Elias see Tripp, Helen

SMITH, John of Gray and Mary A. Monte of Poland Md 4 Nov. 1857

SMITH, John see Skillin, Sophia

SMITH, Hugh see Lawrence, Amanda

SMITH, Johnson see Gleason, Margie

SMITH, Johnson of Gray and Mary M. Barr of Greene PUB. 6 Feb. 1886 Md. 21 Feb. 1886

SMITH, Robert see Allan, Prudence

SMITH, Susan see Pennell, Luther

SNOW, Joshua see Saul, Eliza

SNOW, Nellie see Clark, Joseph B.

SNOW, George see Leach, Jennie

SNOW, Claude L. of Pownal and Villa M. Fogg of Harrison Md 3 Mar. 1915 p.95

SNOW, Velma A. of Gray and Clyde H. Segars of New Gloucester Md. 29 Nov. 1917 in Poland p.109

SNOW, Winfield see Mountfort, Laura

SNOW, Lauris P. of Gray and Edward E. Bragg of Cumberland Md 6 Oct. 1920 p.123

SNOW, Wilmer see Lowe, Eugene

SNOW, Joshua see Saul, Eliza

SOPER, Asa of Gray and Mehitable Lucas of Hebron 13 Mar. 1794 p.151

SOPER, Sarah of Gray and Benjamin Cobb of Windham 13 Mar. 1794 p.151

SOPER, Polly of Gray and Levi Low of Winslow 8 Jan. 1795 p.153

SOPER, Peggey of Gray and Isaac Oakman of Bangor 13 Mar. 1803 p.174

SOPER, Betsy see Latham, Galen

SOPER, Salter see Bailey, Hannah

SOPER, Martha of Gray and Henry M. Chamberlain of Auburn PUB. 19 Nov. 1843

SOULE, Laura see Osgood, William

SPEAR, Margaret see Quint, Earl

SPENCER, Harriet J. of Gray and William O. Ryder of No. Yarmouth PUB. 24 June 1875, Md 24 July 1875

SPENCER, Lizzie see Humphrey, James

SPENCER, Lillian see Richards, John

SPENCER, Lillian see Grant, Alvin

SPENCER, Lydia D. of Gray and John Foss Jr. of Hollis PUB. 3 Apr. 1842

SPIKES, Katie see Black, George

SPILLER, Ella see Foster, Charles

SPILLER, Jennie see Hunt, Delbert

SPILLER, Samuel D. and Ola E. Strout both of Raymond Md 24 Dec. 1890

SPILLER, Freeland J. of No. Raymond and Lena A. Shackford of
　　Poland Md. 6 Aug. 1892 p.5

SPILLER, Susie see Quint, Earl

SPILLER, Vernon W. of Raymond and Beulah A. Thurlow of
　　Poland Md. 12 Oct. 1893 p.9

SPOSEBO, William G. of Casco and Emma Strout of Raymond
　　Md. 26 May 1889

STACKPOLE, Mary see Webster, Joseph

STACY, Marjorie C. of Gray and Robert H. Hamilton of New
　　Gloucester Md. Oct. 28 1925 p.149

STANFORD, Ida see Mayberry, Frederick

STAPLES, Catherine and Samuel Staples Thompson both of Gray
　　18 Nov. 1798 p.157

STAPLES, Sarah see Hunt, Moses

STAPLES, Eunice see Barns, James

STAPLES, Miriam and John F. Weymouth both of Gray PUB. 21
　　Feb. 1818 p.212, Md. 1818 p.217

STAPLES, Susan of Gray and William Loring of Pownal PUB. 25
　　Dec. 1825 p.243, Md 29 Jan. 1826 p.240

STAPLES, Mary see Loring, Isaac

STAPLES, Patience see Libby, William

STAPLES, Mary see Morse, Thomas

STAPLES, Addie see Sawyer, Horatio

STAPLES, Eliza of Gray and Elbridge Loring of Pownal PUB. 8
　　Sept. 1839

STARBIRD, Elizabeth and John Young both of Gray 24 Sept.
　　1789 p.143

STARBIRD, Martha see Symonds, Nathaniel

STARBIRD, Nice see Berry, Peletiah

STARBIRD, John see Gould, Dorcas

STARBIRD, Henry and Joanna Wilson both of Raymondtown 24
　　Sept. 1799 p.160

STARBIRD, Eunice and Robert Starbird both of Gray 25 Oct.
　　1807 p.184

STARBIRD, Robert see Starbird, Eunice

STARBIRD, William see Berry, Olive

STARBIRD, Robert see Small, Apha

STARBIRD, Martha see Libby, Benjamin

STARBIRD, Robert see Haskell, Abigail

STARBIRD, Caroline W. of Gray and Benjamin H. Watson of Levant PUB. 25 Oct. 1835 p.281

STARBIRD, Mary see Haskell, Rev. John

STARBIRD, Sarah see Lawrence, John

STARBIRD, Rhoda see Twitchell, Mark

STARBIRD, Elroy of Gray and Olive A. Wilson of Falmouth PUB. 1 Mar. 1841

STARBIRD, Hannah see Knight, Reuben

STARBIRD, Henry H. of Gray and Hope Cobb of Westbrook PUB. 2 Nov. 1845

STARLING, Joseph see Welch, Susan

STEARNS, William see Porter, Joanna

STEVENS, Joel see Doughty, Martha

STEVENS, Ruth see Doughty, James

STEVENS, Nathaniel see Cobb, Rebecker

STEVENS, Joel see Small, Mary

STEVENS, Nancy see Fogg, James

STEVENS, Joel see Merrill, Mary

STEVENS, Mary see Pride, Alexander

STEVENS, George see Morse, Elsie

STEVENS, John W. of Gray and Nellie E. Redlon of Portland Md 9 June 1906 p.55

STEVENS, Lena see Merrill, Frank

STEVENS, George M. of Gray and Myrtle Thompson of Saratoga, N.Y. Md. 6 Aug. 1913 p.89

STEVENS, Franks. of Georgetown and Irene B. Gilman of Boothbay Md. 8 July 1916 p.99

STEVENS, Mary see Pride, Alexander

STEVENS, James O. of Fairfield and Lavina Parrish of Waterville Md. 30 May 1924 p.143

STEWARY, Mary see Thompson, Joseph

STILES, Eli see Barber, Lucy

STILES, Curtis see Libby, Anna

STILES, Lucy see Stiles Robert

STILES, Huldah see Libby, Willard

STILES, Elizabeth of Gray and John P. Lamb of Harrison PUB. 29 Aug. 1830 p.263

STILES, Fannie see Libby, John

STILES, Stephen see Doughty, Olive

STILES, Ida M. of Gray and George H. Hill of Windham PUB. 12
    Nov. 1875, Md 22 Nov. 1875
STILES, Alice J. of Gray and Samuel S. Pritham of Portland PUB.
    15 Dec. 1875, Md 12 Jan. 1876
STILES, Emma see Libby, George
STILES, Charles see Frank, Hattie
STILES, Caleb C. of Gray and Sarah M. Mariner of Buxton PUB.
    15 May 1883, Md 21 May 1883
STILES, H. see Libby, Simon
STILES, Susie M. of Gray and Orville L. Hanson of Windham Md
    5 July 1902 p.37
STILES, Elizabeth E. of Gray and Stephen A. Libby of Danville
    Md. 28 Nov. 1858
STIMSON, Theophilus, see Allen, Caroline
STIMSON, Naomi see Frank, Alpheus
STIMSON, Theophilus see Lawrence, Mary
STIMSON, Maryann see Libby, George
STIMSON, Woodbury see Maxwell, Mary
STIMSON, Theophilis see Allen, Emily
STIMSON, Horace see Fling, Augusta
STIMSON, Abbie M. of Gray and Melville F. Ingalls of Boston,
    Mass. Md. 26 Dec. 1866
STIMSON, Russel S. of Gray and Delia A. Robbins of Poland Md
    20 Apr. 1877
STIMSON, Hiram C. of Gray and Mamie W. Small of Deering
    PUB. 17 Dec. 1878, Md 25 Dec. 1878
STIMSON, Carrie see Chase, John
STIMSON, Annie see Hamilton, John
STIMSON, Harry O. of Gray and Florence E. Edwards of Otisfield
    Md. 29 May 1899 in Oxford p.27
STIMSON, Mary J. of Gray and William J. Moore of Portland Md
    24 Nov. 1909 in No. Falmouth p.73
STIMSON, Theophilus Jr. see Allen, Caroline
STIMSON, Theophilis see Allen, Ellen
STIMSON, Horace see Fling, Augusta
STINCHFIELD, Oscar see Doughty, Clara H.
STONE, Michael Stone Damon and Mary Tufts both of Gray 14
    June 1812   p.195
STONE, Elwin see Webber, Jennie

STONE, Trueman see Davies, Jessie

STORY, Horace E. of Gray and Tena W. MacLeod of Poland Md 27 Nov. 1907 p.61

STOWELL, Elisabeth see Colley, James

STOWELL, Ebenezear see Russell, Mary

STOWELL, Nabby of Gray and John Farewell of Portland 23 May 1801 p.167

STOWELL, Betsey see Pennell, Joseph

STOWELL, Susan of Gray and Rev. David A. Hill of Cumberland Md. 25 June 1858

STOWELL, Olive see Colley, James

STOWELL, Luther J. of Gray and Mary J. Day of Cumberland PUB. 15 Apr. 1849

STRATTON, Bemis J. of Gray and Vernie M. Grover of So. Portland Md. 15 Nov. 1922 in So. Portland p.135

STROUT, Elizabeth see Cash, Sam'l

STROUT, Sarah see Thurlow, John

STROUT, Silas E. of Gorham and Hattie E. Roggers of Windham Md. 31 July 1889

STROUT, Martha A. of Gray and Arno A. Farwell of Raymond PUB. 15 Apr. 1869, Md 4 Mar. 1869

STROUT, Ellen L. F. of Gray and Lorenzo Crepey of Falmouth Md 13 Dec. 1870

STROUT, Hiram and Sarah M. both of Gray Md 26 Dec 1874

STROUT, Abby see Cary, Albert

STROUT, Abner see Hodgkins, Sophronia

STROUT, Olive see Doughty, Henry

STROUT, Mary see Knight, Charles

STROUT, Ada M. of Gray and Charles May of New Gloucester Md. 25 Nov. 1889

STROUT, Freedom H. and Phoebe Verrill both of Gray Md 16 Dec. 1893 p.11

STROUT, Maria K. and Dwinal Verrill both of Gray Md 22 Feb. 1894 p.11

STROUT, Susan W. see Field, Edwin L. jr.

STROUT, Ephraim P. C. see May, Isabella

STROUT, Dwinal F. and Mary A. Thurlow both of Gray Md 18 Aug. 1900 p.31

STROUT, Cyrus T. and Nancy Thurlow both of Gray Md 1 Feb. 1904 p.45

STROUT, Mary see Edwards, Clarence

STROUT, Charles H. of Gray and Bertha M. Young of New
    Gloucester Md. 23 Oct. 1916 p.103

STROUT, Roberts see Porter, Byron

STROUT, Elmer see Lowell, Mary

STROUT, Alfreda E. and Henry A. Verrill both of Gray Md 1 Jan.
    1923 p.137

STROUT, Clifford E. of Gray and Gladys G. Smith of Oxford Md
    19 Jan. 1929 p.165

STROUT, George see Huston, Alice

STROUT, Caroline see Cambell, John

STROUT, Kedie see Foster, Walter

STROUT, Abby see David, Charles

STROUT, Prince see Dolley, Mary

STUART, Dorcas see Merrill, Richard

STUART, Hannah see Merrill, Joshua

STUART, Deliverance see Hall, William

STUART, Samuel see Frank, Fannie

STUBBS, Howard see Simpson, Etta

STUBBS, Carrie see Jury, Charles

STUBBS, Fred see Cobb, Alice

STUBBS, George A. and Sarah W. Farwell both of Cumberland
    Md. 5 Apr. 1859

STYLES, Salome see Prince, Bela

STYLES, Ann see Hill, Josiah

SUMNER, Willis A. and Martha Steere both of Lewiston Md
    5 June 1922 p.131

SWAN, Sylvester see Brooks, Christiana

SWAN, Emogene see Cummings, Samuel

SWAN, Lillian see Field, Schuyler

SWEATT, Herbert see Higgins, Winnie

SWEETSER, Abagail of Gray and Able Gitchell of Waterville
    3 July 1810   p.189

SWEETSER, Huldah and Andrew Whitney both of Gray 25 June
    1816 p.207

SWEETSER, Nicholas of Gray and Celia Dwinal of New
    Gloucester PUB. 1 Aug. 1824 p.236

SWEETSER, Nancy see Mountfort, Elias

SWEETSER, Jane see Perley, Joseph

SWEETSER, Samuel see Perley, Sarah

SWEETSER, Willard see Whitney, Lenora

SWEETSER, Helen see Martin, Harry

SWEETSER, Mary R. of Gray and Donald C. Chandler of New Gloucester Md. 31 July 1926 p.155

SWEETSER, Alice W. of Gray and Eaton S. Lothrop of Cape Elizabeth Md. 3 Sept. 1927 p.157

SWEETSER, Kathryn W. of Gray and James R. Peck of So. Portland Md. 15 Sept. 1928 p.165

SWININGTON, Elizabeth E. and Frank M. Thompson both of Gray Md. 15 Dec. 1921 p.129

SYKES, Robert see Carey, Theda

SYMONDS, Nathaniel of Bridgtown and Martha Starbird of Raymondston 29 Sept. 1791 p.147

SYMONDS, Abigail see Merrill, Nathan

SYMONDS, Martha F. and Otis Witham both of Gray Md 5 Apr. 1896 in No. Yarmouth p.19

TALBOT, Samuel see Howard, Annie

TAYLOR, Ashman see Nash, Mary

TAYLOR, Orrin A. and Sarah E. Knight both of Poland Md 16 Aug. 1862

TAYLOR, Lizzie see Frank, Granville

TENNEY, Henry see Hayden, Polly

TENNEY, Eliza see Morse, Levi

TENNEY, Susie see Mayberry, Herbert

TERRY, Leslie H. and Abbie Hubbard both of New Gloucester Md 21 Feb. 1914 p.91

THATCHER Rosilla see Black, Abel

THAXTER, Charles see Libby, Mary

THAXTER, Charles see Doughty, Abigail

THAXTER, Sidney see Small, Mary

THAYER, Ruth see Cummings, Joseph

THAYER, William see Nash, Frances

THAYER, Clara see Sawyer, John

THAYER, Augusta see Frank, John

THAYER, Abbie F. of Gray and Frank W. Cragin of Groton Mass. Md. 19 Nov. 1868

THAYER, Charles see Berry, Georgia

THAYER, Henry G. of Gray and Emma J. Oxnard of Freeport, Md 3 Mar. 1873

THAYER, Charles, see Berry, S.J.

THAYER, Fannie see Libby, Herbert
THAYER, Leila see Andrews, Richard
THAYER, Ruth P. of Gray and Charles L. Williamson of Auburn
     Md. 20 June 1916 p.99
THAYER, Capt. Edward see Latham, Abigail
THAYER, Mary see Hall, Cushman
THAYER, Harriet see Durgin, John
THAYER, Deborah see Goff, Samuel
THOMAS, Sarah see Jordan, George
THOMPSON, Pricilla see Pennell, Samuel
THOMPSON, Samuel see Staples, Catherine
THOMPSON, Joseph of Gray and Mary Stewrt of Windham
     26 June 1800   p.163
THOMPSON, William, see Pennell, Rachel
THOMPSON, Mary of Gray and David Bean of Portland 13 Mar.
     1808 p.184
THOMPSON, Nancy of Gray and Jacob Buzzell of Shapleigh
     2 June 1811 p.192
THOMPSON, Joseph see Mountfort, Priscilla
THOMPSON, Rachel see Doughty, Hezekiah
THOMPSON, James see Colley, Sarah
THOMPSON, Laura S. of Gray and Melbourne H. Berry of
     Amesbury Mass. PUB. 4 Feb. 1889, Md 10 Feb. 1889
THOMPSON, Alice L. and Herbert A. Verrill both of Gray Md
     30 Mar. 1889
THOMPSON, Mary A. of Gray and Charles S. Varney of
     Windham Md. 25 Apr. 1870
THOMPSON, Augustus see Hunt, Mary
THOMPSON, Alonzo see Nash, Esmeralda
THOMPSON, Henry see Skillin, Alice
THOMPSON, Royal L. of Gray and Mary E. McGuile of Kings
     County, Nova Scotia Md 29 Oct. 1879
THOMPSON, George see Frank, Mary
THOMPSON, Charles see Mayberry, Alice
THOMPSON, Joseph Jr. of Gray and Nancy F. Huston of
     Cumberland Md. 29 Aug. 1883
THOMPSON, Nellie G. of Gray and Morris P. Barnes of Deering
     PUB. 17 Feb. 1890, Md 8 June 1890
THOMPSON, George see Mace, Alice

THOMPSON, Eben B. and Victoria Verrill both of Gray Md
21 Jan. 1893 p.7
THOMPSON, Cora L. of Gray and John Witham of Raymond Md
21 Aug. 1894 p.13
THOMPSON, Edith see Libby, Charles
THOMPSON, Alice L. and William W. Vinton both of Gray Md
4 July 1906 p.55
THOMPSON, Emma L. and Nathaniel Verrill both of Gray Md
25 Dec. 1907 p.63
THOMPSON, Perley see Hawkes, Ida
THOMPSON, Myrtle see Stevens, George
THOMPSON, Harvey see Cobb, Lilla
THOMPSON, Clara M. of Gray and Francis E. Hayes of No.
Yarmouth Md. 26 Dec. 1916 p.103
THOMPSON, Bertrand of Gray and Mildred V. Prince of Standish
Md. 28 Nov. 1917 p.107
THOMPSON, Frank see Swinington, Elizabeth
THOMPSON, Alice see Rand, John
THOMPSON, George see Berry, Louisa
THOMPSON, Charles see Ramsdell, Hannah
THOMPSON, Joseph Jr. see Gilbert, Nancy
THOMPSON, William of Gray and Joann Leighton of Falmouth
PUB. 20 June 1847
THORNDIKE, Melville see Howard, Martha
THORPE, John H. of Raymond and Alice M. Goodwin of Poland
Md. 10 June 1894 p.13
THURLOW, Emeline see Frank, George
THURLOW, John of Gray and Sarah Strout of Poland PUB.
24 June 1889, Md 18 July 1889
THURLOW, Hannah and William H. M. Tripp both of Gray PUB.
9 Oct. 1868, Md 23 Oct. 1868
THURLOW, David W. and Eunice Verrill both of Gray PUB.
1 June 1869, Md 6 June 1869
THURLOW, Synthia see Hodgkins, Alphonso
THURLOW, William E. of Raymond and Emeline S. Plowman of
Starks PUB. 31 Jan. 1879, Md 25 Feb. 1879
THURLOW, Cora see Hodgkins, James
THURLOW, Clara C. of Gray and Edward Clayton of Gloucester,
Mass. PUB. 7 June 1882, Md 16 June 1882

THURLOW, Stephen see May, Alica

THURLOW, John of Gray and Sarah Bickford of Poland PUB. 24 June 1883, Md 28 June 1883

THURLOW, George see Frank, Mary

THURLOW, Charles H. and Roxie Wing both of Gray Md 27 Jan. 1896 p.17

THURLOW, Annie see Smith, Charles C.

THURLOW, Mary A. see Strout, Dwinal

THURLOW, Fred L. and Georgia A. Vinton both of Gray Md 13 Oct. 1900 p.31

THURLOW, Nancy see Strout, Cyrus

THURLOW, David see Jordan, Ella

THURLOW, Carolus and Mary Pitt both of Worcester Mass. Md 17 Aug. 1914 in Portland p.91

THURLOW, Adaline R. of Gray and Gerald D. Smith of Auburn Md. 3 Aug. 1921 in Auburn p.129

THURLOW, George see Libby, Betsey

THURLOW, Emeline see Frank, George

THURLOW, Augusta see Gore, Moses

THURLOW, Eunice see Benson, George

TIBBETTS, Sarah A of Gray and Charles York of Portland Md 30 Nov. 1854

TIBBETTS, Ann of Gray and Charles York of Portland 30 Nov. 1854

TINKHAM, Ephraim see Cobb, Mary

TINKHAM, Fred see Maier, Christina

TINNEY, Mary and Joshua Young both of Gray 7 Apr. 1802 p.173

TITCOMB, Salley of Gray and Lot Hall of Falmouth 30 Dec. 1804 p.179

TITCOMB, Jane see Doughty, Joshua

TITCOMB, Betsy see Mayo, Thomas

TITCOMB, Jeremiah and Anna Young both of Gray 1817 p.214

TITCOMB, Charity and Elisha Young both of Gray PUB. 7 Nov. 1824 p.237,Md. 26 Dec. 1824 p. 235

TITCOMB, Susan see Allen, Emery

TRENHOLM, Queen see Frank, Walter

TRIPP, Jacob see Fogg, Mary

TRIPP, Lucy see Benson, Edward

TRIPP, Cordelia L. of Gray and Thomas Wing of Bath Md 30 Mar. 1867

TRIPP, William see Thurlow, Hannah

TRIPP, David see Berry, Rozinna

TRIPP, Sarah see Hunt, Sarah

TRIPP, Ida see Farwell, Amos

TRIPP, Bertha E. see McConkey, John R.

TRIPP, Georgia see Hodgkins, Elisha

TRIPP, Fred and Nellie E. Verrill both of Gray Md 14 May 1906 p.55

TRIPP, Gardner E. of Poland and Sadie M. Farewell of Raymond Md. 22 Mar. 1912 p.81

TRIPP, Herbert see Chipman, Julia

TRIPP, William H. and Mamie G. Young both of Gray Md 23 Nov. 1921 p.129

TRIPP, Bertha see Webster, Simon

TRIPP, Pamela N. of Gray and James E. Wagner of Lewiston PUB. 12 Mar. 1856 Md. 9 Apr. 1856

TRIPP, Helen L. of Gray and Elias B. Smith of Lewiston Md 4 Oct. 1856

TRIPP, Ellen see May, Jeremiah

TRIPP, David see Berry, Rosanna

TRIPP, Martha see Benson, George

TRUE, Lyman see Lane, Frances

TRUE, Hannah see Bennett, William

TRUMBLE, Bernice see May, Stephen

TRUMBLE, Samuel see Harmon, Abagail

TUBBS, Joseph see Lyon, Eunice

TUCKER, Hattie see Hunt, Hiram

TUFTS, Mary see Stone, Michael

TUFTS, Sarah see Latham, Eliab

TUFTS, Catherine see Dolley, Jeremiah

TUFTS, Ruby see Goff, Barzilla

TUFTS, Samuel see Caswell, Frances

TUFTS, J. Albert see Dutton, Katie

TUFTS, Lizzie see Merrill, William

TUFTS, Ann see Goff, Lindsey

TUKEY, David see Porter, Lydia

TUKEY, William of Windham and Sarah Low of No. Yarmouth
    Md. 1834 p.280
TUNNEY, Thomas F. and Florence G. Conant both of Hebron Md
    6 Sept. 1911 p.79
TUTTLE, John see Colley, Hannah
TWEEDIE, Emma see Sawyer, Joseph
TWITCHELL, Moses see Dolly, Dorcas
TWITCHELL, Hannah see Berry, Peletiah
TWITCHELL, Jeremiah see Jenks, Betty
TWITCHELL, James of Gray and Mary Haskell of New Gloucester
    12 Apr. 1812   p.199
TWITCHELL, Mark of Gray and Rhoda Starbird of Greene PUB.
    7 Nov. 1840
TWITCHELL, Mary see Humphrey, James
TWOMBLY, Nathaniel see Frank, Belinda
TWOMBLY, Daniel see Osgood, Emma
TWOMBLY, Bertha G. of Gray and Andrew M. Allen of
    Westbrook Md. 8 Apr. 1920 in Portland p.121
TWOMBLY, Bertha see Pollard, Russell
USHER, Elizabeth see Latham, Jabez
VAN, John of Gray and Mary Capen of Canton Md 3 Jan 1871
VanBUSKIRK, Lizzie of Gray and Asa G. Place of Windham
    PUB. 6 Mar. 1884, Md 12 Mar. 1884
VanBUSKIRK, Genie of Gray and William T. McDonald of
    Standish Md. 29 Nov. 1886
VARNEY, John see Frank, Jaob
VARNEY, Charles see Thompson, Mary
VARNEY, Lillian see Pollard, Ira
VARNEY, Walter see Sayward, Kate
VARNEY, Beatrice see Sayward, Carroll
VARNEY, Susan see Elder, Merrill
VARRILL, John see Hodkins, Molley
VELIOURE, Mary see Latham, Fred
VERRILL, Sarah see May, Jeremiah
VERRILL, Hannah see May, John
VERRILL, Charles H. and Agnes Grant both of Westbrook Md
    1 Jan. 1861
VERRILL, Offie see Merrill, Fred
VERRILL, Herbert see Thompson, Alice

VERRILL, Eunice see Thurlow, David
VERRILL, Wardsworth of Gray and Lucinda Russell of
    Cumberland PUB. 30 Mar. 1881, Md 10 Apr. 1881
VERRILL, Lydia see Plummer, Henry
VERRILL, James M. of Gray and Cora E. Berry of New Gloucester
    Md. 12 Aug. 1882
VERRILL, Charles see Day, Carrie
VERRILL, Howard see Libby, Jennie
VERRILL, Joseph of New Gloucester and Hattie Hodgkin of
    Raymond Md. 14 Feb. 1884
VERRILL, Charles see Hodgkins, Cora
VERRILL, Herbert A. of Gray and Lydia A. Huff of Yarmouth Md
    22 Feb. 1890
VERRILL, Ami of Gray and Margaret Mulcurn of Poland Md
    23 Mar. 1891
VERRILL, Victoria see Thompson, Eben
VERRILL, Phoebe see Verrill, Freedom
VERRILL, Dwinal see Strout, Maria
VERRILL, Ransom G. of Gray and Effie Hellen of New Gloucester
    Md. 24 Mar. 1896 p.19
VERRILL, Lewis M. of Gray and Anna O. Verrill of Poland Md
    3 Apr. 1899 p.27
VERRILL, Anna O. see Verrill, Lewis M.
VERRILL, Xena see Humphrey, George
VERRILL, Vergil G. of Gray and Etta M. Brett of Auburn Md
    25 Nov. 1903 in Auburn p.45
VERRILL, Rosetta of Gray and Charles E. Sayward of Windham
    Md. 2 May 1904 in Windham p.45
VERRILL, Villa see Goff, George
VERRILL, Nellie see Tripp, Fred
VERRILL, Jennie M. S. of Gray and William O. Porter of
    Cumberland Md. 17 Nov. 1906 p.59
VERRILL, Rosetta see Bragdon, Gilbert
VERRILL, Nathaniel see Thompson, Emma
VERRILL, Clark L. of Gray and Bessie M. Robinson of Casco Md
    18 July 1908 p.67
VERRILL, Charles L. of Gray and Eliza E. McGowan of Portland
    Md. 23 Nov. 1910 p.77

VERRILL, John see McGowen, Eva

VERRILL, Harlan E. of Gray and Mildred M. Edwards of No. Windham Md. 17 Aug. 1912 p.83

VERRILL, George see Hodgkins, Annie

VERRILL, Sadie see Barker, Herbert

VERRILL, Lillian B. of Gray and Harold C. Fosset of Portland Md 6 Apr. 1914 in Portland p.91

VERRILL, George G. of Gray and Fannie M. Jackson of New York City, N.Y. Md 28 Nov. 1918 p.113

VERRILL, Ernest C. of Gray and Eva I. Edwards of Raymond Md 25 June 1919 in Auburn p.117

VERRILL, Ruth of Gray and Albert J. Larrabee of Gorham Md 19 Oct. 1920 p.123

VERRILL, Albert N. of Gray and Ruth N. Woodman of Yarmouth Md. 4 Feb. 1921 in Yarmouth p.129

VERRILL, Milton E. and Eda Morrill Md 19 May 1922 p.131

VERRILL, Merritt of Raymond and Angie M. Rowe of New Gloucester Md. 13 Sept. 1922 p.133

VERRILL, Myrtle see Brewer, Ralph

VERRILL, Henry see Strout, Alfreda

VERRILL, Eliza see Colley, Richard

VERRILL, Charles H. and Agnes Grant both of Westbrook Md 1 Jan. 1861

VERRILL, Margaret see Farwell, John

VERRILL, Olive see Farwell, Joseph

VERRILL, Lucy of Gray and Nathan Lord of Windham Md 18 May 1865

VERRILL, Joseph of New Gloucester and Hattie Hodgkin of Raymond Md. 14 Feb. 1884

VERRILL, Charles see Hodgkins, Cora

VERRILL, James see Gowen, Cora

VERRILL, John see Frank, Hannah

VERRILL, Eunice and William H. Witham both of Gray PUB. 3 June 1880, Md. 12 June 1880

VERRILL, Lewis and M. Ella Witham both of Gray PUB. 27 Sept. 1880, Md 7 Oct. 1880

VICKERY, Nathaniel see Hill, Jane

VINTON, Clara see Hunt, Lee

VINTON, William see Berry, Martha

VINTON, Georgia see Thurlow, Fred L.

VINTON, William see Thompson, Alice

WAGNER, James see Tripp, Pamela

WAKEFIELD, John of Gray and Susan Weeks of Falmouth PUB.
    15 Jan. 1826 p.244

WAKEFIELD, Nancy of Gray and Peter Gowen of Westbrook
    PUB. 2 Sept. 1827 p.249, Md 21 Oct. 1827 p.252

WAKEFIELD, Addie see Lunt, Neal

WALKER, Fred S. of Scarboro and Alice M. Plummer of
    Raymond Md. 23 Oct. 1890

WALKER, Alfred B. and Florina M. Cobb both of Portland Md
    25 Nov. 1914 p.93

WALKER, William see Geer, Theresa

WALKER, Mary A. of Gray and Randall Mayberry of Standish Md
    16 Dec. 1864

WALKER, Michael of Gray and Mary Brackett of Gorham PUB.
    2 Feb. 1839

WALLACE, Hester see Richards, Orin

WARD, John see Russell, Mary

WARREN, Joseph W. of Standish and Hannah Lamb of Windham
    Md. 1 Jan. 1872

WARREN, William of Gray and Ella Morey of New Gloucester
    Md. 25 Apr. 1883

WATERHOUSE, Freeman and Julia Ann Whitney both of Gray
    PUB. 20 Aug. 1832 p.271, Md Aug. 1832 p.270

WATERHOUSE, Julia A. of Gray and Thomas Carey of Oxford
    PUB. 4 May 1839

WATERMAN, Annah see Anderson, Abraham

WATERMAN, Herbert see McConkey, Thirza

WATERS, Isaac see Libby, Sarah

WATKINS, Eugene R. of Casco and Georgie E. Fairbanks of
    Raymond Md. 26 Oct. 1884

WATSON, Samuel see Morrill, Susanna

WATSON, Elisabeth see Doughty, Elias

WATSON, Benjamin see Starbird, Caroline

WATSON, Lucy see Barbour, Robert

WATSON, Mary see Brown, Oliver

WATSON, Annie see Pennell, Edgar

WAY, Fannie see Hunt, George

WAY, Henry W. of Gray and Josephine E. McElroy of Somerville,
    Mass. Md. 23 Nov. 1930 p.177

WEBB, Lindley see Cobb, Clara

WEBB, John see Whitney, Hattie

WEBB, Roy see Sawyer, Hattie

WEBB, Harriet H. of Gray and Azel W. Faunce of Portland Md
    17 July 1926 in Auburn p.153

WEBB, Iva see Ellinwood, George

WEBBER, John, see Allen, Experience

WEBBER, Margaret see Field, Ulysses

WEBBER, Mary see Field, Edward

WEBBER, Jennie of Gray and Elwin H. Stone of Windham Md
    10 Sept. 1922 p.133

WEBBER, John see Allen, Experience

WEBSTER, Polly see Orne, David

WEBSTER, Jeams see Clark, Jenney

WEBSTER, Joseph of Gray and Mary Stackpole of Durham
    25 Dec. 1806   p.182

WEBSTER, Simon of Gray and Mary Megguire of New Gloucester
    12 Apr. 1812 p.199

WEBSTER, Jane see Maxwell, Ebenzer

WEBSTER, Whitley see Merrill, Mary

WEBSTER, John see Ford, Deborah

WEBSTER, Patience see Farr, John

WEBSTER, Whitley see Merrill, Rebecca

WEBSTER, Simon see Fowler, Isabel

WEBSTER, William and Mary Ann Grant PUB. 6 Nov. 1831 p.268

WEBSTER, William see Barbour, Martha

WEBSTER, Thomas and Sarah E. Webster both of Gray Md
    17 Sept. 1861

WEBSTER, Sarah see Webster, Thomas

WEBSTER, Sarah see Dolloff, James

WEBSTER, Charles see Small, Sarah

WEBSTER, Belle see Goff, Walter

WEBSTER, Frank see Allen, Nellie

WEBSTER, Grace see Morrill, George

WEBSTER, Lucy E. of Gray and Herbert N. Willey of Poland Md
    22 Apr. 1907 p.59

WEBSTER, Harriet B. of Gray and Arthur G. Whittaker of Bar
    Mills Md. 1 Mar. 1917 in Buxton p.103

WEBSTER, Joseph see Dow, Hettie

WEBSTER, Simon and Bertha A. Tripp both of Gray Md 7 June
    1924 p.143

WEBSTER, Bertha see Sayward, Carroll

WEBSTER, Marguerite see Leavitt, Keith

WEBSTER, Simon of Gray and Sarah E. Sawyer of Danville Md
    31 Jan. 1858

WEBSTER, Mary see Small, Almer

WEBSTER, William see Barbour, Martha

WEBSTER, Thomas and Sarah E. Webster both of Gray Md
    17 Sept. 1861

WEBSTER, Sarah see Webster, Thomas

WEBSTER, James D. S. of Gray and Jane Moore of Limington
    PUB. 15 Dec. 1837

WEBSTER, Charles see Hall, Rachel

WEBSTER, Henry S. of Gray and Charlotte Elwell of Oxford
    PUB. 16 Oct. 1842

WEBSTER, James and Ellen D. Purvis both of Gray PUB. 9 June
    1850

WEBSTER, Royal F. of Gray and Olive Emery of Limington PUB.
    29 Oct. 1843

WEEKS, Gardner see Freeman, Narcissa

WEEKS, Joseph of Gray and Sarah Morse of Falmouth pub. 1 May
    1779; 15 May 1779

WEEKS, Susanna of Gray and Jonathan Sanders of Norway 5 Feb.
    1802   p.169

WEEKS, Betsey see Jordan, Calvin

WEEKS, Hannah see Russell, John

WEEKS, Sally see Bennett, William

WEEKS, Isaac see Morse, Mary

WEEKS, Benjamin see Hunt, Hannah

WEEKS, Anne of Gray and William Hamilton of North Yarmouth
    PUB. 20 May 1819 p.219, Md. 8 July 1819 p.224

WEEKS, Benjamin of Gray and Rachel Megguier of New
    Gloucester PUB. 10 Apr. 1824 p. 236

WEEKS, Susan see Wakefield, John

WEEKS, Gardner see Freeman, Narcissa

WELCH, Elizabeth see Libby, Seth

WELCH, Susan of Gray and Joseph Starling of Monhegan PUB.
    8 Sept. 1822 p.231

WELCH, Cora see Hewey, Robert

WELCH, Thomas H. and Olivia W. Farrar both of Yarmouth Md
11 Oct. 1879

WELCH, Rebecca see Blake, Ozias

WELCH, Charles see Shaw, Florence

WELCH, Almeda see Hodgkins, Jonas

WELCH, Nellie see Low, Winfield

WELLS, Cora see Leach, Bela

WELLS, Caroline see Morse, Cyrus

WENTWORTH, William H. and Angie B. Mayberry both of
Westbrook Md. 28 July 1900 p.31

WENTWORTH, Leland see Skilling, Eleanor

WENTWORTH, Sarah of Gray and Alvin Frank of Windham Md
28 May 1865

WESCOTT, John see Humphrey, Charity

WESCOTT, Paul W. and Annie M. Pennell both of Portland Md
11 Sept. 1895 p.15

WESCOTT, Marion see Barker, Philip

WEST, Jenney see Plummer, Elish

WESTON, Mary see Pennell, Henry

WESTON, Augusta see Humphrey, Henry

WEYMOUTH, Eleanor see Colley, John

WEYMOUTH, James see Libby, Eunice

WEYMOUTH, John see Staples, Miriam

WEYMOUTH, Comfort see Libby, Isaac

WEYMOUTH, Timothy of Gray and Mary Merrill of Falmouth
PUB. 30 Jan. 1825 p.237

WEYMOUTH, Martha see Libby, David

WEYMOUTH, Burton D. and Dora E. Plummer both of New
Gloucester Md. 29 June 1889

WEYMOUTH, Nellie see Small, John

WEYMOUTH, Mary E. and Joshua Witham both of Gray Md
22 Apr. 1880

WEYMOUTH, Viola see Barton, Philip

WEYMOUTH, John M. and Edith M. Andrews both of New
Gloucester Md. 2 June 1920 p.121

WEYMOUTH, Capt. T.H. see Humphrey, M.W.

WEYMOUTH, Eunice N. and Wm. Moore of Hebron PUB. 4 Sept.
1844 p.294

WHITE, Mary and Robert York PUB. 18 May 1781; 4 June 1781

WHITE, Deidamia see Hayden, Richard
WHITE, Rebecca see Pray, Edmond
WHITE, Harriet see Dickey, William
WHITE, Nellie see Libby, James
WHITE, Willard F. and Lillian E. Ritchie both of New Gloucester
    Md. 14 July 1924 p.145
WHITE, John see Allen, Harriet
WHITE, Charles see Anderson, Hannah
WHITE, Lucretia see Dutton, Seth
WHITEHEAD, George and Rosa P. Hamilton both of Westbrook
    Md. 27 Dec. 1884
WHITMARSH, Thomas see Dolley, Mary
WHITNEY, William see Frank, Sally
WHITNEY, Andrew see Sweetser, Huldah
WHITNEY, James see Mountford, Lucy
WHITNEY, Amos N. of Gray and Mary M Jones of Falmouth
    PUB. 2 Sept. 1827 p.249
WHITNEY, Julia see Waterhouse, Freeman
WHITNEY, Zachariah see Hayden, Elizabeth
WHITNEY, Peter see Foster, Mary
WHITNEY, Abbie see Blake, Ozias
WHITNEY, Thomas see Campbell, Emma
WHITNEY, James see Foster, Flora
WHITNEY, Ellen E. of Gray and Robert M. Leighton of
    Cumberland PUB. 1 Dec. 1876, Md 17 Dec. 1876
WHITNEY, Hattie M. of Gray and John F. Webb of Windham
    PUB. 17 Dec. 1878, Md 25 Dec. 1878
WHITNEY, Lizzie see Dunn, Walter
WHITNEY, Georgianna see Fields, George
WHITNEY, Orin see Libby, Ida
WHITNEY, Melvin see Bunker, Addie
WHITNEY, Emma see Mountfort, Joseph
WHITNEY, Thankful see Smith, James
WHITNEY, Lenora of Gray and Willard B. Sweetser of No.
    Yarmouth Md. 27 Mar. 1895 p.15
WHITNEY, Carrie T. of Gray and Percy H. Loring of No.
    Yarmouth Md. 28 July 1895 p.15 in No. Yarmouth
WHITNEY, Bertha of Gray and Randall B. Morrill of Raymond
    Md. 28 Apr. 1897 p.21

WHITNEY, Cora M. of Gray and Howard B. Clough of
    Cumberland Md. 26 Apr. 1899 p.27
WHITNEY, Wilbert see Ramsdell, Ella
WHITNEY, Lucy see Sawyer, Hannibal
WHITNEY, Anna see Haskell, George
WHITNEY, Ethel M. of Gray and Guy E. Foye of Windham Md 28
    June 1915 in Windham p.95
WHITNEY, Fred see Colley, Reina
WHITNEY, Thomas see Brooks, Rosezella
WHITNEY, Earl L. of Gray and Margaret E. McIntosh of Lisbon
    Falls Md. 8 June 1917 in Westbrook p.105
WHITNEY, Roland see Sawyer, Eva
WHITNEY, Orin see Libby, Ida
WHITNEY, Melvin see Bunker, Addie
WHITNEY, Lewis W. of Gray and Annie M. Leighton of
    Cumberland PUB. 15 Dec. 1885 Md. 23 Dec. 1885
WHITNEY, Celia see Doughty George R.
WHITNEY, Aurelia see Humphrey, Hiram
WHITNEY, Elmira see Mountfort, John
WHITNEY, Amanda see Lawrence, David
WHITNEY, Julia see Small, Ai M.
WHITTAKER, Arthur see Webster, Harriet
WHITTEN, Eunice see Allen, Andrew
WHITTEN, Bradbury see Frothingham, Eliza
WIGHT, Nathan see Lane, Cyrene
WIGHT, Horace see Morse, Delia
WILCOX, Grace see McCalmon, Edwin
WILEY, Daniel E. and Martha I. Johnson both of Gorham Md
    22 June 1861
WILKINS, Francis see Knight, Emily
WILLEY, Herbert see Webster, Lucy
WILLIAMSON, Charles see Thayer, Ruth
WILSON, Sarah see Nason, Isaac
WILSON, Lucy and James Yeaton PUB. 30 July 1791 p.126
WILSON, Joanna see Starbird, Henry
WILSON, Almira see Low, William
WILSON, Joseph see Ramsdell, Sally
WILSON, Mary see Doughty, Benj.
WILSON, Cornelius and Julia C. Wilson both of Cumberland Md
    17 June 1860

WILSON, Edgar N. of Cumberland and Ella S. Stuart of Windham
        Md. 11 May 1889
WILSON, Lorenzo H. and Sarah F. Morrison both of Cumberland
        Md. 15 Jan. 1880
WILSON, Frank H. and Carrie E. Harding both of Cumberland Md
        21 Mar. 1880
WILSON, Carl A. see Dunn, Alma
WILSON, Ruby see Merrill, George
WILSON, Roderick P. and Frances Emery both of Cumberland Md
        10 Feb. 1928 p.161
WILSON, Floyd S. of Brunswick and Gladys E. Tubbs of Portland
        Md. 29 Sept. 1928 p.165
WILSON, Salmon see Grant, Paulina
WILSON, John see Goff, Sarah
WILSON, Cornelius and Julia C. Wilson both of Cumberland Md
        17 June 1860
WILSON, Lynn of Gray and Jane Emery of Gorham PUB. 18 June
        1837
WILSON, Olive see Starbird, Elroy
WING, Thomas see Tripp, Cordelia
WING, Roxie see Thurlow, Charles H.
WING, Frederick H. of Gray and Costella B. Ryerson of Pownal
        Md. 16 Mar 1926 in Portland p.151
WING, Louise G. of Gray and Raymond P. Peterson of
        Cumberland Md. 21 May 1926 p.151
WING, Everett J. of Gray and Myra E. Chadborne of No.
        Yarmouth Md. 15 Nov. 1926 in Portland p.155
WINSLOW, Lyman Jr. and Eunice M. Hodgkins both of New
        Gloucester Md. 4 Feb. 1898 in No. Raymond p.25
WINTER, Stephen see Humphrey, Hannah
WITHAM, A.R.P. See Barbour, Emma
WITHAM, Joshua see Weymouth, Mary
WITHAM, William see Verrill, Eunice
WITHAM, Ella see Verrill, Lewis
WITHAM, Otis see Symonds, Martha
WITHAM, Orrin see Farwell, Elizabeth
WITHAM, Hattie E. of Gray and Arthur W. Sharp of No.
        Yarmouth Md. 26 Oct. 1904 in No. Yarmouth p.47
WITHAM, Frank E. of Gray and Perley C. Mains of Windham Md
        12 Dec. 1905 p.53

WITHAM, Ada P. of Gray and Sumner P. Perley of No. Yarmouth
    Md. 10 June 1908 p.65
WITHAM, Elizabeth see Nickerson, George
WITHAM, Stanley see Irving, Annie
WITHAM, Eleanor see Sawyer, Arthur
WITHAM, John see Thompson, Cora
WOODBURY, James see Libby, Julia
WOODBURY, John see Colley, Hattie
WOODBURY, William see Libby, Ellen
WOODMAN, Ruth see Verrill, Albert
WOODSOM, Deborah see Marston, Andrew
WREN, Mary see Frank, Joseph
WRIGHT, George see Benson, Hannah
YEATON, James see Wilson, Lucy
YORK, Charles, see Tibbetts, Ann
YORK, Robert see White Mary
YORK, Joseph see Cummings, Abigail
YORK, Ella see Blake, Frank
YORK, Charles see Tibbets, Sarah
YOUNG, Abraham see Cummings, Susanna
YOUNG, Mary see Libby, Joseph
YOUNG, John see Starbird, Elizabeth
YOUNG, Lydia see Hayden, Jonathan
YOUNG, Sarah of Gray and Elisha Allen seaman 30 Dec. 1794
    p.152
YOUNG, Samuel see Libby, Sarah
YOUNG, Joshua see Tinney, Mary
YOUNG, Annie see Blake, Elias
YOUNG, Lydia see Cook, Robert
YOUNG, Hannah see Elwell, William
YOUNG, Nathaniel and Betsey -------- both of Gray   PUB. 13 June
    1813 p.200
YOUNG, Sarah see Humphrey, John
YOUNG, Daniel see Purvis, Betsy
YOUNG, Abraham see Purvis, Susanna
YOUNG, Samuel see Pennell, Mary
YOUNG, Anna see Titcomb, Jeremiah
YOUNG, Abraham of Gray and Rebecca Holmes of Paris PUB.
    22 Feb. 1824 p.234
YOUNG, Elisha see Titcomb, Charity

YOUNG, Jesse see Babb, Eunice

YOUNG, Daniel of Gray and Sarah Plummer of Waterford PUB. 21 Jan. 1827 p.246

YOUNG, Nathaniel of Gray and Hannah Plummer of Waterford PUB. 2 Mar. 1828 p.250

YOUNG, Frances see Lane, Charles

YOUNG, Bridget see Campbell, Alfred

YOUNG, Jane see Shaw, Nicholas

YOUNG, Ketturah see Foster, Jacob

YOUNG, Bertha see Strout, Charles

YOUNG, Mamie see Tripp, William

YOUNG, Calvin see Small, Martha

DEATHS

ADAMS, Jessie 18 Mar. 1898; Gray
ADAMS, John Smith 8 Sept. 1905; Gray
ADAMS, Sarah 20 Feb. 1893; Gray
ADAMS, Sarah H. 8 Feb. 1894; Windham
ADAMS, Silas L. 9 July 1898; Gray
ADAMS, Thomas H. 22 Mar. 1877
ALDEN, Alton R. 18 Nov. 1918; Canada
ALLEN, Andrew 3 Dec. 1894; Gray
ALLEN, Charles E. 30 Mar. 1921; Gray
ALLEN, Clarence E. 30 Nov. 1925; not listed
ALLEN, Cynthia J. 27 Jan. 1900; Gray
ALLEN, Emery 5 Mar. 1895; Windham
ALLEN, Eunice W. 16 Feb. 1912; Gray
ALLEN, George P. 11 Nov. 1924; Gray
ALLEN, Ida Emma 20 Apr. 1930; Cumberland
ALLEN, Jennie O. 23 Sept. 1928; P.E.I. Canada
ALLEN, John H.16 July 1894; Gray
ALLEN, Josiah W. 6 June 1930; Gray
ALLEN, Lizzie 8 Aug. 1865
ALLEN, Minnie I. 19 Sept. 1902; Cumberland
ALLEN, Mrs. Andrew 28 Feb. 1877
ALLEN, Robert Adams 6 Mar. 1904; Gray
ALLEN, Sarah E. 18 Mar. 1909; Gray
ALLEN, George S. 9 Sept. 1895; Augusta
ANDERSON, A. W. 24 Mar. 1876
ANDERSON, John D. 29 Sept.1924; Gray
ANDERSON, Kate A. Leslie 7 July 1907; Gray
ANDERSON, Susan M. 1 Sept. 1914; Gray
ANDERSON, Willis 21 July 1905; Niagara Falls, N.Y.
ANDREWS, Anson M. 2 Oct. 1926; Gray
ANDREWS, Emily C. M. 8 Jan. 1894; Readfield
ANDREWS, Margaret 12 May 1899; St. David, N.B., Canada
AUSTIN, Arthur D. 9 Apr. 1901; Kansas
BACHELDER, Amos 16 July 1898; Nova Scotia, Canada
BAILEY, Dura L. 26 Dec. 1898; Minot
BAILEY, George Allen 23 Oct. 1908; Gray
BAILEY, Jane 18 Jan. 1920; Gray
BAILEY, Joel S. 7 Nov.1907; Gray
BAILEY, Mary E. 26 Dec. 1903; Gray
BAILEY, Sarah A. 4 Dec. 1905; Gray

BAKER, Eugene 17 Mar. 1929; Windham
BAKER, Huldah 1874-75
BALDWIN, Charles A. 2 June 1916; Charlestown, Mass.
BARBERICK, Theophilus 11 Mar. 1906; Boston, Mass.
BARBOUR, Emerson S. 21 Dec. 1897; Gray
BARBOUR, Emma M. 20 Aug. 1897; Portland
BARNEY, Rosey 29 Nov. 1902; Canada
BARROWS, Margaret P. 28 May 1910; Spy Harbor, N.S.
BARTON, Mary H. 14 Feb. 1923; Gray
BEASLEY, Infant of, Percy 11 June 1917; Gray
BEATTY, William 17 July 1901; Manchester, England
BENSON, George W. 27 Feb. 1914; Gray
BENSON, Hannah E. 31 July 1893; Gray
BENSON, Major 30 Jan. 1929; Gray
BENSON, Maria A. 22 Aug. 1915; Raymond
BENSON, Woodbury 7 Jan. 1910; Gray
BENSON, Zilpha 29 Feb. 1892; Gray
BERRY, Eunice 14 June 1878
BERRY, George Freeland 27May 1930; Poland
BERRY, Laura S. 7 Apr. 1909; Gray
BERRY, Louisa 2 Jan. 1877
BERRY, Lucinda 23 May 1898; Gray
BERRY, Melbourn H. 24 Nov. 1930; Buxton
BERRY, Wilson P. 6 Sept. 1899
BICKFORD, G. Earl 7 Sept. 1893; Sabattus
BLACK, Gorge F. 5 Dec. 1909; Gray
BLAKE, Abbie E. 17 Oct. 1899; Gray
BLAKE, Daniel H. 1874-75
BLAKE, Ozia 11 Aug. 1892; Gorham
BLAKE, Thomas 25 Jan. 1900; Brownfield
BOHNSEN, Albert N. 17 Oct. 1899; Cumberland
BOHNSEN, Ellen M. 2 Feb. 1930; Denmark, Europe
BOHNSEN, Peter C. 11 Mar. 1901; Denmark, Me ?
BOWIE, Etta 22 Sept.1903; No. Windham
BRACKETT, Alice E. 17 June 1909; Cambridge, Mass
BRACKETT, Lewis E. 17 Feb. 1898; Gray
BRACKETT, Louise 21 Feb. 1898; Gray
BRAGG, Edward E. Jr. 14 Aug. 1921; unknown
BREEN, John 24 May 1920 Portland
BRIGGS, Naomi E. 10 Dec. 1912; Paris

BROOKS, Christiana 26 June 1876
BROOKS, Samuel N. 2 Apr. 1895; Woodstock
BROWN, Clara 15 Nov. 1878
BROWN, Elizabeth M. 15 Oct. 1929; Augusta
BROWN, Harriett A. 4 Oct. 1922; Kennebunk
BROWN, Lina A. 25 Oct.1900; Readfield, Me
BROWN, infant of Frank, 0 days 30 Oct. 1916; Gray
BURLEIGH, Mary S. 21 Feb. 1904; Gray
BURNS, Clifford M. 12 Aug. 1897 Gray
BURROWS, Edward M. 9 Mar. 1918 Brewer
BURROWS, Julie E. 31 Oct. 1922 Falmouth
CAMBELL, Alfred 14 May 1923 Scotland
CAMPBELL, Charlotte 5 May 1906 Prince Edward Is. Canada
CARY, Albert T. 6 June 1927 Gray
CARY, Bina 9 Mar. 1917 Scarboro
CASWELL, Charlotte B. 16 Jan. 1900 Gray
CASWELL, Edgar S. 5 Dec. 1925 Gray
CHAMBERLAIN, Susan M. 28 Oct. 1905 Boston, Mass.
CHIPMAN, Ella A. 30 Mar. 1920 Poland
CHIPMAN, William A. 1 Aug. 1926 Poland
CHURCHILL, Demerit 27 Feb. 1903 Poland
CLARK, Amie F. 22 Aug. 1904 Gray
CLARK, Jennie 17 Jan. 1908 Monmouth
CLARK, Lucetta 30 Aug. 1898 Gray
COBB, Annie M. 19 Jan. 1905 Gray
COBB, Chipman 4 Sept. 1900 Otisfield
COBB, Clara Apr. 1878
COBB, Daniel Sylvester 11 Jan. 1919 Falmouth
COBB, Eliza J. 20 Apr. 1903 Gray
COBB, George F. 20 Dec. 1895 Westbrook
COBB, Gladys M. 25 Sept.1903 Gray
COBB, Laura 20 Feb. 1901 Freeport
COBB, Lucinda A. 8 Oct. 1910 Gray
COBB, Mabel 8 Oct. 1903 Gray
COBB, Mary M. 19 Mar. 1914 Waterboro
COBB, Rosabelle 14 July 1899 Poland
COBB, Rosilla 18 June 1904 Gray
COBB, Rotheas O. 2 Aug. 1902 Falmouth
COBB, Ruben S. 6 Mar. 1902 Gray
COBB, Sylvester B. 30 Apr. 1919 Gray

COBB, William H. 2 June 1864
COBB, William H. 18 June 1896
COFFIN, Abigail M. 19 July 1892 New Gloucester
COFFIN, Jane G. 3 Mar. 1916 Ireland
COFFIN, Martha A. 12 Feb. 1907 Gray
COFFIN, Silas A. 5 Mar. 1916 Freeport
COLE, Elizabeth A. 26 July 1913 Cumberland
COLE, Leonard C. 9 Jan. 1909 Gray
COLLEY, ? 26 Oct. 1878
COLLEY, Dora L. 19 July 1924 Chelsea
COLLEY, Eliza J. 29 Feb. 1908 New Gloucester
COLLEY, Helen A. Feb. 1879
COLLEY, James H. 28 Feb. 1915 Gray
COLLEY, Lottie H. 24 Jan. 1879
COLLEY, Lucy E. 11 Feb. 1929 Gray
COLLEY, Martha S. 29 May 1878
COLLEY, Nancy 19 Nov. 1893 Hartford
COLLEY, Amos 11 May 1899 Gray
COLLEY, Infant of True M., prem. Birth 11 Feb. 1920 unknown
COLLEY, Richard 13 Feb. 1922 Gray
COOLBOURGH, Edwin 5 Dec. 1918 Allentown, Pa.
CORSON, Albert 8 Dec. 1922 Raymond, NH
CORSON, Henrietta 11 Feb. 1915 Yarmouth
COTE, Omer W. 8 Sept. 1913 Gray
COTTON, infant of, Albert 2 June 1926 Gray
COWDREY, Abbie A. 17 Oct. 1899 Rumford
CRECY, Walter 25 Aug. 1896 Gray
CROCKETT, Lucy 1875-76
CROOKER, Nathaniel 4 Apr. 1864
CROSBY, Julie E. 1 Aug. 1923 Whiting
CROSS, Cornelia R. 15 Oct. 1897 Falmouth
CROWELL, L. Maj. 12 Dec. 1893 Nova Scotia, Canada
CUMMINGS, Eliza I. 11 Oct. 1865
CUMMINGS, Leonard F. 10 June 1876
CUMMINGS, Martha 26 Oct. 1876
CUMMINGS, Samuel 20 Nov. 1899 Gray
CUMMINGS, Samuel M. 5 May 1906 Porter
DAVIS, Augusta 25 Sept. 1907 Gray
DAVIS, Benjamin 13 July 1907 Poland
DAVIS, Emily Elizah 14 Jan. 1923 London, England

DAVIS, George W. 10 Mar. 1918 Gray
DAVIS, Joseph E. 21 Oct. 1897 Falmouth
DAVIS, William 26 June 1913 Wales, Great Britain
DOLE, Annie V. 1 Jan. 1930 Auburn
DOLE, James R. 22 Aug. 1897 Gray
DOLE, John T. 15 Sept. 1927 Portland
DOLE, Willard W. Oct. 1878
DOLLEY, Daniel H. 17 May 1904 Gray
DOLLEY, Eliza 1874-75
DOLLEY, George 19 Feb. 1921 Mexico
DOLLEY, Thirza 20 Sept. 1894 Gray
DOLLOFF, Albert W. 23 Apr. 1896 Paris
DOLLOFF, Dorothy I. 15 June 1925 Gray
DOLLOFF, Robert E. 9 Nov. 1916 Gray
DOLLOFF, Sarah A. 18 Sept. 1910 Windham
DOTEN, Persis R. 6 Dec.1927 Minot
DOUGHTY, Albert H. 19 Dec. 1924 Gray
DOUGHTY, Alvin S. 11 Nov. 1928 Gray
DOUGHTY, Amy G. 6 May 1898 Gray
DOUGHTY, Bathsheba 5 Mar. 1892 Turner
DOUGHTY, Catherine L. 22 Jan. 1907 Scarbourgh
DOUGHTY, Cellia E.W. 21 May 1916 Gray
DOUGHTY, Charles H. 14 June 1925 Windham
DOUGHTY, Daniel A. 19 Nov. 1895 Gray
DOUGHTY, Emily J.S.F. 27 Sept. 1901 Gray
DOUGHTY, Enoch M. 14 Apr. 1897 Gray
DOUGHTY, George W. 3 Dec. 1897 Gray
DOUGHTY, George W. 28 May 1900 Gray
DOUGHTY, Hannah F. 21 Sept. 1881
DOUGHTY, Henry P. 9 Apr. 1922 Gray
DOUGHTY, James 7 Nov. 1895 Gray
DOUGHTY, John R. 26 Nov. 1912 Gray
DOUGHTY, Olive 25 May 1929 Poland
DOUGHTY, Sarah 2 Oct. 1907 Gray
DOUGHTY, Sarah A. 22 Jan 1901 Gray
DOUGHTY, William E. 4 Nov. 1926 Gray
DOUGLASS, Leander M. 23 Sept. 1908 Gray
DOUGLASS, Mary E. 7 Mar. 1914 Poland
DOW, Greenleaf G. 27 Sept. 1920 Woodstock
DOW, Martha M. 9 Aug. 1911 not known

DOW, Mehitable T. 10 Jan. 1913 Gray
DOW, William H. 17 Oct. 1924 Lewiston
DOW, William M. 20 Feb. 1902 Sumner
DREW, Maurice M. 6 June 1928 Vinalhaven
DUFF, Sophronia A. 12 Nov. 1917 West Falmouth
DUNN, Caroline B. 1 Sept. 1906 Buxton
DUNN, Elizabeth F. 30 June 1909 Gray
DUNN, Mary C. 15 Jan. 1902 Gray
DUTTON, Betsey J. 25 Apr. 1874
DUTTON, Emeline L. 7 Sept. 1923 Windham
DUTTON, Thomas 17 Jan. 1866
EDGECOMB, John E. 6 July 1928 Biddeford
EDWARDS, Addie J. 14 Dec. 1920 Rockland
EDWARDS, Ephraim 26 Sept. 1902 Poland
EDWARDS, Mary A. 4 Apr. 1876
EDWARDS, Sewall 12 Mar. 1876
ELDER, William 10 Jan. 1899 Gray
ELDRIDGE, William H. 17 Sept. 1920 Wells
ELLINWOOD, Harriet M. 12 Aug. 1914 Munro
ELLINWOOD, Helen M. 8 Feb. 1898 Williston, VT.
ELLINWOOD, Ralph 14 Aug. 1910 Thorndike
ELLINWOOD, George A. 3 Apr. 1930 Thorndike
ELLINWOOD, infant, Geo.A. stillborn 23 June 1929
EMERY, Albert Leroy 25 Oct. 1929 Portland
ESTES, William S. 5 Jan. 1903 Poland
EVANS, Henry M. 13 Oct. 1913 Gray
EVELETH, Emeline 4 May 1900 Gray
EVERETT, Eliza E. 6 June 1930 Falmouth
FAIRWEATHER, Carrol C. 5 July 1924 Portland
FARRINGTON, Mary 1874-75
FARWELL, Joseph 26 Sept. 1895 Limington
FARWELL, Martha A. 26 May 1894 Limington
FARWELL, Olive 3 Jan. 1910 Ripley
FARWELL, Samuel S. 4 Sept. 1895 Portland
FAVOR, Charles H. 18 Sept. 1922 Bennington, NH
FERGUSON, Anna 16 Mar. 1892 Gray
FIELD, Addie E. 21 June 1897 No. Raymond
FIELD, Callie A. 14 Apr. 1909 Gray
FIELD, Charles A. 25 June 1913 New Gloucester
FIELD, Edward E. 23 May 1917 Gray

FIELD, Edward J. 18 Apr. 1914 Windham
FIELD, Edwin L. 21 June 1916 Falmouth
FIELD, Frank L. 24 June 1897 Raymond
FIELD, Hyman W. 1874-75
FIELD, Jennie G. 3 Nov. 1907 Gray
FIELD, Margaret E. 31 May 1896 Portland
FIELD, Wendall 8 Feb. 1900 Gray
FIELD, infant of Edward E., one hour 27 Apr. 1914 Gray
FLAGG, Ronollo 23 Nov. 1913 Mexico
FLING, Betsey M. 6 Feb. 1912 Gray
FOGG, Ai S. 17 Oct. 1893 Limerick
FOGG, Charles F. 2 Dec. 1925 Gray
FOGG, Sarah E. 30 Dec. 1903 Searsmont
FOGG, Scammon 10 Apr. 1899 Gray
FORTANE, Caroline E. 12 May 1892 Londonderry, N.S., Canada
FORTIN, Anthony 9 Jan. 1929 Fort Kent
FORTUNE, William A. 26 July 1920 Nova Scotia
FOSTER, Alice J. 10 June 1893 Gray
FOSTER, Angie B. 15 Sept. 1923 Paris
FOSTER, Ann H. 4 Mar. 1897 Gray
FOSTER, Caroline M. 3 Apr. 1894 Gray
FOSTER, Clarence M. 3 Feb. 1897 Gray
FOSTER, Daniel A. 21 Nov. 1922   Gray
FOSTER, Edna F. 7 Sept. 1929 Danville
FOSTER, Eliza A. 8 Feb. 1892 Gray
FOSTER, Elizabeth D. 13 Aug. 1911 Gray
FOSTER, Elwood G. 29 Aug. 1897 Gray
FOSTER, Eunice R. 28 June 1894 Gray
FOSTER, Horace C. 3 June 1917 Gray
FOSTER, Jacob 11 Feb.1918 Gray
FOSTER, James N. 2 May 1901 Gray
FOSTER, John 13 July 1896
FOSTER, Jonathan R. 3 Jan. 1897 Gray
FOSTER, Justice S. 24 Sept. 1864
FOSTER, Lena M. 25 Mar. 1894 Gray
FOSTER, Margaret E. 22 June 1903 Gray
FOSTER, Marshall 22 Mar. 1930 Gray
FOSTER, Mildred L. 8 Apr. 1919 Gray
FOSTER, Nora E. 3 Feb. 1919 Windham
FOSTER, Perley W. 4 Mar. 1910 Gray

FOSTER, Samuel J. 16 Feb. 1919 Gray
FOSTER, Silas W. 13 Mar. 1906 Gray
FOSTER, Wilma F. 30 Mar. 1918 Gray
FOUNTAIN, Annie V. 1 May 1925 New Gloucester
FOWLER, John H. 3 Oct. 1900 Gray
FOWLER, Mark F. 10 Sept. 1894 Gray
FOWLER, Martha L. 2 Mar. 1901 No.Yarmouth
FOWLER, Thomas 1 June 1902 not listed
FRANK, Alpheus 6 Oct. 1876
FRANK, Alpheus Jr. Oct. 1878
FRANK, Annette C. 16 Feb. 1909 New Gloucester
FRANK, Augusta 27 Nov. 1913 Gray
FRANK, Elizabeth S. 29 Aug. 1909 Gray
FRANK, Frances E. 5 July 1900 Gray
FRANK, George 31 Oct. 1917 Gray
FRANK, Greenleaf 25 Feb. 1902 Gray
FRANK, Harry E. 18 Jan. 1911 Gray
FRANK, Hersey A. 25 Apr. 1926 Gray
FRANK, James E. 5 May 1904 Gray
FRANK, John N. 30 Dec. 1923 Gray
FRANK, John S. 9 Aug. 1907 Gray
FRANK, Josiah 22 Dec. 1893 Gray
FRANK, Mary Ann 1 June 1912 Gray
FRANK, Orrin L. 4 Mar. 1898 Gray
FRANK, Rebecca D. 27 Feb. 1909 Naples
FRANK, Ruth Vinton 11 May 1893 Gray
FRANK, Samuel Jr. 18 Oct. 1864
FRANK, Sarah 4 May 1896 Gray
FRANK, Sarah Jane 18 Jan. 1901 West Gray
FRANK, Sewall 12 Feb. 1899 Windham
FRANK, Stephen 28 Aug. 1893 Gray
FRANK, Virginia H. 3 Mar. 1895 Gray
FRANK, Wilburn 5 Dec. 1903 Gray
FRANK, William H. 24 July 1911 Gray
FREEMAN, George H. 24 Oct. 1915 Gray
FREEMAN, Louisa July 1878
FRYE, Mary S. 15 Mar. 1918 Cumberland
FURBISH, Stephen 1 Nov. 1896 Gray
GARRETT, Joseph H. 11 Dec. 1918 Nova Scotia, Canada
GIBBS, Charlotte 24 July 1892 Gray

GILPATRICK, Charlotte S. 11 Feb. 1907 Gray
GILPATRICK, Thomas 21 Feb. 1903 Limerick
GLINES, Mary L. 29 Oct. 1898 Charlestown, Mass.
GLINES, Samuel R. 8 Sept. 1912 Gray
GLOSS, Roland H. 30 May 1929 St. John, NB Canada
GODEY, Sally 1874-75
GOFF, Anna 22 Mar. 1895 New Gloucester
GOFF, Eugenia A. 30 Nov. 1899 Gray
GOFF, Frank P. 19 Nov. 1898 Gray
GOFF, Hannible W. 17 May 1925 Gray
GOFF, Herbert 20 June 1907 Gray
GOFF, Jennie Etta 16 May 1864
GOFF, Joseph H. 23 Jan. 1898 Gray
GOFF, Lindsey 3 Jan. 1877
GOFF, Lucius S. 23 Aug. 1898 Gray
GOFF, Sarah A.P. 26 May 1921 Gray
GOFF, William H. 5 Dec. 1864
GOFF, William H. 24 Dec. 1894 Gray
GOLDEN, Kate B. 3 July 1907 Quebec, Can.
GOLDEN, Luella 2 Nov. 1917 Minot
GOLDING, Henry F. 12 June 1926 England
GOODWIN, Elsie D. 3 Sept. 1926 Springfield
GORE, Edwin L. 18 May 1893 Gray
GORE, Jesse 17 Jan. 1892 New Gloucester
GOULD, Helen S. 2 Jan. 1904 Lisbon
GRANGER, Ella S. 10 Mar. 1927 Lewiston
GRANT, Grant 3 Nov. 1913 Gray
GRANT, James P. 6 Jan. 1896 Gray
GREEN, Susanna 23 Feb. 1900 Otisfield
GROVER, Abagail J. 24 Jan. 1909 Portland
GROVER, Betsey J. 30 Oct. 1876
GROVER, infant of Frank C.,0 days 8 Mar. 1911 Gray
HAINES, Eben M. 10 Sept. 1897 Windham
HAINES, Juliette 5 Mar. 1895 Gray
HAINES, Sarah Nov. 1878
HAINES, Louis H. 2 Apr. 1909 Gray
HALE, Charles R. 25 June 1906 Maine
HALE, Jennie B. 3 Dec. 1903 Danville
HALL, ? 18 Aug. 1878
HALL, Bertha F. 5 Jan. 1903 Sabbath Day Lake d. Portland

HALL, Carolin H. 19 Sept. 1917 Gray
HALL, Charles C. 23 Dec. 1905 Gray
HALL, Clara 17 Oct. 1876
HALL, Florence A. 3 Apr. 1907 Boston, Mass.
HALL, Herbert B. 21 Oct. 1912 Gray
HALL, Jennie J.18 Mar. 1920 Portland
HALL, Joseph W. 29 Apr. 1884
HALL, Lillian G. 21 Dec. 1918 New Gloucester
HALL, Lucy C. 5 Feb. 1908 Gray
HALL, Martha Josephine 7 Jan. 1904 Rumford
HALL, Mary S. 3 Mar.1902 Falmouth
HALL, Matilda J. 24 Nov. 1926 P.E.I. Canada
HALL, Roscoe G. 10 Jan. 1920 Gray
HALL, William T. 5 Apr. 1881
HAMMON, Roxanna C. 30 Dec. 1920 Peru
HANCOCK, Elizabeth P. 21 Dec. 1918 Raymond
HANCOCK, Harriet F. 16 Apr. 1913 Gray
HANCOCK, James T. 4 May 1912 Gray
HANCOCK, Lois A. 12 Feb. 1922 Dayton
HANCOCK, Ronald W. 11 Mar. 1916 Gray
HANNA, Annie J. 19 July 1916 Gray
HANSCOME, Effie 1874-75
HARMON, Elizabeth H. 22 June 1924 Gray
HARMON, Henrietta J. 27 Feb. 1923 Windham
HARMON, Marie E. 11 Feb. 1923 New Gloucester
HARMON, Peletiah 12 Feb. 1875
HARMON, William 17 Feb. 1896 Scarboro
HARRIS, Chase M. 6 Mar. 1903 Poland
HARRIS, Fannie J. 13 Feb. 1921 Gray
HARRIS, Julia 16 June 1864
HASKELL, Emily F. 7 Mar. 1894 Cumberland
HASKELL, John 11 May 1902 New Gloucester
HASKELL, Lizzie E. 19 Apr. 1897 No. Yarmouth
HASKELL, Lizzie H. 14 May 1897 Gray
HASKELL, Martha P. 13 Apr. 1910 New Gloucester
HASKELL, William P. 2 July 1900 New Gloucester
HAWES, Josiah T. 22 Oct. 1892 Yarmouth, Mass.
HAWKES, Eben 26 Feb. 1909 Windham
HAWKES, Ellen 19 July 1917 No.Yarmouth
HAWKES, Mary B. 26 Nov. 1895 Gray

HEAD, Arthur P. 24 Nov. 1894 Poland
HEAD, Charles C. 27 Dec. 1914 Gorham
HEAD, Ralph 7 Sept. 1913 Gorham
HENDERSON, Herman W. 24 Mar. 1866
HENRY, Annie V. 24 Nov. 1927 Scotland
HENRY, Thomas 23 Nov. 1930 Scotland
HERRICK, Azore 19 Jan. 1892 Greenwood
HERRRICK, Eliza B. 27 Sept. 1904 Woodstock
HERRICK, Linnie 22 Dec. 1893 Gorham
HIGGINS, Charles H. 1874-75
HIGGINS, Henrietta 7 Apr. 1930 Gray
HIGGINS, Orrin S. 18 July 1910 Gray
HILL, Abbie F. 29 Sept. 1876
HILL, Albert 21 Dec. 1902 Gray
HILL, Ardelia M. 3 Apr. 1911 Gray
HILL, Irma A. 24 May 1915 Gray
HILL, Josiah 23 July 1876
HILL, Luther W. 22 Jan. 1922 Buxton
HINES, Bridget 29 May 1918 Ireland
HODGKINS, Alphonso 11 June 1896 Poland
HODGKINS, Emeline H. 1 July 1895 Gray
HODGKINS, Flora Belle not known Temple
HODGKINS, Flossie E. 13 Feb. 1901 Winthrop
HODGKINS, George B. 21 May 1902 Gray
HODGKINS, Harland, infant son of 4 hrs old 11 Dec. 1906 Gray
HODGKINS, Helen Louisa 9 Sept. 1908 Gray
HODGKINS, Herman H. 16 Jan. 1906 Gray
HODGKINS, Irving 6 June 1899 Gray
HODGKINS, Jonas R. 6 Feb. 1905 Gray
HODGKINS, Joseph E. 10 June 1902 Gray
HODGKINS, Leon M. 19 May 1909 New Gloucester
HODSON, Eliza M. 13 Dec. 1925 Pownal
HOPKINS, Mary E. 15 Aug. 1892 Windsor VT
HOULE, Henry 8 Oct. 1930 Canada
HULIT, James E. 18 Apr. 1917 New Gloucester
HULIT, Willard F. 8 July 1925 New Gloucester
HULME, James 28 Mar. 1911 England
HULMES, Phoebe C. 7 July 1907 Gorham
HUMPHREY, Abbie L. 7 Mar. 1927 Gray
HUMPHREY, Alford 15 Feb. 1896 Gray

HUMPHREY, Daisy 15 Dec. 1921 England
NUMPHREY, James C. 24 Feb. 1927 Gray
NUMPHREY, Shadrach G. 15 Apr. 1922 Gray
HUNT, Charles 27 Jan. 1915 Gray
HUNT, Cynthia P. 28 Dec. 1898 Gray
HUNT, Edith L. 11 Nov. 1896 Gray
HUNT, Eliza J. 9 Dec. 1898 Limerick
HUNT, Elnathan 14 Feb. 1894 Gray
HUNT, Fannie S. 6 Oct. 1926 Cumberland
HUNT, George 2 Aug. 1916 Windham
HUNT, Harriet N. 12 Apr. 1908 Milton, Mass.
HUNT, Hiram P. 17 July 1903 Gray
HUNT, James H. 18 Dec. 1907 Gray
HUNT, Julia E. 4 Feb. 1928 Gray
HUNT, Lee B. 21 May 1923 Albany
HUNT, Lewis B. 26 Mar. 1924 Gray
HUNT, Phoebe 16 Apr. 1921 Nova Scotia
HUNT, Susie Lee 1 Feb. 1929 Gray
HUNTLY, Marian G. 30 Dec. 1910 Portland
HUSTON, Augusta H. 2 May 1925 Gray
HUSTON, Caroline E. 25 Jan. 1925 Derby, Vt.
HUSTON, David F. 6 Sept. 1925 Gray
HUSTON, Edward 25 Mar. 1911 Falmouth
HUSTON, Edwin E. 15 Oct. 1924 Gray
HUSTON, Elijah 1 Oct. 1895 Cumberland
HUSTON, Frances 23 Jan. 1876
HUSTON, Frank 18 Aug. 1878
HUSTON, Helen 30 Apr. 1920 Gray
HUSTON, Joseph F. 18 Sept. 1918 No.Yarmouth
HUSTON, Moses 25 Feb. 1892 Gray
HUSTON, Stephen 4 Feb. 1901 Windham
HUSTON, Willard H. 21 Sept. 1916 No. Yarmouth
JACKSON, Sarah E. 3 Oct. 1905 Lincoln, Me.
JAQUES, Ellen T. 13 Oct. 1897 Charlestown, Mass.
JEWETT, Hannah M. 25 Apr. 1928 Standish
JONES, Annie V. 12 July 1929 Gray
JONES, Charles T. E. 31 Jan. 1897 Paris
JONES, Ellen C. 14 Nov. 1920 Gray
JONES, Emma B. 25 Nov. 1910 Gray
JONES, Roxalana A. 28 Nov. 1909 New Gloucester

JORDAN, Lilla M. 8 June 1895 Brunswick
JORDAN, Rueben B. 24 Feb. 1899 New Gloucester
KING, Augustas H. 12 Dec. 1865
KING, Edward Oct. 1878
KING, infant 10 Aug. 1896 Lewiston
KIRSCH, Anton 10 Jan. 1922 Germany
KIRSCH, Windel 28 May 1924 Germany
KNAPP, Lucy A. 2 Apr. 1905 Gray
KNAPP, Charles O. 5 Sept. 1899 Gray
KNIGHT, Effie 1 May 1906 Gray
KNIGHT, George F. 9 Oct. 1917 Gray
KNIGHT, John R. 15 Sept. 1915 Gray
KNIGHT, Maria Allen 2 May 1905 Gray
KNIGHT, Patrick H. 13 June 1896 Gray
KNIGHT, Sarah J. 24 Mar. 1865
KNIGHT, Susan M. 24 Dec. 1917 Standish
KNOWLES, Fred A. 24 May 1902 Corinna
LATHAM, Cyrus 16 Apr. 1900 Gray
LATHAM, Ernest L. 9 Dec. 1893 Cape Elizabeth
LATHAM, Hannah H. 2 Dec. 1898 Raymond
LATHAM, Jabez L. 17 Mar. 1893 Cape Elizabeth
LATHAM, Jabez M. 4 Dec. 1905 New Gloucester
LATHAM, Leslie E. 11 Dec. 1910 Gray
LATHAM, Levi B. 22 June 1881
LATHAM, Samuel S. 24 Sept. 1903 Gray
LATHAM, Woodward 28 Sept. 1865
LATIMER, William G. 30 June 1906 Washington, D.C.
LAUGHTON, John 28 Oct. 1916 Bristol
LAWRENCE, Amanda 14 Mar. 1920 Cumberland
LAWRENCE, Charles H. 26 July 1929 Gray
LAWRENCE, Ephraim 20 Sept. 1874
LAWRENCE, Henry L. 7 Jan. 1929 Gray
LAWRENCE, David 11 Jan. 1899 Gray
LEACH, James H. 1 Nov. 1904 Raymond
LEAKE, Charles R. 6 Oct. 1929 Charlestown, Mass
LEAVITT, Daniel W. 3 Jan. 1907 Gray
LEAVITT, Hatie E. 27 Mar. 1929 Raymond
LEAVITT, Libeus H. 18 Sept. 1916 Gray
LEAVIT, Loantha 8 May 1930 Gray
LEAVITT, Mary E. 25 Dec. 1901 Gray

LEGROW, Charles W. 11 May 1924 Portland
LEIGHTON, Aphia S. 6 Apr. 1893 Gray
LEIGHTON, Celia H. 2 Feb. 1902 Falmouth
LEIGHTON, Daniel 15 Aug. 1899
LEIGHTON, Edward G. stillborn 21 Dec. 1920 unknown
LEIGHTON, Flora A. 1 Feb. 1899 Troy
LEIGHTON, Frank 16 Feb. 1901 Falmouth
LEIGHTON, Hattie E. 28 Dec. 1895 Gray
LEIGHTON, Percy A. 13 Oct. 1899 Gray
LEIGHTON, Sarah J. 26 Oct. 1915 Gray
LEIGHTON, Silas 3 Apr. 1893 Norway
LEIGHTON, William H. 24 Mar. 1918 Gray
LESLIE, Mand B. 25 Feb. 1893 Gorham
LIBBY, Abbie P. 18 Mar. 1921 Gray
LIBBY, Adeline B. 29 Oct. 1894 Gray
LIBBY, Alfred 25 Apr. 1897 Gray
LIBBY, Almer 9 Dec. 1893 Gray
LIBBY, Ann A. 16 May 1896 Johnson, VT.
LIBBY, Augustus F. 29 Oct. 1903 Gray
LIBBY, Charles 13 Feb. 1865
LIBBY, Charles E. 4 Aug. 1905 Gray
LIBBY, Charles E. 14 June 1917 Gray
LIBBY, Donald W. 31 Mar. 1914 Gray
LIBBY, Dorothy 16 Aug. 1913 Gorham
LIBBY, Edward H. 24 Jan. 1907 Gray
LIBBY, Elizabeth 18 Mar. 1914 Nova Scotia
LIBBY, Elizabeth E. 30 May 1924 Auburn
LIBBY, Emeline 24 Aug. 1894 Gray
LIBBY, Emma M. 11 Feb. 1898 Gray
LIBBY, Ephraim Oct. 1878
LIBBY, Esther A. 23 Sept. 1915 Gray
LIBBY, Evelyn 10 Aug. 1927 Gray
LIBBY, Fanny T. 11 Apr. 1897 Gray
LIBBY, Frances T. 18 Dec. 1902 Gray
LIBBY, Freeland E. 13 Apr. 1903 Gray
LIBBY, George W. 6 Nov. 1907 Yarmouth
LIBBY, Herbert M. 18 Dec. 1909 Gray
LIBBY, Herbert W. 6 Oct. 1893 Gray
LIBBY, Hettie W. 15 Mar. 1907 Gray
LIBBY, Huldah 26 Apr. 1896 Harrison

LIBBY, Isaac 10 May 1893 Gray
LIBBY, James P. 2 Nov. 1908 Gray
LIBBY, Jedeiah 10 July 1910 Gray
LIBBY, Jennie E. 9 Aug. 1898 Gray
LIBBY, John H. 16 Mar. 1902 Gray
LIBBY, John M. 29 May 1901 Gray
LIBBY, Laura Margaret 4 Oct. 1909 Gray
LIBBY, Martha A. 28 Jan. 1900 Gray
LIBBY, Mary 9 July 1865
LIBBY, Mary 21 May 1910 Gray
LIBBY, Mary A. 8 Aug. 1878
LIBBY, Mary F. 26 Nov. 1893 Gray
LIBBY, Mary W. Feb. 1879
LIBBY, Molly P. 14 Apr. 1910 Gray
LIBBY, Rebecca C. 27 Feb. 1898 Gray
LIBBY, Sally 2 Apr. 1864
LIBBY, Shirley T. 18 Apr. 1930 Gray
LIBBY, Simon 31 Aug. 1928 Gray
LIBBY, Stephen A. 6 Oct. 1903 Gray
LIBBY, Sumner 23 Apr. 1920 Gray
LIBBY, Thomas L. 19 Mar. 1901 Gray
LIBBY, Viola Jennette 4 Feb. 1903 Gray
LIBBY, William H. 15 July 1864
LIBBY, Infant of J. R., 4 hours old 17 Sept. 1917 Gray
LIVINGSTON, Leroy 5 Nov. 1918 Bangor
LORD, Clara B. 22 Feb. 1914 Gray
LORD, Isaac H. 30 Dec. 1920 Brownfield
LORING, ? Nov. 1878
LOW, Francis L. 16 Mar. 1908 Gray
LOW, Herbert 6 Mar. 1864
LOWE JR., Charles F. 10 June 1926 Gray
LOWE JR., Frank H. 31 May 1896 Gray
LOWE JR., Mary Eilena 21 July 1930 Yarmouth
LOWE, Mary Elizabeth 17 Mar. 1915 Gray
LOWE, Nellie J. 13 June 1920 Gray
LOWE, infant son of Eugene H. 6 hours 17 May 1924 not known
LOWE JR., Eugene H. 21 Aug. 1922 Gray
LUNT, Ellen 25 Oct. 1876
LUNT, Marion C. 14 Jan. 1906 Gray
LUNT, Meshach H. 2 Feb. 1921 Gray

LUNT, Ruth I. 26 Jan. 1911 Gray
MANCHESTER, George B. 19 Oct. 1926 Portland
MAPES, David B. 13 June 1911 not known
MAPES, Jacob 27 Jan. 1912 not known
MARKS, James Hewey 26 May 1912 Malaga Islands, Portugal
MARSTON, Mildred 26 Apr.1898 Windham
MAUSISE, Miranda F. 10 July 1930 Cumberland
MAXWELL, Delmar H. 30 Dec.1928 Gray
MAXWELL, Eben 11 Mar. 1893 Windham
MAXWELL, Elizabeth A. 5 Mar. 1901 Gray
MAXWELL, John 10 Dec. 1899 Windham
MAY, Albert G. 29 Apr. 1894 Gray
MAY, Anna C. 23 May 1902 Raymond
MAY, Edwin G. 26 Jan. 1929 Gray
MAY, Julia Tripp 30 Jan. 1929
MAY, Lucy E. 25 Dec. 1916 Gray
MAY, Rufus 22 July 1894 Raymond
MAY, Sadie E. 14 June 1896 Gray
MAY, Thomas L. 23 Apr. 1910 Raymond
MAYBERRY, Charles T. 15 July 1911 Gray
MAYBERRY, Cynthia J. 18 Dec. 1896 Gray
MAYBERRY, Leforest 24 June 1898 Gray
MAYBERRY, Mary E. 6 Jan. 1904 Gray
MAYBERRY, Nancy 3 Feb. 1903 Dixfield
MAYBERRY, Thomas J. 17 June 1909 Windham
McCANN, Herbert L. 16 Mar. 1930 Rollingdam, NB Canada
McCONKEY, George 22 Dec. 1900 Ireland
McCORRISON, Earl F. 7 Nov. 1918 Kenduskeag
McDONALD, Flora E. 3 Mar. 1909 Gray
McDONALD, Fred S. 30 June 1901 Gray
McDONALD, Joseph 14 Jan. 1898 Gray
McDONALD, Sarah A. 24 Dec. 1912 Falmouth
McGOWEN, James 26 Feb. 1892 Perry
McINNIS, Clayton F. 24 Mar. 1927 Gray
McINNIS, James H. 8 May 1915 Gray
McKEEN, infant son of John, 0 days 30 Aug.1910 Gray
McQUARRIE, Sarah 2 Jan. 1879
MEGGUIER, Lewis 7 Sept. 1865
MEGGUIER, Salome 10 Sept. 1865
MEGQUIER, Lois E. 12 Dec. 1900 E. Corinth

MEGQUIER, Martha A. 1 Nov. 1909 New Gloucester
MERRILL, Ansel W. 7 Nov. 1910 Brownfield
MERRILL, Eliza Wentworth 20 Mar. 1916 Bridgton
MERRILL, Elizabeth 11 May 1876
MERRILL, Elizabeth T. 22 Nov. 1928 New Gloucester
MERRILL, Emeline 14 Apr. 1897 Falmouth
MERRILL, Enoch 26 June 1908 Brownfield
MERRILL, Frances H. 18 Oct. 1922 Gray
MERRILL, George Dwight 8 Sept. 1929 Gray
MERRILL, John T. 7 Apr. 1910 Poland
MERRILL, Martha A. 11 Sept. 1897 New Gloucester
MERRILL, Mayhew C. 17 Oct. 1900 Woodstock
MERROW, Louis S. 29 Feb. 1908 Belfast
MESERVE, Almira D. 14 Feb. 1901 Lyman
MESERVE, James 6 Mar. 1913 Hollis
MESERVE, Mary M. 7 Feb. 1902 Hollis
MICHAUD, Raphael 22 July 1923 Winn
MITCHELL, Emily J. 15 Dec. 1916 Falmouth
MODES, Annie 31 May 1916 Russia
MODORL, John 2 Nov. 1918 Wallagrass
MOODY, Eliza 1874-75
MOODY, Lillian E. 28 June 1904 Gray
MOREY, Harriett W. 26 Aug. 1926 Portland
MORRILL, Annie F. 8 Apr. 1909 Halifax, N.S.
MORRILL, Charles R. 3 Dec. 1895 Portland
MORRILL, Hugh P. 7 June 1896 Raymond
MORRILL, Jacob P. 10 Apr. 1901 Gray
MORRILL, Julia A. 25 Feb. 1909 Raymond
MORRILL, Lydia A. 4 Feb. 1892 Boothbay
MORRILL, Margaret E. 5 Jan. 1896 Gray
MORRILL, Mark C. 19 Oct. 1906 Windham
MORRILL, Mary E. 13 Aug. 1904 Portland
MORRILL, Matthew C. 21 Feb. 1926 Raymond
MORSE, Charles M. 21 May 1914 Gray
MORSE, Ellen L. 24 July 1904 New Gloucester
MORSE, Frank W. 17 Mar. 1879
MORSE, Horace L. 28 Nov. 1898 Gray
MORSE, John 1874-75
MORSE, Lucy A. 13 Dec. 1925 Wilton
MORSE, Maria C. 26 June 1908 Gray

MORSE, Marshall 18 Apr. 1902 Gray
MORSE, Mary E. 22 May 1896 New Gloucester
MORSE, Sarah Jane Loring 23 Oct. 1918 Gray
MORSE, William H. 18 Oct.1902 not listed
MORSE, William R. 28 Nov. 1903 Gray
MORSE, Verona W. 20 July 1908 Derby Line, Vt.
MOUNTFORT, Joshua M. 28 Mar. 1865
MOUNTFORT, Louisa 20 Aug. 1897 Gray
MOUNTFORT, Roland 1875
MUZZY, June N. 18 Jan. 1914 Dummer, N.H.
NASH, Hannah 31 Mar. 1866
NASH, Hannah F. 13 June 1906 Gray
NASH, James 3 Aug. 1896 Gray
NASH, Joshua M. 2 Jan. 1892 Gray
NASH, Mary S. 20 Sept. 1897 Boothbay
NASH, Sophia A. 23 Aug. 1895 Gray
NEWBEGIN, Mary E. 2 Mar. 1910 Brunswick
NEWBEGIN, Salome S. 24 Mar.1924 Buxton
NEWMAN, Marion 28 Sept. 1894 Bangor
NICKERSON, Dora E. 10 June 1905 Gardner
NOYES, Alvin A. 12 Sept. 1919 Portland
O"CONNELL, Ella F. 8 Dec. 1921 Cumberland
OSGOOD, Elmer L. 16 Mar. 1921 Gray
OSGOOD, Emery 20 Feb. 1905 Durham
OSGOOD, Ina A. 7 Feb. 1908 New Gloucester
OSGOOD, Martha A. 29 July 1904 Portland
PARKER, Cynthia A. 15 Feb. 1927 Baldwin
PARKER, Martha J. 10 Oct. 1911 Gray
PARKER, Sarah 9 Nov.1874
PARKER, Alonzo S. 9 Feb. 1923 Bridgton
PENNELL, Albert 19 July 1916 Harpswell
PENNELL, Elizabeth J. 21 Jan. 1899 Gray
PENNELL, Joseph F. 10 Feb. 1865
PENNELL, May B. 21 May 1896 Gray
PERLEY, Cyrus J. 2 June 1917 Gray
PERLEY, George 30 Mar. 1875
PERLEY, George W. 9 Sept. 1905 Gray
PERLEY, Roscoe 28 Nov. 1919 Gray
PERLEY, Sally 17 Jan. 1892 Gray
PERLEY, Susan D. 5 Aug. 1895 Gray

PERVES, Adam 18 Feb. 1892 Gray
PETTINGALL, Susan S. 24 June 1864
PIERCE, infant of Willis 23 Oct.1925 Gray
PLUMMER, Mary 24 June 1856
POOL, Naham A. 20 Oct. 1915 Minot
POOLE, Sarah S. 3 July 1892 Gray
PORTER, Eliza 25 Dec. 1874
PORTER, Elizabeth 14 Mar. 1864
PRATT, Elva M. 1 Jan.1924 Canton
PRATT, Lucy E. 28 Apr. 1928 Martha's Vinyard, Mass.
PRATT, infant of Ernest, 0 days 4 June 1912 Gray
PRAY, Sarah 28 Mar. 1864
PRINCE, Anna S. 29 Oct. 1912 Sherman
PRINCE, Johanna 12 Jan. 1910 Poland
PRINCE, Sewall B. 15 July 1901 Gray
PRITHAM, Alice J. 8 Feb. 1917 Gray
PROCTOR, Martha A. 16 July 1892 Portland
PURVES, John F. 4 May 1903 Gray
PUTMAN, Henry L. 25 Apr. 1913 Winthrop
QUINT, Frank A. 19 Apr.1916 Newburyport, Mass.
QUINT, Jennie E. 24 June 1897 Casco
QUINT, Thomas 27 Mar.1902 Sanford
RACKLEY, Alice G. 20 May 1919 Portland
RAMSDELL, Grace P. 16 Feb. 1925 Gray
RAMSDELL, Abbie 18 June 1912 Gray
RAMSDELL, Benjamin F. 11 Feb. 1865
RAMSDELL, Charles 19 Dec. 1913 Gray
RAMSDELL, Eliza J. 23 Ap   9 Gray
RAMSDELL, Elizabeth R. Aug. 1878
RAMSDELL, John D. 2 Aug. 1865
RAMSDELL, Joseph H. 15 July 1895 Gray
RAMSDELL, Mary P. 1 Nov. 1899 Gray
REED, Althea D. 3 June 1892 Gray
REED, Charles R. 3 Aug. 1916 Deering
REED, Henry F. 20 June 1910 Scarboro
RICH, John B. 13 Oct. 1874
RICHARDS, infant son of John 1 Apr. 1905 Gray
RICKER, Anna 8 Oct. 1864
RICKER, infant of Basil F., 0 days 3 Feb. 1928 Gray
RING, Charles 21 Oct. 1904 not listed

ROGERS, George L. 3 May 1929 Pittsfield
ROWE, Rebecca 8 Apr. 1901 New Gloucester
ROWE, Hannah T. 2 Apr. 1912 New Gloucester
ROWE, Hattie E. 11 Mar. 1909 New Gloucester
RUSSELL, Hiram 28 Feb. 1910 Gray
RUSSELL, Martha Merrow 18 Feb. 1923 Gray
RUSSELL, Mary M. 1 Apr. 1900 Gray
RUSSELL, Mary Merrill 16 Feb. 1923 Gray
RUSSELL, William L. 9 Oct. 1920 Cumberland
RYDER, Andrew S. 3 Apr. 1923 No.Yarmouth
RYDER, Amanda S. 10 Oct. 1904 Gray
RYDER, child of Sumner 1875-76
SAUCIER, Sarah G. 3 Sept. 1930 Canada
SAVOY, Henry G. 13 May 1921 Gray
SAVOY, Mary S. 15 Aug.1913 Gray
SAWYER, Annie M. 2 July 1919 Gray
SAWYER, Charles A. 21 Dec. 1916 Gray
SAWYER, Clara A 7 May 1925 Gray
SAWYER, E. 1 Sept. 1896 Gray
SAWYER, Greenleaf 27 Nov. 1918 Gray
SAWYER, John D. 19 Dec. 1917 Gray
SAWYER, John F. 11 May 1897 New Gloucester
SAWYER, John M. 5 Feb. 1920 New Gloucester
SAWYER, Joseph P. 10 Jan. 1898 Gray
SAWYER, Lewis M. 9 Mar. 1917 Gray
SAWYER, Lydia R. 29 Sept.1896 Danville
SAWYER, Malinda P. 16 Nov. 1903 Gray
SAWYER, Martha J. 20 Nov. 1922 Ireland
SAWYER, Mary E. 24 Jan. 1920 New Market, N.H.
SAWYER, Mary Louise 17 Apr. 1930 Gray
SAWYER, Mildred E. 25 Feb. 1918 Gray
SAWYER, Parker L. 21 Feb. 1903 Gray
SAWYER, Parker W. 19 May 1900 Gray
SAWYER, Phoebe E. 7 May 1925 Cumberland
SAWYER, Willard F. 4 Dec. 1928 Gray
SAWYER, Infant of Arthur, 0 days 15 Sept. 1928 Gray
SAYWARD, Dorothy M. 11 Aug. 1928 Gray
SAYWARD, Johns H. 8 June 1917 Windham
SEARS, Warren D. 27 Mar. 1914 Gray
SEELY, Sadie C. 24 Oct. 1928 Monson

SHAW, ? A. 19 Sept. 1878
SHAW, Abbie F. Aug. 1878
SHAW, Alva M. 31 Jan. 1927 Cumberland
SHAW, Frank J. 24 Feb. 1927 Buckfield
SHAW, Robert D. 1 Sept. 1892 Gray
SIDLINGER, Carrie A. 8 Sept.1907 Kennebunk
SIMPSON, Harry F. 20 Apr. 1925 Gray
SIMPSON, Lowell B. 16 Dec. 1909 Deer Isle
SIMPSON, Sarah A. 11 Nov. 1897 Westport
SIMPSON, William R. 5 Apr. 1903 Poland
SIMPSON, William W. 1 May 1914 Gray
SKILLIN, Albion 27 Mar. 1875
SKILLIN, Clara A. 19 July 1865
SKILLIN, Clifford E. 7 July 1896 Gray
SKILLIN, Edna E. 30 June 1899 Gray
SKILLIN, Esther M. 5 Nov. 1864
SKILLIN, Esther M. 18 Oct. 1894
SKILLIN, Josiah 25 Dec. 1874
SKILLIN, Margaret A. 15 July 1900 Gray
SKILLIN, Thomas 17 Aug. 1895 Gray
SKILLING, Samuel T. 17 Dec. 1908 Gray
SKILLINGS, Addie F. 25 Oct. 1915 Buxton
SKILLINGS, Edwin S. 26 Aug. 1909 Gray
SKILLINGS, Ellen L. 31 Mar. 1907 Gray
SKILLINGS, Harriet L. 9 Dec. 1927 Cumberland
SKILLINGS, Hewett Chandler 6 Sept. 1920 Gray
SKILLINGS, Hiram 16 Mar. 1893 Gray
SKILLINGS, Kate E. 3 Jan. 1907 Gray
SKILLINGS, Martha E. 13 June 1897 Windham
SKILLINGS, Otto W. 9 Jan. 1897 Yarmouth
SKILLINGS, Pamelia M. 21 Feb. 1914 Cumberland
SKILLINGS, Sarah S. 29 Feb. 1916 Gray
SMALL, Addie J. 9 Jan. 1898 Boston, Mass.
SMALL, Addie P. 23 Aug. 1897 Gray
SMALL, Asenath 27 Nov. 1921 Alfred
SMALL, Bernice G. 23 Oct.1900 Gray
SMALL, Christiana 20 May 1874
SMALL, David 23 Oct. 1898 Gray
SMALL, Elisha 22 Jan. 1879
SMALL, Eunice M. 31 Dec. 1901 Gray

SMALL, Freeland M. 21 Feb. 1920 Gray
SMALL, Hannah T. 14 Aug. 1894 Woburn, Mass.
SMALL, Irene 18 Aug. 1897 Gray
SMALL, Issac 29 Jan. 1908 Windham
SMALL, John H. 25 Dec. 1915 Gray
SMALL, Joseph F. 8 Apr. 1878
SMALL, Levi G. 31 Dec. 1912 Casco
SMALL, Lois B. 14 Feb. 1911 Gray
SMALL, Louisa 3 June 1900 Poland
SMALL, Mabel Edith 28 Jan. 1929 Gray
SMALL, Richard A. 18 Aug. 1878
SMALL, Sophia A. 16 July 1898 Gray
SMALL, Sylvanius C. 28 Apr. 1930 Island Falls
SMALL, William 4 Apr. 1903 Windham
SMITH, Abbie J. 1 June 1912 Liberty
SMITH, Clar M. 22 Aug. 1904 Gray
SMITH, Hannah ? May 1878
SMITH, Hugh 19 Feb. 1909 Gray
SMITH, Ivy H. 18 Jan. 1911 Gray
SMITH, James E. 24 Mar. 1923 Poland
SMITH, Johnson 6 June 1896 Raymond
SMITH, Lucinda L. 18 May 1900 Gray
SMITH, Margaret D. 12 Oct. 1928 Scotland
SMITH, Marieta A. 15 Oct. 1913 Dover, N.H.
SMITH, Orland 1874
SNOW, Abbie J. 26 Nov. 1923 Litchfield
SNOW, Jennie L. 5 Nov. 1902 Raymond
SNOW, William S. 25 Sept. 1897 Poland
SNOW, Forest B. infant28 June 1906 Gray
SPENCER, Julia A. 22 Apr. 1915 Gray
SPILLAR, Delia ? Feb. 1878
STAPLES, Adrianna L. 7 May 1892 Mexico, Me.
STARBIRD, Nellie N. 23 Apr. 1876
STEVENS, Ellen M. 6 Apr. 1905 Raymond
STEVENS, Elsie Morse 15 May 1906 Andover, Mass
STEVENS, John W. 23 Dec. 1921 Poland
STEVENS, Lorna 22 Aug. 1892 Sanford
STEVENS, Moses 10 May 1897 Chatham, N.H.
STEVENS, infant of L.O., 0 days 7 Oct. 1914 Gray
STILES, Abbie4 Dec. 1902 Gray

STILES, Charles W. 13 Mar. 1914 Gray
STILES, Cushman C. 22 May 1892 Auburn
STILES, Hattie E. 4 Feb. 1898 Gray
STILES, Stephen W. 13 Oct. 1906 Danville
STIMSON, Augusta M. 11 Aug 1910 Gray
STIMSON, Caroline M. 20 Nov. 1860
STIMSON, Horace O. 5 Mar. 1916 Gray
STIMSON, Russell S. 20 May 1917 Gray
STOREY, John R. 22 Mar. 1897 Carlisle, England
STROUT, Abner T. 19 Apr. 1923 Gray
STROUT, Barbara 31 May 1910 Melvill, N.S.
STROUT, Iva N. 9 Sept. 1895 Gray
STROUT, Marshie 16 July 1900 Gray
STROUT, Nancy 20 Sept. 1915 Raymond
STROUT, Oretta A. 24 Oct. 1921 Gray
STROUT, William 7 Apr. 1906
STROUT, William H. 22 Oct. 1897 Raymond
STROUT, William H. 30 June 1911 Raymond
STROUT, Samuel C. 1 Dec. 1929 Windham
STUBBS, Orin H. 16 May 1864
STURGIS, Infant of Frank O., 5 days old 6 Jan. 1917 Gray
SWEETSER, Frances E. 21 Sept. 1897 Casco
SWEETSER, Sarah A.P. 15 July 1920 No.Yarmouth
TENNEY, Alice A. 30 Aug. 1895 Gray
TENNEY, Mary E. 27 Nov. 1898
THAYER, Georgeanna 1874-75
THAYER, Harriett A. 16 Nov. 1918 Gray
THAYER, Mary A. 6 Mar. 1895 Gray
THAYER, Sarah Josephine 23 Jan. 1929 Gray
THAYER, Warren 3 Mar. 1900 Gray
THOMAS, Agnes H. 17 Nov. 1929 St.George, NB Canada
THOMPSON, Bessie E. 29 Jan. 1907 Gray
THOMPSON, Charles H. 3 Aug. 1907 Paris, Me
THOMPSON, Charles L. 19 Nov. 1928 Mechanic Falls
THOMPSON, Elisha 5 Mar. 1904 Buckfield
THOMPSON, Elizabeth H. 25 Oct. 1924 Gray
THOMPSON, George L. 1 Oct. 1913 Gray
THOMPSON, George W. 4 May 1929 Gray
THOMPSON, Joan 22 Feb. 1897 Cumberland
THOMPSON, Martha I. 12 Nov. 1930 Windham

THOMPSON, Roger S. 14 Apr. 1921 Cumberland
THOMPSON, infant of Perley, 5 days old 27 Apr. 1921 Gray
THURLOW, Charles 25 Aug. 1892 Riley Plantation
THURLOW, George W. 26 Dec. 1899 Gray
THURLOW, John 13 Nov. 1899 Raymond
THURLOW, Mary L. 16 June 1897 Raymond
THURLOW, Sophronia M. 7 Nov. 1913 New Gloucester
TINKHAM, Fred 1875-76
TOLE, Mary E. 20 July 1902 Lawrence, Mass.
TRIPP, Charles F. 4 Nov. 1917 No.Yarmouth
TRIPP, David G. 28 Dec. 1894 Gray
TRIPP, Frank 16 July 1908
TRIPP, Georgianna P. 23 Apr. 1924 Limington
TRIPP, Glenn M. 21 Jan. 1920 Gray
TRIPP, William H. 11 May 1916 Gray
TROWBRIDGE, Charles S. 14 Sept. 1903 Raymond
TRUE, Edward H. 26 Apr. 1915 Portland
TWITCHELL, John 11 Jan. 1866
TWOMBLY, Daniel H. 1 Dec. 1903 Bangor
VANNAH, Ambrose L. 20 Mar. 1922 Jefferson
VARNEY, Augusta F. 9 Jan.1919 Portland
VEASEY, Lucinda M. 20 July 1920 Stark, N.H.
VERILL, Abraham 23 Mar. 1921 New Gloucester
VERRILL, Andrew 26 Jan. 1902 Gray
VERRILL, Bela 12 Sept. 1900 Gray
VERRILL, Bela 11 July 1911 Raymond
VERRILL, Benjamin F. 16 Aug. 1899 Portland
VERRILL, Catherine 6 Dec. 1924 Gray
VERRILL, Charles N. 12 Sept. 1900 Gray
VERRILL, George G. 8 Dec. 1919 Gray
VERRILL, James 14 Mar. 1909 Raymond
VERRILL, Joseph 25 June 1899 Gray
VERRILL, Lewis M. 9 Aug. 1929 Raymond
VERRILL, Mary B. 5 Mar. 1901 Cumberland
VERRILL, Ramsom 1874-75
VERRILL, Vera E. 22 July 1899 Gray
VERRILL, Wardsworth 24 Sept. 1894 New Gloucester
VERRILL, William Henry 1 Dec. 1908 Poland
VERRILLE, Henry J. 9 May 1926 Canada
VINTON, Harriet L. 28 July 1895 Gray

VINTON, Martha H. 13 Nov. 1900 Gray
VINTON, Warren H. 13 Mar. 1907 Paris
VINTON, William W. 7 Apr. 1930 Gray
WALKER, Harriett A. 23 Oct. 1920 Hampden
WAY, Mary Olive infant, 18 hours 25 Mar. 1923
WAY, Sarah A. 31 May 1922 Gray
WEBB, Fred L. 26 Dec. 1918 So. Windham
WEBSTER, Charles R. 22 Dec. 1895 Gray
WEBSTER, Eliza J. 3 Aug. 1898 Minot
WEBSTER, Isabell 13 July 1865
WEBSTER, Maria C. 28 Sept. 1922 New Gloucester
WEBSTER, Martha A. 24 Jan. 1915 Gray
WEBSTER, Nellie L. 7 May 1926 Gray
WEBSTER, Simon 7 Feb. 1926 Gray
WEBSTER, William H. 26 Mar. 1902 Gray
WEEKS, Benjamin F. 25 Dec. 1878
WEEKS, Harriet O. 11 Feb. 1892 Gray
WESTON, Jennie P. 26 Dec.1904 Wiscasset
WEYMOUTH, Miriam H. 7 Jan. 1892 Raymond
WHITE, Charles W. 17 Dec. 1919 Dresden
WHITNEY, Alfred S. 29 July 1892 Cumberland
WHITNEY, Edward 17 Aug. 1908 Portland
WHITNEY, Emma R. 27 Feb. 1916 Brownfield
WHITNEY, Flora I. 5 Dec. 1926 Gray
WHITNEY, Helena P. 13 Jan. 1925 Gray
WHITNEY, Hezekiah 12 June 1895 Cumberland
WHITNEY, James 19 Apr. 1894 Cumberland
WHITNEY, Maria F. 7 Oct. 1909 Gray
WHITNEY, Mary Agnes 27 Apr.1930 Auburn
WHITNEY, Mary Ellen 31 Oct. 1908 Falmouth
WHITNEY, Mary Hannah 14 Oct. 1929 Gray
WHITNEY, Oren F. 30 Jan. 1925 No.Yarmouth
WHITNEY, Peter S. 5 Jan. 1909 Raymond
WHITNEY, Thomas G. 20 Apr. 1917 Casco
WHITTEN, James 23 Jan. 1876
WILCOX, Sadie McN. 26 Oct. 1923 Portland
WILSON, Carl C. 30 Aug. 1896 Gray
WILSON, James L. 26 Feb. 1894 Gray
WILSON, Jane 5 Apr. 1904 Gorham
WILSON, Loemma 8 Mar. 1924 Cumberland

WING, Dorothy E. 16 Oct. 1910 Gray
WING, Willis R. 2 Dec. 1908 Leeds
WINTER, Samuel 16 Apr. 1927 Switzerland
WITHAM, Harold O. 16 Dec. 1914 Gray
WITHAM, Hazel Clifton 19 July 1906 Windham
WITHAM, Joshus 22 Nov. 1922 Alfred
WITHAM, Mary E. 25 Nov. 1907 Gray
WITHAM, Mial 13 Feb. 1918 Raymond
WITHAM, Nancy 9 Jan. 1892 Sanford
WITHAM, Dilys M. 28 June 1922 Gray
WOODBURY, Flora 4 Aug. 1907 Levant
WOODBURY, John P. 12 Aug. 1896 New Gloucester
WOODBURY, William P. 27 Sept.1904 Westbrook
WREN, Stephen B. 10 Jan. 1926 Sumner
YARNEY, John 12 Sept. 1900 Medford, Ma.
YOUNG, Calvin W. 18 Aug. 1900 Gray
YOUNG, Martha H. 20 Sept. 1899 Gray

9 781585 498864